My Childhood on My Shoulders

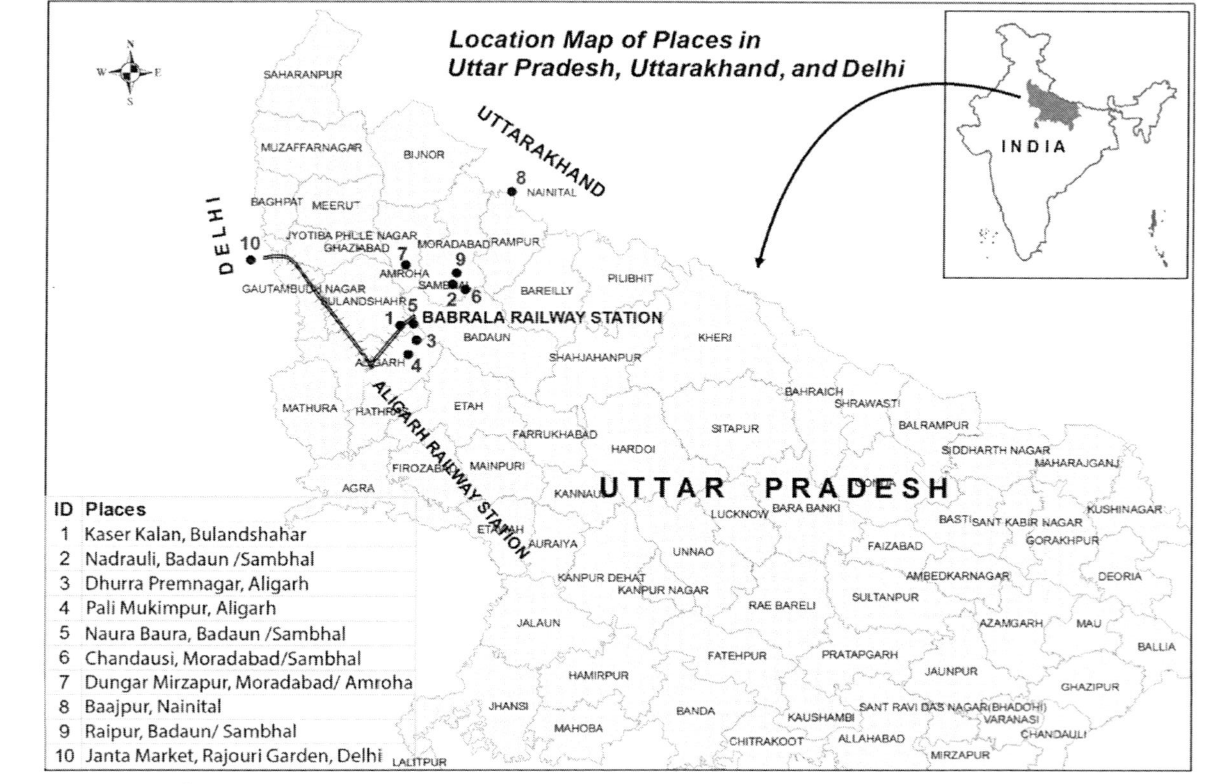

Source: J.P. Singh.
Note: Map not to scale and does not represent authentic international boundaries.

My Childhood on My Shoulders

SHEORAJ SINGH BECHAIN

Translated from Hindi by

Deeba Zafir and Tapan Basu

Oxford University Press is a department of the University of Oxford. It furthers the University's objective of excellence in research, scholarship, and education by publishing worldwide. Oxford is a registered trademark of Oxford University Press in the UK and in certain other countries.

Published in India by
Oxford University Press
2/11 Ground Floor, Ansari Road, Daryaganj, New Delhi 110 002, India

First published in Hindi by Vani Prakashan, India, in 2009
This English translation published by Oxford University Press in 2018

ISBN-13: 978-0-19-947929-0
ISBN-10: 0-19-947929-1

Typeset in Berling LT Std 10/13.5
by Tranistics Data Technologies, New Delhi 110 044
Printed in India by Rakmo Press, New Delhi 110 020

To my children
Ajatika and Ayush

Contents

Acknowledgements

First and foremost we thank Vani Prakashan, New Delhi, the publishers of the original manuscript in Hindi, for granting permission for the publication of the translation.

I wish to thank Mini Krishnan for discovering me and persisting with me over the years. I shall remain forever obliged to her for the keen interest she has shown in my work and the Dalit cause. As a matter of fact, Miniji read the first translation of the extracts of my autobiography which featured in a serial form in the *Tehelka* weekly, even before it was brought out by Vani Prakashan as a book. Thanks are due to Amitsen Gupta too for introducing my work to an English readership. I am also thankful to my translators, Tapanji and Deebaji, for their dedicated efforts in bringing out this English version. I wish to also acknowledge my wife Rajat Rani Meenu, my companion since 1990, for her understanding and cooperation.

—Sheoraj Singh Bechain

Both of us would also like to acknowledge Mini Krishnan, friend and mentor, who introduced us to the book and its author, and encouraged us with the conviction that we were the best people to undertake the task of translation. We owe much to Mini for her expert tips as well as sage advice to us on the intricacies of translation, particularly of a Dalit text from its original language into English.

To Sheorajji, for believing in our capacity to undertake this task.

—Deeba Zafir and Tapan Basu

Individually, I would like to thank Tapan, for his magnanimity in letting me be a part of the book that he had begun. I gratefully acknowledge Ammi for her prayers, Naghma for her strength, Tarun for his constant encouragement, Preeti for her support, and all those who stood by me. And Sanaa and Najam for their forebearance.

—Deeba Zafir

To Deeba, for stepping in to retrieve and put in shape a project that had been proceeding, for several years, in fits and starts.

To Rekha and Bonny, my closest companions, who therefore have to bear each day of their lives, the brunt of my moods and dispositions, pleasant and unpleasant.

—Tapan Basu

Introduction

Written in Hindi, and already translated into Punjabi and Urdu, Sheoraj Singh Bechain's autobiography, *Mera Bachpan Mere Kandhon Par*, is a paradigmatic life story of a member of one of India's numerous Dalit castes. Bechain's book is an extended narrative of his struggle against social disabilities imposed on him by birth. Born into a family of Chamars (animal skin and leather workers), and, therefore, stigmatized as an 'untouchable' within the framework of India's caste society, all through his childhood Bechain was constrained to also bear the burden of acute economic hardship. Indeed, it is the image of a young boy weighed down by manifold pressures of life that gives Bechain's book its title.

A whole new world of the Chamars stands revealed in Bechain's life narrative, in all its 'terrible beauty'. The gruesome task of dealing with dead cattle upon which the sustenance of his community depends is hereditarily determined but the forced nature of this labour renders it reprehensible even to its practitioners. Notwithstanding the inhuman levels of poverty to which the community is reduced, the author brings out the inherent dignity of this labour of skinning and tanning, which work is referred to as both 'art' and 'science' on account of the skill and care required in carrying it out. As the author points out, 'No negligible expertise was in order to fulfil these chores. These tasks did not require bookish knowledge, even though society looks up to book-learning as respectable while regarding the task of lifting carcasses as reprehensible. Any Brahmin would fail in this test.'

The author also highlights the conundrum faced by the Chamar community, of which many gave up their hereditary professions and began calling themselves Jatavs but had no alternative means of livelihood to fall back on. Despite being as impoverished as the rest of the Chamars, these Jatavs practised a form of untouchability against those who continued to lift dead cattle, creating yet another sub-caste amongst the Chamars themselves. The othering impulse, which is innate to the caste system, produced yet another set of outcastes, among whom the author's family itself featured. Even though the author, in the ten-year period that this narrative covers, tries his hand at many professions in order to sustain himself, he often turns to lifting carcasses and skinning them on the sly to earn a bit of money on the side. One of the many episodes that leave a deep impression on the reader is when, as a schoolgoing child, the author hides a scraper that he uses for skinning inside his schoolbag. He is unable to concentrate on his studies and his mind is thrown into a conflict that stems from the fear of its discovery by his classmates, which would result in his expulsion as also his belief that the goddess of learning might make an exit from his books.

Although a minor presence in the narrative, it is the centenarian Kaare Baba, a distant relative of the author, whose views prevail. As Kaare Baba, who worked as a tanner all his life and prospered through this profession to not only go on to acquire land but also educate his children—all of whom are well settled—tells the author, 'If I change my profession, will my caste change? ... Processed leather is now being exported by Brahmins and Banias. Now the owners of Bata Company are not declared Chamars, nor are they treated as untouchables by the Brahmins.' He concludes by reciting an interesting rhyme:

Does anyone call Tata a Luhar, or Bata a Chamar?
The hatred of our own leather work has kept us below par.

Thus, Bechain's book is an attempt to reclaim Chamar pride and tracks it through the first stirrings of self-respect that the author as a child begins to experience when confronted with the scourge of untouchability.

This chronicle of his early experiences, which has been endorsed as an extremely powerful example of protest literature by Mahasweta Devi, the eminent Jnanpith Award–winning author and public intellectual, commences with the tragic loss of a parent which afflicts the already trouble-torn existence of the child called Sauraj and his siblings. Suddenly rendered fatherless, the three children are left to the mercy of an adverse fortune in the shape of their dislocation from their ancestral homestead in Nadrauli, in the Badaun district of western Uttar Pradesh. Their mother is married off by her father, in quick succession, to a second husband, Ramlal, and then to a third husband, Bhikarilal. In Bhikarilal's household, comprising him and his two unmarried brothers—Daalchand and Chhotelal—the three children are subject to much suffering. Sauraj is all but recruited as an apprentice to a gang of robbers by his criminally inclined step-uncle, Daalchand. His stepfather, Bhikarilal, a leather worker, like many of Sauraj's blood relations, enrols him, along with Roop Singh, his own son by his first marriage, in the local school in the village of Pali Mukimpur in Aligarh district. However, since Roop Singh does not display the academic promise that Sauraj does, Sauraj invites upon himself the wrath of his stepfather, who one day summarily burns all his books. His books destroyed, Sauraj nevertheless looks for opportunities to resume his studies. Indeed, his sheer desperation in this regard prompts him to steal one rupee from the kurta pocket of Daalchand, who is a small-time gambler. Unfortunately, the crime is discovered and attributed to Sauraj's mother. The poor woman is thrashed mercilessly for a misdeed of which she has no knowledge at all.

The child Sauraj does not admit to it for the fear of meeting with a similar fate. Even as he daubs turmeric on her back, Sauraj notes, 'I felt as if the letters of the alphabet were imprinted on my mother's back and Amma herself became transformed into a text.' In what seems to be a syncopated moment in the narrative, the author fuses two perspectives that are separated over a period of time. For the child, who is obsessed with the thought of learning, even the bruises on his mother's back remind him of the book he hoped to purchase. For the adult narrator though, the 'text' becomes a metaphor for the patriarchal inscription in which he also sees himself as implicated. It is the mother who along with him bears the brunt of his aspirations. He holds himself guilty not only in this case but also later, for his inability to look after her in his single-minded pursuit of acquiring an education. As he mulls over her death, he interrogates his own motives:

> And then there was me. Was I any different from her? ... We were both victims of circumstances in our own ways but even then I continue to reproach myself. On what grounds could I keep my morale high? Should I reason that had I not given up wage labour, there would have been no beginning to literacy in our family? Or should I say that had I not done what I did, neither I nor Amma would have survived? Whatever I could make of myself after I left Amma to die, and have been able to speak on behalf of the Chamar community in the form of this narrative, should I be proud of it? Or should I believe that my life narrative poses a question about the entire Chamar community to which there is no answer in this century?

This self-questioning foregrounds not just the author's individual predicament but also that of his whole community who have been bypassed by the entire narrative of progress in independent India and of which the women of the community have been the worst victims.

Given the overall social context of patriarchal domination within which he was born and brought up, it is remarkable that Bechain's personal narrative provides the space it does to women, particularly those who played important parts, big or small, in his life. His account of the past records a deep sensitivity towards women's struggles, despite occasional lapses into stereotypical male sentiment. Most noteworthy is the description of gender-centric hardships of the two women closest to him, his mother and sister, their utter dependence on their husbands, and the crises of survival when they find themselves without supportive male companions.

There is hardly any help proffered to either woman by their extended families, not because kinship ties have loosened but because of the deprivations which dog the lives of all untouchables alike. The silver lining in the shape of his sister's marriage to a man of some property is soon clouded over by the unexpected death of her husband. The poignant description of the sense of despair of the relatives as they arrange for the last rites of the deceased in the face of their lack of resources in the impersonal city of Delhi is among the most touching portions of the record.

In fact, the travails of poverty sharpen the torments of discrimination on the basis of caste. Bechain inimitably remarks upon the accentuation of caste divisions hand-in-hand with the increase of economic disparities in Indian society despite the enactment of an egalitarian constitution of the nation. Even in this era of democracy, past the last post of the twentieth century, Bechain avers that his family still remains moored in a sixteenth-century cultural milieu. His aspirations to education abruptly aborted, Sauraj is sent to work as a labourer at a brick kiln. On the trajectory of downward mobility in his career during this phase of his existence, the narrator of this piece of life writing observes: 'After Independence, the condition of Dalits worsened in direct proportion to the increase of the affluence of the savarnas as has the hostility between castes. Along with caste distinctions, economic faultlines have also grown deeper.'

A few years later, Sauraj returns to Delhi to earn a livelihood after several unsuccessful attempts at sustaining himself in the countryside where, as an agricultural labourer, he did not even receive subsistence wages and was subjected to the direst of denials. In Delhi, to use Sauraj's own words, he finds himself treading with 'small steps in a large world'. He takes up employment as an assistant to skilled masons at construction sites but is unable to tolerate the high-handedness of his overseers. He quits the job and becomes a newspaper delivery boy. This assignment too does not last very long. He endeavours to make both ends meet by becoming a hawker of lemons and eggs, at the same time tries to educate himself by attending a night-shift school. A philanthropically inclined Sikh couple proposes to his mother that they will finance his studies but they are met with stiff resistance from the hapless, unlettered woman. A childhood spent travelling in search of work, Bechain recounts the several escapades and adventures, in which he narrowly escapes being sexually assaulted and is, at one point, nearly killed. As he points out, 'Education was the birdfeed, in reaching out for which, I, like a pigeon, would always be ensnared in one or the other mesh of exploitation.'

Failing to fend for his family and for himself through his meagre income in the city, he returns to Nadrauli, his native village, yet again. His schooling is suspended till, providentially, his uncanny talent for weaving words into rhymes, a manifestation of his potential for learning, catches the attention of a village schoolmaster named Prempal Singh Yadav. A landed farmer as well, Prempal Singh offers to enlist Sauraj as a student at his school if he would stay at his house and help with the chores on the fields. The deal is struck, though on terms entirely in favour of the shrewd Prempal Singh, who exploits Sauraj's industriousness to the hilt while enjoying the gratitude due to a mentor.

Of Prempal Singh, the author states, 'His contribution in my own life was of a contradictory nature. He had set me in the direction of acquiring an education and that was a debt I could not repay. All the same, it cannot be forgotten that he thoroughly exploited my physical labour.' Though the Arya Samajists in the village encourage him to pursue studies, mere sustenance remains a challenge throughout. Even Prempal Singh's homilies about the ascetic condition of a scholar's life begin to sound hollow to the author, who is made to work hard on his fields and at home, and yet his requirements are never fully addressed. As he points out, 'Eventually, my exploitation began to be disagreeable to me. Why was it not a sin to exploit labour? How could oppression coexist with devotion to God? Why could I not find a solution to my problem in Dayanand Saraswati's *Satyartha Prakash*?' However, even in these difficult circumstances, Sauraj—renamed Sheoraj by his 'Massaab'—resumes his schooling, starting now at class six and notwithstanding many hurdles, pulls on till the tenth class. He finally clears his matriculation examination in 1978 at the age of eighteen and signs off with a generous gesture towards Prempal Singh: 'A remarkable teacher had unconsciously laid a good foundation for the future.'

This saga of a Dalit child's quest for education is rendered in a diction which derives from the folk language of the territory in and around his native region. Sauraj's blind Tau is a seminal presence and also a formative influence on the author. He is an exemplary exponent of the orality of the subculture of the Chamars. It is significant that the Chamars offer prayers to a different pantheon of gods and goddesses, and the subversive potential of the lyrics and ballads which Tau sings harks back to an anti-Brahminical strain embodied in the verses of Kabir and Raidas. It is this tradition that Bechain imbibes from the Tau, which leads him to question, 'I wondered at what ultimately was the measure of the so-called wisdom of the Brahmins? What kind of tree of Brahminical knowledge was it that had only produced the fruit of inequality?' Tau's song is a case in point:

O Peers! The Brahmins ruined our garden.
Neither any wisdom imparted,
Nor any reforms started,
O Peers! The Brahmins ruined our garden.

At another level, the narrative also recounts the tentative beginnings of the making of the author and the literary influences that shape Bechain's writings. Later, it is through his role model, Bhai Saab, that he gains exposure to communist literature and the writings of the Progressive Writers, especially those of Urdu, which leave a lasting impression on his literary idiom. Thus, the child protagonist's quest for an education not only makes him literate but also paves the way for him to become an exponent of literature.

The overall structure of Bechain's autobiography gives the impression of a journalistic account with its use of headings and subheadings, which may well be seen as the principle of selection of what is essentially a memory text. Memory plays a key role in which the adult narrator attempts to recreate a child's experiences of a largely peripatetic life. The early traumatic loss of his father and its lasting consequences for the author and his family, along with the people and places that leave an indelible mark on his memory, are recorded in all their blurred and vivid details. Not just at an individual level but also in terms of collective memory, Bechain takes up the issue of the complete absence of a history of his people and the need to write one. The author attempts to chart a lineage and establish a sense of legacy, even if it is one of exploitation and destitution.

Perhaps the ultimate compliment to Bechain's book has been paid by Dr Dharamvir, fellow Dalit writer from the Hindi belt, who has penned an entire book on it, entitled *Baalak Sheoraj: Maha Shilakhando ka Sangram*. Apart from the applause which he heaps on this extraordinary bildungsroman of a subaltern subject, he points out that Bechain is able to hold up for his readers a mirror through which they might see images of the everyday existence of the Chamars. In this sense, *Mera Bachpan Mere Kandhon Par* is no less than a rich archive of material on the life and times of one of the most significant under-caste communities. Through the text, Sheoraj Singh Bechain has brought into focus not only the emergent genre of the Dalit autobiography in Hindi but also a powerful and prolific tradition of writing by Chamars whose lineage can be traced back to the beginnings of Dalit print culture in the United Provinces and its contiguous territories since the early decades of the twentieth century. No wonder, Bechain has more than once, in his discursive writings, acknowledged his debt to this tradition, especially to the writings of Swami Acchutanand 'Harihar', the doyen of Dalit Hindi writers from north India, on whose extensive corpus of work Bechain has penned an entire monograph. Bechain is thus both a product as well as an embodiment of a vibrant Dalit literary culture in the so-called Hindi heartland.

Bechain's autobiography occupies a prominent place in the rich counter-canonical body of Dalit writing that has carved out for itself an oppositional and alternative discursive space by contesting established representations in the dominant Hindi literary tradition. Badri Narayan's formulation of the making of Dalit public in north India was later developed by scholars like Sarah Beth Hunt and Laura Brueck into considering Dalit literary production as the construction of a counter public, of which this book forms an important cornerstone. Having entered into the mainstream and now prescribed in the syllabi of many universities across the country, the 'consumption' of Bechain's autobiography by metropolitan readers in itself involves an act of translation. Bechain's book chips away at our received notions of reading literature and exposes the insularity of urban-middle-class perceptions. Redefining the very parameters of what constitutes literature, Bechain's book is part of the Dalit literary movement that has militated against the authority of the hegemonic Hindi literary world. Therefore, the translation of this text involved not just a representation of the original in another language but also a representation of an excluded segment in the traditionally insular sphere of 'literature'.

Translation often entails a transformation which has been construed as involving, in a small or large measure, a quantum of 'loss'. In the case of translating a Dalit text, however, the gains, as suggested by Sharmila Rege in the introduction to her book *Writing*

Caste, Writing Gender: Narrating Dalit Women's Testimonios, far outweigh the deficit. The translators found their task akin to a form of activism wherein an intervention is made into the public sphere by introducing a text that has no parallel in the target language. It must, however, be added that the translators' activism is largely derived from the nature of Dalit writing itself, marked as it is by a strident expression against the long history of exclusion from domains of knowledge, both in terms of its access and forms of production. Thus, this content-driven choice of text shifts the emphasis for the translators from regarding their role as merely involving a linguistic transfer. Bechain's book is a compelling account about his hard-won right to self-articulation, and, therefore, its translation not only places his struggle in a larger cultural field but also enables the furtherance of the Dalit agenda of an alternative vision of human liberation.

It would be redundant to state that a source text in Hindi would have a completely different register than one in English, especially if substantial portions of it are in a dialect and also include folk songs. The double-frame narrative device that Bechain employs plays out two different voices; one of the adult Sheoraj, who uses standardized Hindi in a stark and simple prose, interspersed by poems that mark the turning points of his journey. The other voice is that of the child Sauraj, who speaks the language of his people—the Khadar Boli, a dialect spoken in the areas surrounding Badaun. The folk songs and ballads which the blind Tau recites will appear in this dialect and it is to them that the author traces the origins of his poetic sensibility. However, the switch of registers from standardized Hindi to dialect is lost in translation. Nevertheless, it is hoped that some of the cadence and rhythm has been captured and conveyed in the translated text.

The one term that confounds translation and recurs consistently is 'savarna', a word which literally means of the same colour, form or appearance, kind, race, articulation, or spelling, and, more importantly, as belonging to the same caste. It has come to be a shorthand to refer to the 'upper' castes in general. Often translated as the dominant or privileged caste, in the context of this autobiography, the author uses the term 'savarna' to refer to those castes that belong to the Hindu fold, clearly seeing himself as an outcast who falls outside it. While having little to do with Brahmins per se, the author's experience of untouchability as well as exploitation at the hands of the Yadavs of the village, compounded by the outcasting by his own community, constitutes the core of this text. However, the Yadavs themselves belong to the 'other backward castes' category and yet, as the author points out, they were 'more hypocritical, superstitious, and greater exponents of savarna culture than Brahmins'.

The other terms that remain untranslated in the text are those which are either region-specific or for which no English equivalent could be found. These include food items, names of trees, fish, utensils, customs, measures, and sundry other items, whose meanings, it is hoped, are clearly brought out by the context itself. The references to mythological characters and texts, religious movements and related personages, and poets and literary works are presumed to be familiar to any reader of Indian literature. The terms that relate to tanning, skinning, and leather work, as well as agricultural implements and technique, have been translated as best as possible so as to not impede comprehension.

The translators have worked in close collaboration with the author who has sanctioned the excisions, editing, and even minor restructuring of what was originally a vast and digressive narrative in order to produce a more condensed and concise English version. It is hoped then that the exercise of translation, which is often addled by the vocabulary of 'loss', has, in this case, been more about gain.

DEEBA ZAFIR
TAPAN BASU

An Untimely Death

'O the gardener departed before his time'

It has been almost thirty years since my paternal uncles, Beedhe Phupha and Gangawasi, earned their livelihood through petty business in scavenging, skinning carcasses of cattle, and trading in the remains of the dead beasts. Well into the twenty-first century, Gangawasi continues to be engaged in very much the same occupations and his home is still the same ramshackle, dilapidated dwelling in which my father had passed away. Nothing seems to have changed. The brothers had a small, ancestral mud hut outside the village, surrounded by the larger pukka homes of Jats with much bigger courtyards. Phupha took care to conduct his dealings in cattle skins in a very clandestine manner because the Hindus resented his practice. In order to prevent the stench of the skins from spreading, he would sprinkle salt on them. Despite such precautions, he found it necessary to stack his goods outside the precincts of the village.

The Chamars who had given up picking carcasses had begun to regard themselves as belonging to a higher social stratum, whereas their economic condition was as bad as ours. These Dalits were in favour of finding new possibilities by changing their occupation. The savarnas had neither the experience nor the compulsions to drive them towards these occupations. Indeed, the very reference to these chores was considered contaminating. In the immaculate surroundings of their daily lives, this was an inconvenient element.

To further their own vocation, the two brothers and their father erected a tiny mud hut in the jungles far removed from the habitation of their village. Near the hut, a small well was dug and a hovel-like home had been set up. Gangawasi, who was newly married, began to live in this house with his wife, Maanti. Gangawasi and Beedhe

Phupha's sister was about to get married. We at Nadrauli village had been invited to join the festivities. My Tau, Baburam, was blind, as were my two Babbas, Gangi and Bhagirath. Bidharam Babba was lame; my father and Baburam Tau were his sons. The children of my other Babbas had died prematurely. Of my two Dadis, the elder one had taken refuge in her mother's house and the younger one was no more. Thus, the only able-bodied member of the household, apart from my Tai and Amma, was my father Radheyshyam. Therefore, it was his responsibility to take the ceremonial gifts or '*bhaat*' for the wedding.

As soon as my father, whom I called 'Chacha', along with my uncles, started from home with a bundle on his head, I threw a tantrum demanding that I be allowed to accompany him. My sister Maya also cried a lot but was persuaded to stay back, while I remained adamant. As the eldest male child, I was considered to be the bearer of the family name and was, therefore, treated with more indulgence than Maya, although she was older to me. My father resolved to take me along with him and handed over his bundle to Pyare Chacha to put me on his shoulders. Amma followed us for quite a distance, grumbling, trying to tempt me with all sorts of things that might allure a child. Even Tau supported her. However, my father assured him, 'We are all going together. We shall take turns in carrying Sauraj. He will see the wedding and meet his Choti Bua as well. He has not met her for many years and she too is extremely fond of him.'

Many years have passed since then. Now I myself am the father of two children—a daughter, Ajatika, who is twelve years of age, and a son, Ayush, who is ten. I was approximately half his age at that time. Yet, even today the affection-filled outline of my father's face is recorded very clearly in my memory. The details of his features are perhaps lost to me, but I still retain a sense of what he looked like. The story of the loss of my father is one of devastation and destruction. A tall man of thin frame, my loving father carried me on his shoulders all the way to Bua's village. I do not know why I remember that ride on his shoulders, considering that I have forgotten so many things, including experiences most bitter. The short-lived bonding with my father on that occasion remains indelibly stamped on my mind. Like every other child, I probably valued parental love more than anything else. Perhaps, it was from my childhood onwards that I grew more sombre and responsible, as love and affection were snatched away from me and I was deprived of the barest necessities of life. I cannot recall the exact date or year of this event and there is no way to find out the details. My aunts, uncles, and other members of my extended family, including their children, are all unlettered; so are my Bua's in-laws. Her extended family earns its subsistence through the traditional occupations of the Chamars. Bypassed by literacy and literature, culture, and civilization of a developing world, they inhabit a separate, extremely backward world which has for centuries been outcaste and denigrated by society.

In those days, we journeyed by foot as we did not own bullock-carts like the privileged castes of our village and it took a whole day to reach my Bua's village. Everything we did then—even a dip in Ramghat Ganga—aroused my childish curiosity. Today I can relive those moments only in my imagination, or recreate them by recovering a few threads from their texture. These include my first-ever journey by boat.

On reaching Dhurra Premnagar that evening, we put on our new clothes and waited for the *baraati*s to arrive. The ceremonies were to be performed on the outskirts of the village in the mud hut in which Maanti and Gangawasi lived. I sat on my father's lap under its thatched roof and he was served a drink laced with sugar. As someone carrying the *bhaat*, my father, according to ritual, was fasting that day. I was looked after by my Bua who washed my feet, hands, and mouth, and fed me some sweets. By the time the marriage had been solemnized, it was quite late. I cannot recollect at what point in my slumberous condition I was put to bed and near whom. On waking up around midnight, I searched for my father but could not find him. I began howling when I saw several people gathered around my father. He had taken ill very suddenly through exposure to the night air. He had gone out to relieve himself when suddenly he started to throw up and found it difficult to speak. Both my Bua and Phupha were with him but there was no medical help at hand. My Bua was in a state of acute panic. Weeping aloud, she protested that my father had been forced to drink when he had no wish to.

The dark night on which it happened seemed long and terrible and we witnessed it fade away in the light of a clay lamp. I had lost my sleep altogether and had begun to cry as I watched my father repeatedly overcome with sickness. Sitting close, I clung to him. Even in his discomfort, he stroked my head affectionately. My Bua took me in her arms. It was the hour of daybreak. My Phupha had instructed that I should be taken away but I did not want to be separated from my father and refused to sit with anybody else.

My father was throwing up continuously and by morning his condition was critical. As a mere child of five or six years, I could only be a helpless and horror-stricken onlooker of this scene. The fear which gripped me that night still remains. There are several such fears that are deeply entrenched within me but this has seeped into my consciousness. The customary remedies were tried—the usual charms, incantations, and appeasement of deities. Not one appropriate modern measure was taken to cure him. To suggest that this was deliberately done would be to charge them with neglect. The fact was that these villagers were victims of utmost ignorance and obscurantism. A majority of them contended that my father had been possessed by the evil spirit who inhabited the crossroads outside the house when he was in the act of relieving himself there and that he would not be rid of his torture till an accomplished exorcist invoked a mightier spirit to counter the spell cast upon him. Pyare Chacha was sure that the evil spirit could be exorcised by Makhan and Khacheri, the renowned 'wisemen' of Nadrauli. If only they could be fetched, the most formidable of spirits would be defeated. We believed that our gods were more powerful than any other and these misconceptions persist in our community even today.

The next day a team of exorcists from a neighbouring village was called. As soon as he saw my father, the team leader declared that the patient was in the clasp of no ordinary spirit. The evil spirit who haunted the crossroads was an adversary to reckon with and in this instance was also accompanied by a few she-demons. Hence, an incessant beating of *thali*s for two to three days by the congregation and whipping of the afflicted person was prescribed. Immediately, a thali was fitted to the mouth of an earthen pot and its beating matched with the notes of devotional music intended to drive away the evil spirit. This form of exorcism has been prevalent among the Chamars of our region for centuries.

Three exorcists, in unison, had invoked the spirits upon themselves. Swaying wildly and with strange gesticulations, they swept their arms through the air to plant the soundest of slaps on my father's cheeks. Imagining the slap to be directed against the evil spirit in possession of my father, my Bua and Phupha repeatedly thrust my ailing and bedridden father towards the exorcists. The spectacle of their blind faith in the spirits and the extreme cruelty towards the afflicted was moving enough to melt the hardest of hearts. Although Kalavati Bua had intervened to plead, 'Take my brother to town', no one heeded her pleas. She always held that it was Beedhe's obduracy that had killed her brother. As time elapsed, my father's condition deteriorated further. He needed prompt and correct medical attention; instead a team of exorcists were inflicting a series of physical torments on him. My father had been pulled out of bed and laid on the ground. It was the general opinion of the crowd which had gathered around him that it was the spirit that haunted the crossroads which was being thrashed by the exorcists and not my father. Not one among the gathering could appreciate the import of the tears which the dreadful pain brought to my father's eyes. I was his flesh and blood, but was in no position to come to his aid. As I watched my father being repeatedly slapped by the exorcists and sometimes whipped by them, I clung to him. He kept repeating, 'I have not been possessed by any spirit. Get me a doctor. Don't kill me while I'm still alive.'

Instead of listening to his appeal, the exorcists silenced him by slapping and whipping him harder. My father would open his eyes hoping to find some support, only to have them brimming with tears of agony as a result of the pain that was being inflicted upon him. This sequence continued not merely for a couple of hours but for full three days. Dhurra and its neighbouring villages were agog with the news that exorcists were in full play against a spirit that had invaded a Chamar home. Ordinarily, the other castes would not intervene in our affairs, deeming us to be inhabitants of another universe. Nevertheless, on this occasion, all and sundry came together to watch what was happening in the Chamar locality. This congregation of people, who shared a belief in the supernatural would hardly pay attention to, let alone be convinced, by arguments to the contrary.

Bua's brother-in-law, Gangawasi, had been hidden away behind the verandah, lest those who were haunting my father find their next victim in him. Ultimately, he was sent off to Nadrauli under the pretext of getting my mother to Dhurra. Pyare Chacha instructed, 'Get Khacheri and Makhan from our village so that together they might rid our Radhey of the spirit of the crossroads.'

For three days, the extended family of my Bua, including her in-laws, provided full hospitality to the team of exorcists. These men, if incensed, could themselves become the spirits incarnate, as awful and cruel as the invisible spirit they had been engaged to outwit. As it was, they were venting their spleen on my father's person. I had neither the foresight nor the agency to stall the disaster that they were about to usher into my life. Each time my Bua or some other relative attempted to draw me away from the scene. I rushed back to my father's side. In the name of offering prayers, the exorcists kept adding various sacred ingredients such as cloves and desi ghee to the little fires they had lit. Offerings were prepared and distributed in accordance with the stature of the deities.

My second Bua, Mano, on learning about my father's precarious condition had also come over from Pali. Of an overly sensitive disposition, she was deeply affected by the tragic turn of events. On the evening of the third day, Gangawasi returned with the report that quite a few members of our family were also going to arrive. Only the last few breaths were left in my father's body. I felt utterly dejected by the inhuman atmosphere that had been generated in the house over the last three or four days. How I wished that somebody would retrieve my father's life from the hands of these murderers who were operating in the guise of physicians. I hoped that my mother and others of my family would rescue him once they came from the village. With this eager expectation, I would sometimes rush out to await the prospect of aid and sometimes run in to observe my father. Maanti endeavoured to placate me and even though nobody was yet in sight, I came and whispered into my father's ear, 'Amma will be with us soon', and promptly ran outdoors again.

It was night by the time Dayaram Chacha and Baburam Tau arrived with Khacheri and Makhan. Amma was to follow later, as my younger brother Rambharose had been born just a few weeks before. She also had to look after the other child, Neksingh, who was barely a year old, apart from the other physically impaired members of her family. Given their limitations, they were incapable of doing a journey by foot, and a bullock-cart journey was beyond their means. In the face of this emergency, however, they had to somehow make their way to Dhurra. That evening, the exorcists, sensing that their patient, far from being freed of the spirit of the crossroads, was nearly at the point of death, discreetly collected the tools of their trade as well as the wages for three days of labour and, one by one, disappeared from the scene. Even at this point, Phupha did not make any effort to call a doctor to examine my father. What his constraints were I do not know, except that he had no faith in the system of modern medicine.

In the evening, the sun had set and darkness descended. Fearing an inauspicious interruption in the celebrations, the *baraat*, which was to leave after breakfast the following day, was given a hurried send-off. The bride would be blighted for life if something untoward were to befall my father. People were more concerned about the ominous consequences of my father's apprehended demise than his terrible plight. In the moment of parting, with tension hanging in the air, as the bride crossed the threshold of her dwelling with the faintest of steps, with like unwillingness, from the same thatched cottage, my father's life ebbed out of him.

Even as my mother walked into the premises at the hour of nightfall, the sun of our family had all but set as my father's body was lifted out of the charpoy and laid on the floor. Every member of the family felt the descent of darkness in the room. A two-fold shroud of darkness had begun to envelop me. A few gasps of breath were still left in my father's body. Its shell was bloodied and swollen due to the assaults on it by the exorcists. 'My brother died due to Beedhe's foolishness,' Kalavati Bua had announced. Sitting near my father, the sightless Baburam Tau kept on grasping my father's arm, while my nerve-wracked mother hung on to his neck. Bereft of speech though he was, he expressed a desire to look at me one last time. To gratify his wish, Pyare Chacha led me to him.

But even as my father tried to communicate to Amma through the language of tears, his end had come. It was as if a flourishing garden had been blighted before the arrival of spring, with the passing away of the gardener. As the import of what had happened came home to her, Amma fell prostrate on the ground. Her loud laments were echoed by my Tau and Babba. My Bua's mother-in-law took charge of my younger brother from Amma, whose bangles were removed and broken. The spectacle of children weeping was not unfamiliar to me, but this was the first time I saw so many adults in tears. The eldest of my three grandfathers too was sobbing pitifully. But strangely enough, no one seemed to be directing any of their ire at all towards the exorcists. Their ignorance prevented them from holding the exorcists responsible for my father's untimely death. I had come to the wedding happily astride the shoulders of my father but now after his death was returning from here bearing my own childhood on my shoulders.

In the morning, the corpse was to be taken to the Ramghat adjoining the Ganga. All that I had witnessed over the previous couple of days had so terrorized me that my mind was benumbed with dread. For several months afterwards, according to Amma, I would mutter in my sleep, 'Don't kill my father. Please leave him alone.' I frequently relived the horror in my dreams. Probably, the malady of incontinence too, which afflicted me for many years, started during that period.

It was a gloomy morning the next day, one which I have been never able to forget. In the interlude of forty years, there have been many mornings and evenings and not all of them were full of joy either, but somehow that morning imprinted itself on my consciousness as a morning just gone by. I wonder why that melancholic and distressful morning has become so deeply entrenched in my memory! Why am I still enveloped in its darkness? But then, why must I rely on someone else's account? Don't I have my own memories of the past? Perhaps they are shadowy but at least they belong to me. So what if they are only fragments that I have managed to retrieve from the ruins of my past?

My father's body was lifted by the men on their shoulders. The same man on whose shoulders I had travelled to Dhurra four days ago was now going on his last journey on the shoulders of others.

The feet of the corpse were supposed to face the Ganga, where the cremation ground was situated. It was believed that the demons which had possessed the dead would also take leave in that direction and not come back. A Jat Choudhary's bullock cart was hired and firewood for the cremation was loaded onto this vehicle. Amma with Rambharose in her lap and I perched atop the firewood. For me, it was an indelible spectacle. It was not that death itself was a novelty or that this was a unique fate; the poignancy centred upon the fate of the dependants that the dead had left behind. Amma seemed to have lost her laughter for all times to come and remained sombre till the end as she battled the crises of her life. For months afterwards, she would weep while remembering my father, almost singing out her woes in the manner of a dirge, 'Who will tend to your garden now, o gardener? The flowers will wilt before their time and scatter hither, thither, o gardener!'

As per custom, Bidharam Babba sat with his face turned away from the body of his son at one corner of the bullock-cart. Although we were considered outcastes by our community, the funeral procession was nevertheless accompanied for a while at least by some junior and senior members, including womenfolk of the Dhurra community. 'Radhey has died young, he will surely return to haunt us as a ghost,' Phupha continued to talk in this vein for several years thereafter. Like us, Phupha and his brothers had been excommunicated in their village, since they continued to work with animal carcasses and they had no truck with those Chamars who had become Jatavs by giving up leather work. The Chamars had as many dissensions between themselves as did the dominant castes, but from the point of view of the dominant castes we were all equally untouchable. Yet a handful of them from our village came for the last rites of my father, to show their solidarity with us in this critical moment of death.

At Ramghat the hearse was untied so that the deceased could be given a final bath, after which everyone was asked to take a final look. Bidharam Babba's eyes were filled with extreme pathos, while Bhagirath Babba, Gangi Babba, and Baburam Tau, being sightless, had to be led to the dead man's face. They felt his features with the touch of their palms, stroking his ears, nose, and lifeless cheeks, and bidding his soul rest in heaven in a final farewell. Traditionally, funeral processions did not include women, as it was believed it would bring ill-fortune to all concerned, but Amma set aside convention and stood in our midst, after which nobody insisted that she leave the scene.

Somebody made me place an ember in one of the hands of the corpse. Holding me close to himself, my Tau passed on to me a flaming torch, intoning, 'Son, now light your father's pyre. Do not cry while doing so, or else your father will descend to hell.' It was the popular belief that a father whose pyre had been lit by his son would ascend to heaven and his soul would rest in peace. With a heart filled with sorrow, I lit my father's pyre, and having done so sat with the others staring wordlessly at the heart-rending spectacle. I saw the body of my father wither away in front of my eyes, but my eyes were totally dry. I stood aghast. This sight was stamped in my memory for years afterwards. People die and their invaluable persons are consigned to flames by their own people—this realization was borne out by my first and most personal experience. On the sands of the Ganga, at that moment, Amma's lap was my only refuge. A measure of how horror-stricken I was by all that I had been enjoined to perform, and how strangely affected my mind had become by the turn of events, is that till today I am unable to expunge the traces of those occurrences from my memory. Often, when I relive my moments of loneliness, the memories of that unfortunate day appear before me in all their glaring clarity. It seems to me that it was only the other day that I cremated the body of my father. Very often on occasions of other cremations attended by me, it has happened that when I suddenly recall the cremation of my father, I grow extremely restless.

At that time, my mother was wailing aloud as Babba counselled, 'Mukhi Beta, you need to steel your heart. My son has left behind three miniatures of himself. It is your responsibility to safeguard their interests. There is a lifetime ahead of you to shed your tears. Think of your children instead.' He was, of course, counting only sons, although Maya, my sister, was the eldest child.

After the cremation, everyone present went for a dip and all other social obligations were fulfilled. Before we left the cremation site, Mano Bua ensured that the clothes taken off from my father's body were immersed in the waters of the river. It was believed that if the clothes were passed on to someone, the demons which plagued Radhe would settle on that person and if they were burnt, the evil spirits would get angry and return to destroy others.

A few days later, my mother and I travelled almost twenty kilometres on foot, pausing to rest at intervals, to reach Rajghat Narora. Her face had lost its glow and she walked with despondent steps. The very sight of her weeping related her tale of woes. I remember the rite involving the lighting of a lamp in my father's memory, which I was made to perform. A lamp was lit and set afloat on the waves of the Ganga. Even though it was a mere lamp, it was believed that the distance it travelled on the waters would determine the brightness of the fortunes of the deceased's descendants in the years to come. After our return to our village, on starry nights my mother would point her finger at the sky and say to me. 'Look Lalla, one of those stars shining up there is the soul of your father. See carefully how brightly he shines in the house of God.' In due time, all the formalities of bidding goodbye to the dead were over, and many a fanciful tale was spun to assist me in reconciling myself to my lot.

As the news of my father's demise spread, a procession of visitors started to arrive to condole with us in our hour of grief. My Nani, maternal and paternal aunts, and all those of the neighbourhood, along with all their children, visited us to proclaim their sympathy. Some even stayed on for a week. Subsequently, my mother would lament that the guests had devoured all of the one-and-a-half months of rations that she had managed to hoard for our family. In these troubled times, we had nobody to lean upon and despite the scarcity of resources, the people of our *basti* forced us to host a ritual feast for them on the thirteenth day after the death of my father. Even those Chamars who shunned us because we continued to deal with dead animals extracted from us the provisions due to them on this occasion and they cooked for themselves a separate meal with them. This further increased the burden of debts which we carried on our already-weak shoulders. Even my maternal relatives went away without pondering about how we would survive. Apart from lip-sympathy, no help of any kind from anybody was forthcoming.

I would wait everyday at the roadside to spot my father's face among the many faces of the people returning from the market at Junabai, but he was no longer among them. As dusk fell, Amma would come through the darkness looking for me. 'There you are, once again waiting for your father! How many times have I told you that your father is dead, and he will never come back? Nobody ever comes back from the dead. Death has claimed even gods such as Ram and Krishna. From now on, son, think of ways to feed yourself, take whatever work you get, eat whatever leftovers you find, wear whatever rags come your way, but never ask anybody for anything. Remember, no one will give you anything without extracting something in return.' Words of wisdom fell from my mother's lips, but I listened to them indifferently. Giving up on me, Amma would slap me hard on the cheek and drag me home by the hand, saying 'Did you not light the pyre with your own hands?'

My father had left behind a few pieces of jewellery that he had inherited on his marriage to my mother along with some implements for carrying and cutting the carcasses of cattle as well as the sundry tools used by a cobbler. He also left for us a ramshackle hut in which he processed leather from the skins of dead animals. By way of land, there was a plot of two bighas of barren soil, of which half belonged to my Tau. The produce from this field was worth less than even the seeds sown into it. Under these circumstances, agriculture was but an exercise in building castles in the air. This was the sum total of the legacy bequeathed to me by my late father, Shri Radheyshyam. It was as if he was challenging me. 'Pick up as many as you can of all the carcasses of the dead beasts of our village, waiting to be borne by your tender shoulders. If you are hungry, there is enough substance in these carcasses for you to fill your stomach. And if you want a pittance for wages, slave unconditionally for the zamindar, draw water for him and his family by driving bullocks round his well. Gather dung for their use and clear their garbage. So, you find yourself incapable of doing such chores? Then why stay on in this village? Except that your roots are entrenched here, in your ancestral home within the Chamar territory. But a mere home will not sustain you. To survive, you must flee. Why blame your ancestors? They have merely passed on to you the collective misfortunes they suffered.' Eventually, the little hut which could have been developed into a leather factory also collapsed and, like my father's body, turned into dust.

It was in this situation that my helpless, widowed mother reached her parental home in Chandausi with the three of us. My disabled Babbas and Tau could not support her for more than a few months. As I have mentioned earlier, the plot of land which we had to our name had been, over a period of time, divested of the unclaimed borders. Nevertheless, the field did produce some harvest which neighbours such as Amar Singh Yadav or Ramvir would either steal at night or set their cattle loose to graze upon. In sheer violation of boundaries, they poached upon our premises and continue to do so even today.

Now the pace of events quickened to hurl us to our ruin. Everybody was anxious about our future but its remedies were out of everybody's grasp. My father had been wedded before his teens and had not survived his early twenties. It was during this period of crisis that my younger brother, Neksingh, took sick and could not receive medical treatment. Medical treatment was a far cry indeed since he did not even get minimum nourishment in the shape of an adequate diet. Amma's own family was impoverished and ever on the verge of bankruptcy. All she could do by way of attending to my brother was to take him around to some local quacks, but to no avail. In the end, Neksingh passed away, painfully, bit by bit, in front of our eyes. Amma, invoking all her maternal love, had addressed his corpse thus, 'Son, forgive me. You remained unhappy while you lived. May you have a happy life in your next birth. May God bring peace to your soul. For us here, there is no difference between being dead or alive.'

During those days, we would stealthily collect the grains of wheat which stuck to the dung of bullocks in the process of treading. Even after washing and sifting the grains from the dung, the yellowness would make it difficult for us to consume it. My father's death, like the setting of the sun, had shrouded all the planets which revolved around him under a cover of darkness. Indeed, our poverty was so dire that my blind Babba was forced to scour around the village for any kind of work that he might have got—grinding grain, operating the straw-chopping machine or weaving twine for charpoys—sometimes for as meagre a wage as a jug of *mattha* and two rotis for work disproportionate to the payment.

All that time, it was only Dori Tau who continued to be a tanner and for lifting of carcasses he would require a couple of assistants, among whom he would inevitably marshal our Gangi Babba. His labour was cheap and he would shoulder the greater part of the weight than the others. In the lifting of a carcass on a pole, the lighter portion of the weight falls on the one whose shoulder carries the longer end than the one who carries the shorter end. Gangi Babba, being blind, was always loaded with the shorter end of the pole. And then, huffing and puffing, the old man would bear his burden, like a donkey accustomed to his chore. There and then, the carcass would be skinned and its flesh carved out. Apart from our own family, the extended family of Dori Tau sustained itself on the flesh from carcasses. After keeping for themselves the choicest portions, they would dispense the rest to us. At times, just the meat curry cooked by Dori Tau's wife, whom we called Mausi, would be passed on to us. Leaving aside our two families, the other Chamars we knew had ceased to trade in the carcasses of animals.

Now Babba, Tau, and I would, every morning, station ourselves in front of our house like saleable commodities. Perhaps somebody might hire us for a day—either as a field hand or as a coolie. Anything was fine as long as it gave us something to fill our stomachs with and also of those old and young at home. My delicate shoulders could not take the weight of the poles, so I helped the grown-ups by lending my support to the horns, legs, and tails of the dead animal in the hope of getting some of its flesh in return. I do not even recall when I graduated to putting the poles on my shoulders, thanks to the additional aspiration of earning a few annas. Thus began my informal apprenticeship in the line.

It was a most difficult task to transport the carcass of an animal from the home of its owner to the jungles far away. You could not drag it because dragging would damage the skin by leaving marks upon it, which would reduce its price by half. The risk of marks persisted till the skinning was finally done. Absolute care was observed so that no scar tarnished the skin. It was an extremely demanding and skilful job. If skinning was an art, then the job of processing the skin was a science in itself. No negligible expertise was in order to fulfil these chores. These tasks did not require bookish knowledge, even though society looks up to book-learning as respectable while regarding the task of lifting carcasses as reprehensible. Any Brahmin would fail in this test. Notwithstanding the fact that Chamars provide an essential service, society rewards them with incalculable contempt. A doctor who submits a human body for post-mortem receives social esteem, then why should it be withheld from those who skin animals? Why should those who cleanse society of its pollutants be repaid with the ignominy of untouchability? I too have suffered this humiliation and I know what it feels like to eat inedible food and be at the receiving end of social discrimination.

Like crores of Dalit children in our country, I never celebrated my birthday, even though, like other children, I too considered it a festive occasion. My date of birth was unknown to Amma, since, after all, she never got the opportunity to be literate.

Amma told me that I did not have a naming or *naamkaran* ceremony conducted by a pandit, either. She was against the derogatory names that pandits imposed on the likes of us—names such as 'Durjana', 'Khachera', 'Khuba', and so on. So the name Sauraj, given to me by my Choti Bua, stuck and was accepted by other members of my family.

To my knowledge, there is no scripted history in existence of either my village or my community. This being so, how can I expect my family to have a sense of its past? What happened to that chapter of our history? Among my acquaintances in the village, there was only one person who knew something of its past. This was the Gandhian freedom fighter Raghunath Shastri. Shastriji had authored a long poem about our village entitled '*Nandnandini Nadrauli*', and presented it to me. The poem highlighted the village's scenic beauty and was, from an aesthetic perspective, no doubt, praiseworthy, but it had a sub-text of self-advertisement that one finds in the compositions of courtier poets. But these poets were dependent on the patronage of the monarch, whereas Shastriji wrote for his own pleasure. The seamy side of village life—the curse of untouchability, the pitiable existence of its subaltern groups such as Dalits and women, group rivalries born out of unenlightened attitudes—did not find any mention in his text. Since Shastriji himself belonged to the dominant Yadav caste within the village, he was not anchored within the dynamics of oppression that operated in village society. His verse exuded the magic of words and imaginative excellence, conjuring up a village in which everybody was privileged and prosperous. In response to my criticism on this score, he had promised to also write about the actualities of village life but had never done so. He did not ever recognize the crimes against the rights of Dalits for which the privileged castes owed a duty of repentance. The Gandhian stance was one of compassion towards Dalits, and the discourse of rights did not feature within its ambit. There are other writings similar to those of Shastriji, which refrain from the depiction of rural India with all its blemishes, in particular with reference to the evil of caste by which it is plagued.

This reform-minded Gandhian was more broad-minded than most of the Yadavs of our village. His deportment was gentle and he was not given to observing the norms of untouchability. The so-called untouchables were permitted to embrace him on festive occasions and he returned their hugs as well. He even allowed them to touch his feet by way of paying their obeisance to him. Yet neither he nor anybody else has ever wondered why the untouchables leave the village en masse year after year to go to the cities. The only prospect for them in the village is to subsist by selling their labour cheaply for various menial chores. Nobody has contemplated land reforms as a mode of affording a basis for self-reliance to the untouchables. Even the land deeds awarded to them by the government are routinely confiscated by savarna bullies under false pretences; their proprietorship passed on to non-Dalits although on the documents themselves the grants of land are meant for needy Dalits. The effort of the Gandhians to tackle this scourge through personal example and eloquent homilies abjuring untouchability fall short of concrete measures to eradicate the evil. However, the Gandhians of my village were able to at least write in a certain idiom, whereas I was not even informed about the history of my close relations.

Be that as it may, time passed as it usually does. Following the death of my father, our family found itself devoid of the wherewithal for self-preservation. As his children, we were ready to embark upon child labour, but in our village even opportunities for labouring were few and far between. An illiterate mother, a landless home, minor children, and no source of income, the death of the man of the house had left the house itself in disarray. What was left for us in the village? Every night our old Gangi Babba would lie on his cot and sing out an impromptu song. Revising and improvising upon it at will, he would give it a new construction each time he sang it. Originally a song about the separation of lovers, I found an image of the declining fortunes of our household in it. To suit my aim, I too have overwritten upon it quite thoroughly, though to what exact extent, I cannot say. All that I can say is that my poetic sensibility has sanctioned its modifications and one of its versions was rendered thus:

The broken branch has shed its leaves.
How helpless it was, after all!
A storm of troubles God sent its way,
For nature's sustenance its flowers pray.
Held as it is, in a heartless season's thrall,
To whom can it turn to or call,
To guard it from a ruinous fall.
O the gardener departed before his time!
Newborn sprouts will now not come of age,
Weakened by the foul weather's rage.
Devoid of the food and drink they need,
They will surely go to seed.
Disaster looms over their roofless heads,
Penury resides in their homesteads.
O the gardener departed before his time!
All shops are shut down, well-booted
Traders, once prosperous, feel looted.
Gone is all the glitter and shine.
O the gardener departed before his time!
Words come to an end, but the message is clear,
Out of our sorrows, we ourselves must steer.
Our own guardians we must be, o hear!
O the gardener departed before his time!

Whither Home?

Ram Lal: A Bare Shelter

Ultimately, my Nanaji married off my mother to Ramlal Chamar, a resident of the village of Naura-Baura, thus making him our second father. Ramlal was an extremely poor man who dealt in the remains of dead cattle. After collecting their bones and horns, he would sell them at the market in Sambhal. It was the manufacturing centre for items such as combs made from cattle remains. In sending us to Naura-Baura, my Nanaji had not consulted my father's kin. City folk habitually consider their country cousins to be ignorant. Their ways, speech, attire, and everyday behaviour are all a source of amusement. Nevertheless, when they seek alliances for their daughters, the same city folk not only prefer but give primacy to sons of families from the countryside. Tanners, in particular, do not marry outside their caste, nor, for that matter, do they have social contact with those who are not their caste fellows. The tanners are a diminishing community, so they count themselves fortunate to find girls suitable for their boys. The situation is the same today. It is a popular notion as well as true that if a girl is married to a tanner, she will at least be well fed on meat and fish and, therefore, never starve.

The news had somehow reached our Babba in the village that Surajmukhi, Sauraj, Maya, and Rambharose had been dispatched to Naura-Baura. With the aid of a stick, Babba managed to cover the distance to Chandausi village on foot. On meeting my grandfather, he had questioned Nana's decision.

Nanaji replied shortly, 'My daughter is but in her early twenties. What has she seen of life? We are not Brahmins or Banias that we can afford to keep our widowed daughters unmarried, nor are we Chaudhuris whose daughters can feed off the fat of their lands. We are Chamars. This is our custom. On whose support can we keep our daughters at home? Is there any prospect of sustenance to be provided from your end? You and your brothers are yourselves in dire straits. Two of you are blind and the third lame. Given the circumstances, whatever has been done is after due consideration. There is no other way of ensuring the upbringing of the children. You go back home, this is the best course of action.' Nanaji was, of course, the girl's father, but he also turned out to be a crafty city dweller for a simple denizen of the countryside such as Babba. Villagers are customarily held in contempt by folk from the city, yet today I have no hesitation in asserting that the individuals who have understood the Dalit predicament in its entirety and provided leadership to the Dalits, from Dr Ambedkar to the respected Kanshi Ram, have had their roots in the villages. Town people hardly have the capacity to endure the corresponding risks. I cannot claim this to be a statement of a general principle, though on first impression it does seem so to me.

Instead of returning home, my lame grandfather walked directly to Naura-Baura to meet us. Ramlal was not at home then. On entering our lane, he was spotted by Amma who, on her way back with water from the well, recognized him from under her veil and brought him home. Seeing him in a state of penury, with a dirty *angocha* tied round his waist and a patched-up shirt, Amma burst into loud sobs. The revival of memories from bygone days had brought tears to my mother's eyes. Babba too wept with her in commiseration for her troubles. Our ramshackle tenement reverberated with sounds of sorrow rather than with voices in conversation.

Babba was more worried about our misfortunes than about his own adversities. He wished that we go back home with him. 'Merely wishing on your part won't serve us. Be reconciled to this and just pray that I am able to bring up my children,' Amma said amidst sobs. Babba sat for a long time in the courtyard and when we returned from play, he drew us to his breast and showered us with his love. He took out some batches of *jalebis*, dried of their syrup, from the folds of his angocha and handed them to us. Today such rustic delicacies are not likely to appeal to my own children, but the memory of the sweetness of that old man's affection has stayed with me and is sweeter than anything I have tasted to this day. After all he was our grandfather.

That was indeed the last occasion on which we met our loving Babba. About three weeks later, we learnt that our Babba had taken to bed instantly upon his return from his journey. He got out of his bed only to be lifted on to his bier. We at Naura-Baura were not able to participate in his last rites or any ritual related to his passing away. Nor were we present at the feast that formally marked the end of mourning for him. The story of his privations is remembered even today by his neighbours.

Ramlal could provide only for a wife and not for three children, nor was he keen to look after those that were not his own. He wanted a couple of his wife's children to be sent off to their paternal or maternal grandparents. Amma was not prepared to concede this demand. In fact, my mother and Ramlal fell out with each other within six months of our stay at his house. I have no recollection about the nature or source of their quarrel. Amma had never felt it necessary to discuss the matter with me. Hence, that event did not get transferred to my memory from hers.

But I do remember that she brought us back to Chandausi from Naura-Baura. The main cause of her discord with her husband was their poverty and mutual incompatibility. However, I do believe that in this context my Nanaji and my Phupha from Dhurra had a role to play. My Phupha had come up with a new proposal, which involved three brothers who were tanners in Pali Mukimpur, namely, Bhikari, Chottelal, and Daalchand. Phupha himself was originally from that village and was related to them. Bhikarilal had wedded the sister of our neighbour, Dori Gangasai. The girl had died a couple of years ago after giving birth to a son. Daalchand and Chottelal were yet unmarried. My Phupha's Birbal Chacha too was a resident of Pali. His house was across the road from Bhikari's house. He and Phupha plotted together to get my mother married to Bhikari.

Remarriage, widow remarriage, and marriage by mutual consent of partners are common social practices among us. Even today we are not as fastidious as the Brahmins; their widows remain forever burdensome on their families. The example of the widowhood of my mother and my sister is clearly etched in my mind. In my own social milieu, Dalit women have never faced resistance to widow remarriage nor has the practice of Sati ever been imposed on them.

Habbu Aheriya's Advice

In Pali, the mohallas of Chamars, Bhangis, Dhobis, and Aheriyas were adjacent to each other. The Aheriyas of this village sustained themselves by petty thieving, burglary, and pick-pocketing in trains and buses. These petty transgressors of law were poor people who would often be caught by the villagers and handed over to the police after being brutally beaten up.

I must have been barely twelve years old at the time I settled in Pali-Mukimpur with my mother. Habbu Aheriya would visit us now and then because of his acquaintance with Daalchand. On Daalchand's advice, he called me to his side one day and addressed Amma, 'Bhabhi, I have a request to make to you—hand over Sauraj to us. We can share fifty–fifty of what he collects in one night. As a child he will be able to break into houses with ease. He will become adept at evading arrest and denying guilt.' Amma was aghast, 'What are you saying? Here I want to protect him from evil influences, and you want me to enlist him for training into theft. That's out of question!'

I was well aware of their trade and its rewards. They would conspire to apprentice youngsters like me into their business. I could not take to such an enterprise. In any case, Chamars do not thrive upon dishonest means. They sustain themselves through the fruits of their toil. I too was destined to likewise use the wages of my industry to meet my day-to-day necessities for survival.

At Pali

Pali-Mukimpur is a big village in the Atrauli division of Aligarh district. Here, in those days, I would join Amma and my sister in taking up sundry jobs such as the peeling of sugar-cane, separating grains of wheat from chaff, digging out potatoes from the ground, and so on. Most of the women in the neighbourhood, along with hordes of children, would come out to work. Frequently, there would be altercations between us as we worked. Once, while peeling sugar-cane, Phoolchand had teasingly called me a 'calf', by which he meant that as someone staying in a stepfather's house, I could no longer be considered a human offspring. I must now be counted among the animal species—the calf of a buffalo that had come along with it. I often wonder at the plight of illegitimate children when even stepchildren face such humiliation as I did. How much more they would have to bear the brunt of social discrimination!

Within our neighbourhood, Amma was 'Bhabhi' to Phoolchand, but in age he was only two or three years my senior. His entire attitude was one of trying to provoke and humiliate me. Therefore, one day I retaliated by throwing him on his back, a situation which he found intolerable. He resolved to take revenge through covert means and hid himself to aim a pebble directly at my earlobe, which tore through the tender skin, spilling blood all over my face. Screaming, I ran to Amma and complained.

Amma cleaned the blood off my face and took me to Phoolchand's mother, who was a stout and tall woman, blindly devoted to her sons. Seeing us come, Phoolchand had, of course, fled from the scene. His mother heard Amma out and replied, 'I shall talk to him about it, Mukhi, but it befits step sons to behave like stepsons. Your son did fight with mine in the morning. Tell me whether he did or not.' In this manner, she tried to turn the tables on us. Amma came away, grumbling to herself. As far as my stepfather and his brothers were concerned, far from taking my part, they warned my mother, 'He will be beaten up if he persists in speaking out of turn. If you want to stay on in Pali, you have to mind your ways.'

Time passed and my relations with Phoolchand did not mature into either a steady hostility or a friendship. After all, we children do not bear grudges like adults do. We are more inclined to maintain amiable equations. Things returned to normal. But the hole in my earlobe, to this day, has kept the episode fresh in my memory. It was fortunate that this episode did not cause any emotional damage. Unlike physical injuries, the wounds of the heart are different, deeper, and more painful, caused by the discriminations inherent in our systems. For example, the slur of being a stepchild and hence of an inferior status, made me the object of much derision and contempt.

It seemed as though one and all in Pali thought I belonged to a lesser species. Just as girls were discriminated on grounds of gender, so too was second-class treatment meted out to me by my own contemporaries. I got lesser time to play and endless chores were piled upon me at home and in our *basti*. If nothing else, I was asked to replenish the hookahs of the men as they dragged upon their pipes at the village square. Sometimes I would station myself at Komal Singh's cycle repair shop. If I sat on someone's charpoy, I felt that my presence was unwelcome and that people ignored me. I could not feel comfortable in their company nor were they easy in their interactions with me. I found their conduct towards me to be oppressive. Therefore, I had but few friends, perhaps no more than one, called Laturia. Gradually, I became more and more sombre in my disposition.

Unlike other children, I could not demand favours from my kith and kin. Throwing tantrums was out of the question. Initially, if I asked my mother for something or the other, she would catch hold of my hands and give me a shake, 'Listen Sauraj, your father is dead and I will not be able to fulfill any of your demands. From now on, you have to fend for yourself with your own earnings. Leave your tantrums and learn some trade. If nothing else, learn to mend cycle punctures at least.' In this manner, my burdensome childhood became the load which my weak shoulders learnt to carry. I could not forgo my childhood or rush through it to escape its travails. The destinations of my life beckoned me to come forward. The road ahead was uncharted and uncertain. There were no means of survival available to me in Pali. I was an unwanted thing here and had to shoulder the responsibilities of my childhood all by myself.

Hunger Pangs: Poison for Food

An event transpired a month prior to the wedding of my sister Maya. Amma had been at Nadrauli for five to six months. After the peasants had harvested the grain, the soil would break into cleavages. Some grains of rice would remain stuck to these gaps. We would be allowed to collect these leftovers as part of our share. After picking the grains from these gaps and sweeping the entire field, we would winnow the chaff from which only a small quantity of rice would be recovered in the process. This rice, which was reddish in colour and remained so even after cooking, was called *saati*. It was on this rice that we sustained ourselves but would soon run out of stock.

Now what were we to eat? The other Chamar families in our village had at least one male wage-earner. Most of them also had some arable land in their names. In almost every house at least one member had taken to masonry; the traditional occupations of the Chamars had been abandoned. The cobblers were the first to do so. Instability of income had compelled them to change their occupations.

It was at this point that I noticed a number of *darayan* trees growing around the fields and I suggested that we try cooking their seeds which were available in such abundance. Amma wondered, 'If it were worth eating, why would the Yadavs leave it untouched?' Amma was right. Yet I insisted, 'Who knows why the idea has not struck people before? It does not follow that those who have land will also have wits. What is wrong if we tried eating?' I thought I was being very clever.

After some deliberations, we picked up the fruit and took it home. Maya, Rambharose, and I hovered impatiently around the broth. Though I was not sure that my discovery could be the solution to our basic problem of food, I definitely nurtured hopes in this direction. We had slept on empty stomachs the previous night. Amma found it particularly difficult to starve because she was nursing my infant brother who was but five- or six-months old. The tasteless darayan seeds bore no resemblance at all to rice apart from the fact that the fruit sprouted on rice fields. Inedible though it was, we quickly ate it up out of a torturous need to fill our stomachs.

We were not aware of the poisonous potency of the fruit we consumed. Even a hundredth portion of a mouthful, transmitted to the bowels with sediments of rice, would cause havoc to a digestive system, and here we had devoured the poison undiluted. As the hot gruel settled in our stomach, those with least resistance to its toxins began to pass out the quickest. One by one, the four of us were soon lying prostrate on the ground. I had slumped down in the courtyard. Amma lost consciousness on the cot itself with Tej Singh still sucking milk from her breast. Maya was lying nearby, her face sunk into the floor.

It was Tai who first came to our aid while Amma was sure that we were all virtually dead. It was my flawed judgement that had brought all the members of my family at death's door. Overpowered by the fear of being close to death, we clung close to Amma. Would we be casualties to the consumption of inedible food or to the compulsions of starvation to which we had all been reduced? Was it not gnawing hunger which had driven us to this point of desperation? I suffered on two counts—the after effects of consuming poison and the guilt of such an ill-advised move. Tej Singh too was in a stupor. He had been breast-fed by my mother but a few minutes ago.

Our sightless Gangi Babba groped his way towards our room and grabbing his stick proceeded to fetch the *vaid*. Apart from the physical effects of consuming darayan, the psychological impact became greater when everyone around us began to speak of it as a poisonous fruit. We became pale with repeated retching and only a person who has had a brush with death would be able to see it on our faces. Amma hugged all four of us and lamented our fate, and when Babba got back he too joined in the lamentation. Who knew better than him the trauma of losing a close one before one's time? In a space of three years, his aged shoulders had borne the bodies of two sons, a young nephew and three grandsons. A blind old man, he was witness to the many mortal woes to which his family had been subject.

Our neighbours got us to drink water and throw up by putting our fingers down our throats to eject the poison. Raghunath Shastri, the vaid, was either genuinely unavailable, or it was made out to be so. None of us was dead, but each of us was almost lifeless. We were desperate with hunger and Babba brought out half a *ser* of rice which he had saved in a bundle. Tai cooked the rice for us, and we had shared it amongst ourselves after sprinkling salt on it for taste. The food hit our hollow palates, as water strikes a hot tawa; in other words, made our hunger more acute.

As the hours of the night passed, our neighbours slept in peace since we had been saved from the jaws of death. This was enough for everybody. Tai and Tau, too, had bolted their door and gone off to bed. It was at this moment that a new problem cropped up. Tej Singh developed high fever and in no time lost consciousness. During the day, our family had struggled through one encounter with death. We had not eaten to our fill. Therefore, sleep eluded us.

The next morning, Dori Tau's family visited us but the sympathy they brought was without substance. The next day too we lacked the capacity to go out on the hunt for food for ourselves and there was little scope for asking for a loan in our kind of neighbourhood. By sheer coincidence, that same evening our stepfather Bhikarilal unexpectedly made his appearance in the village, despite the fact that for the past seven to eight months he had neither come to fetch my mother nor exhibited any interest in his newborn son, Tej Singh. On that particular day, he had come to take them home. He was stunned to find our home in such an utterly miserable condition. Seeing our state, he quickly set out for the provision store of the village and returned with good quantities of corn flour and lentils. How can I forget how tasty our meal was that night! The dal seemed no less than nectar to our tongues.

My mother had no option but to leave me behind after spending a couple of days at Nadrauli. She took off to Pali-Mukimpur with Bhikari, as before, with my youngest siblings. I would grow restless, melancholic and wander anxiously for many days whenever she left me thus. However, I understood Amma's compulsions. From the very next day itself, I would have to start looking for work.

On the occasions of Bhikari's visit to our village, the people of our neighbourhood would refuse to socialize with him or even sit near him. People maintained a distance from him just like the privileged castes maintain a distance from those whom they deem to be untouchables. This was so because the nails of his hands and feet had acquired a red colour due to the process of tanning. Bhikari did not have gloves for this kind of work, and on account of his red nails could be identified from afar. He too was an outcast, like us.

Some of our neighbours would tease Gangi Babba by saying, 'Gangi, your son-in-law has come. So, when are you bidding farewell to your daughter?' Gangi Babba would be immediately reminded of the untimely death of my father, 'Say whatever you like, if God had not snatched my Radhey away, you would not have laughed at me. If these children had but a few bighas of land to their names, the poor woman could have raised them in our own village.' As it happened, Bhikari's own in-laws lived in our neighbourhood—Dori and Gangsai were brothers of his first wife. Earlier, even Babba would have considered him like a son-in-law but now the term had a double meaning and concealed a sense of mockery. Amma would feel harassed by Bhikari but at the same time, as the illiterate mother of several children, was dependent on him too. Amma, Tau, Tai, Babba, and indeed everybody else, wished that I would forthwith tell Bhikari to leave our village and order him to never return. But how was I to do so? On the one hand, this man was my mother's husband. On the other, the two had their mutual human needs. I understood the situation very well. One night I was sleeping with Babba while Bhikari slept in the covered verandah nearby. I had heard Bhikari speak in a soft voice to my mother. In the morning, Amma started berating him in the same manner as the neighbours. Addressing me, she said, 'Why don't you chase him away? But how will you see the back of him? You are such a shameless creature! There is no impact on you of what the neighbours say about him!' I got annoyed and blurted out, 'If you wish to see him go, why did you allow him to come?' Giving up her aggressive posture, Amma muttered, 'Should good children comment on the private affairs of their parents?' How else would Amma have sustained herself but by joining her husband? I was incapable of earning much. There was no livelihood for women in those days in our village. In our rural life, there was no greater source of bondage than landlessness. Landowners, on the contrary, could justify all excesses—terrorizing, bullying, injustices were all permissible. During harvest season and at the sweet potato-digging time, there was enough to eat; otherwise having one meal a day was the routine order.

Amma was never happy at Pali. Most torturous for her were the beatings that Bhikari inflicted on her with lathis, sticks, rods, and whips. That she always remained anxious about me and my sister's well-being was also one of his reasons to harass her. After spending a couple of months in Pali, she would return for a week or so to tend to our needs. Sometimes she would set out on foot, with us in tow to the home of Buddho, my Tai's sister in the village of Ahmadpur. In Buddho's house and in those of her in-laws, the men performed the tasks of lifting animal carcasses and processing the skins into leather. The family would eat the dried meat of the dead beasts. The meat would be dried in the open courtyards in front of the house. Perhaps even now this practice persists. Only two categories of 'untouchable' people have been able to improve their lot—those who acquired land and those who secured government employment. Indeed, those who have secured government employment are those very ones who have acquired land. Buddho's family members had neither.

There are many incidents from during the period of my stay alone at Nadrauli which are still etched in my memory. I remember distinctly that once, during the year 1969–70 or thereabouts, I was returning from my sister's village. On the way, I encountered a person who was singing a folk-song. This was a folk-song version of a folk-romance called *Malua*. I walked along with the singer for almost 24 kilometres till I reached my village. All through the journey he sang his 'Malua'. I kept on listening, and by the time I reached home, I knew it by heart, well enough to sing it to my kith and kin. The story went thus. A servant named Malua used to work for a wealthy aristocrat. The aristocrat's daughter fell in love with the servant and professed her love, offering him several allurements to become hers. But the servant declined, saying, 'You are my master's daughter and so I regard you as my sister. I cannot think of any other relationship with you.' At this, the lady got annoyed and began to threaten the servant, 'I'll skin you alive, Malua, and fill your hide with straw. Then I'll set your straw figure on fire.' From that time onwards, Malua became a kind of role model for me.

◆

Fake Devotion

The scene of our departure from our village is still fresh in my memory. A few tattered clothes and some utensils had been wrapped in a bundle which Amma carried on her head. Rambharose was in Amma's arms. Maya and I walked by her side. We were to undertake a long journey on foot. Amma was prevented from taking her silver armbands, bracelets, and sundry brass kitchenware along with her and though she did feel bad at that time about the manner in which they had been taken away, it was with these items alone that sister Maya's marriage was later arranged. Dressed in new clothes, we left for Pali in the afternoon. An unknown man, tall and slim, named Bhikari walked ahead of us. My mind was full of speculations—what would my new home be like? How would we relate to the new people whom we would meet through our new father? Mano Bua too was a resident of this village. This in itself was a source of comfort for us. Amma had told us, 'You will be able to eat two meals a day there. Make sure you work hard in the house. Obey your elder brother, Roop Singh.' And so on.

We had been coached and compelled to accept and address Bhikarilal as 'Dada', a term that was used for father in the local dialect of that village. It did not seem natural because we knew that there can be no substitute for one's own father. In course of time, Bhikari proved to us the truth of this axiom. It is not possible to express how we felt because Bhikari never treated us as his own children and in its stead always bore us much ill-will. Till his death, he continued to harbour evil thoughts about us.

On reaching our new home that night, we began to hope for a fresh start in life. Bhikarilal's son by his first marriage, Roop Singh, was a couple of years older to me. I remember my first meeting with him. As soon as we had arrived, he had taken me out to play with him. His pockets were jammed with peanuts. Without any frugality, he shared the peanuts with me and we became friends. My guess is that this must have been around the year 1966. The people of the neighbourhood looked at us curiously and quipped about our status as stepchildren, 'Bhikari has a new bride and readymade, grown-up kids.' Even we began to sense the forced nature of our relationship to Bhikari, never to find any spontaneity in it. Every Sunday, Bhikari would take dip in the Ganga and at the same time he was most oppressive in his treatment towards Amma. She would find a deep contradiction in his behaviour and his observance of religious rites. Amma would tell him, 'If you wish to go to heaven, take care of your deeds. The fake devotion with which you bathe in the Ganga every Sunday will not wash away your sins.'

A few days after we had arrived at Pali, Ramlal reached our home with the police in tow. The pradhan of the village was a privileged Brahmin landlord and it would have been impossible for the police to arrest anybody, without his permission. The Chamars provided their services to the villagers and were an organic part of the village community, even if only in name. Therefore, their problems were made out to be linked to the issue of the prestige of the village as a whole. The savarnas were habituated to making deals with the police to rescue or harass the Dalits as and when it suited them and then exact obligatory dues from the Dalits. Indeed, many Dalits paid the interest they owed to their savarna benefactors through lifetimes of labour performed for them. The capital, of course, would remain overdue for generations. The modes of exploitation have certainly changed a little over time, but the basic structure is still intact. The burden of debts on the Dalits is on the increase while the savarnas continue to grow more prosperous.

A panchayat was held and everybody knew that the police had come to take away Bhikari's wife from him. The news had brought in a throng of gossipmongers and idlers onto the scene. The Jats and Brahmins sat on cots and charpoys, while people from the other sundry castes squatted on the ground. My sister and I stood fearfully at one corner of the gathering and watched the proceedings. Amma sat with the mien of one who is guilty, head bowed and face covered with her saree. All kinds of pointless questions were being fired at her. 'What kind of a widow is she, with two husbands at her disposal? She is a Chamarin after all.' Amma had no replies for such queries, nor was anybody ready to listen to her answers. It had already been decided that the police would be bribed and the verdict would be in favour of the village. Poor Ramlal sat despondent, having been duped of all his resources. Our own fortunes were tied to that of Amma, and like helpless cattle we would follow her to whomsoever the panch sent her.

According to the pradhan, the ultimate verdict depended on Mukhi. On being asked, Amma said she would not go with Ramlal. The pradhan declared, 'We will not allow him to take her forcibly. It is an issue of the dignity of the village. She might be a Chamar's wife, but she is also the daughter-in-law of the village.'

Ramlal was saddened by this judgement. He had paid hard-earned hundred rupees to the police in the hope of getting Amma back. He told the pradhan about it who eventually persuaded Bhikari to give Ramlal fifty rupees, after which he left.

Bhikari was now my stepfather. It was my mother's need to remarry that had put him in that position. My sister, brother, and I were burdens on him, which he started resenting within the first five or six months of marriage. Though he pretended to conduct himself like our real father, stepfatherly feelings were revealed time and again. In the gatherings of adults as well as among children, I began to perceive myself as inferior to others. Many would make me feel as if my mother had committed a crime.

Roop Singh was a good kid. To begin with, he and I hit it off together. In our friendly wrestling matches, I would defeat him easily, although he was a few years older than me. This convinced his father and uncles, Chotta and Dalla, that Roop needed extra nourishment. Therefore, while he was plied with buffalo milk, *pedas* and the like, I ate the ordinary food like other members of the family. Nevertheless, I was not to be out-wrestled by any other boy but my friend Laturia, who was broad-chested and well-built. His father and uncle were trained wrestlers. I could never lay him flat on the ground nor was ever overthrown by him. As far as our skills in wrestling were concerned, Laturia and I were more or less equals. During that period of my childhood, Laturia was my only good friend. I felt a sense of parity in my dealings with him. He was an exception among the children I knew in those days. At his home too his mother always made me feel welcome even though his family had given up tanning.

The Jatavs who had taken up tanning or working at brick kilns were landless, whereas those who owned a little land were engaged only in farming and agricultural work. The Chamars who tilled the land and those who did not lived in separate bastis. They do so even today. They draw water from separate wells, and conduct their marriage ceremonies separately. We were a family of tanners, and, therefore, drew water from the tanners' well. As we bathed at the edge of the well, I would see children of my age being bathed by their fathers. This practice put Bhikari in a grave dilemma. Had he helped Roop Singh alone with his bath, he would be accused of discriminating against his stepson. Hence, he gave me a bath as well, but one which was more a spectacle than for real. He would clench his teeth tight and scrub my body so hard that I would squirm with pain. His scrubbing carried the force of his stepfatherly feelings towards me. There was such harshness in his rubs as if a carpenter was scraping filings off a piece of wood. If I tried to run away from him, he would get an excuse to smack me on my face. If I ran to my mother, half-bathed, and complained about Bhikari, she would quarrel with him. This sequence of events repeated itself on numerous occasions.

After a year and a half of our arrival at Pali, Amma gave birth to another son who was called Tej Singh. This event added to Amma's stature in the household. Some of the older boys from our neighbourhood who attended school were Narottam Singh, Bhimsen, Badan Singh, Kalicharan, Komal Prasad, and Om Prakash. Bhikari and his brother were often asked by neighbours and other enlightened persons from the privileged castes. '*Arre*, why don't you send the children to school?' The Chamars, Aheriyas, and Dhobis were not inclined towards educating their children. These three castes occupied the margins of the village. The Dhobis and Chamars lived in mixed localities but the Aheriyas had fallen into ruin. Among the Valmikis, the few who were lettered had taken up jobs in the big cities. They would come back to their villages once in a while, but the propagation of education was not on their agenda. It was in such a milieu that I came of age. The savarna looked down upon me as an untouchable and the people of my own caste considered me inferior on account of being a stepchild.

In those days, I was incapable of performing hard labour but would do various odd jobs on the fields along with Roop Singh, including those tasks beyond the capacity of a child like me. Our household was so full of contention and abusive exchanges that, far from improving its lot, it hardly knew a moment of stability or peace. This situation was similar to the household of Rukmani and her partner Munni Chamar, who fought with each other day in and day out. Their altercations were more audible to their neighbours than to each other. The woman, it was believed, could not raise her hand against her husband and to be beaten up by him was a matter of tradition. After a beating, she would go down the lane grumbling to herself, very much a replica of my own mother after she had similarly suffered at the hands of Bhikari. Rukmani was not wedded to Munni but my mother's plight was worse than Rukmani's since Bhikari was a much more cantankerous, cruel, and selfish man than Rukmani's partner. He lost his temper frequently and was capable of doing anything and everything in a fit of rage. It would take others a couple of hours to argue him back to his senses and pacify him. But the very next day, he was back to being his old self.

Cracking the Alphabet

Compelled by social pressure, Bhikari managed to do the one good deed in our favour. He got us admitted to school. Along with my stepbrother Roop Singh, I attended primary school in Pali. In a short time, I was able to recognize the first letters of the alphabet in the primer. Although Roop Singh was a year and a half or two years older to me, both of us had been enrolled in the same class. Hardly a year had lapsed when this journey took a new turn. It all happened because Roop Singh could not master the letters of the alphabet of even the first primer. He would steal away from school to go to visit his Chachas and they indulged him by feeding him snacks and allowed him to stay at home if he complained that the teacher had caned him for not being able to follow the instructions. On the other hand, I never played truant to my classes and my perseverance established me more firmly into the school routine while Roop Singh became detached from it. But this served neither of us well. Our teacher, Harprasad, was a local Aheriya of the village and knew the Bhikari brothers personally. To a query from Bhikarilal, during a chance meeting on the road about how we were faring, the teacher had bluntly replied, 'Look here, Bhikarilal, to tell you the truth, your elder son takes no interest in studies nor puts in any effort but your younger son Sheoraj is good at studies. He can study ahead and you must encourage him to pursue his education. I'm sure he'll make a mark for himself in future.'

On receiving this unexpected report from the teacher, Bhikarilal and his brothers became extremely worried. The teacher's prediction seemed like a prophecy to them and it wrecked the peace of our house. The three brothers received such a jolt that they began to worry more about it than their usual struggle for existence. They could have borne these unfortunate tidings a little better if the teacher had said the same thing for both of us.

The three brothers went to the teacher again, who merely repeated his earlier assessment. It was then that Bhikarilal revealed to the teacher that I was his stepson and that he was being compelled by my mother to send me to school. The teacher understood his line of thinking and advised him to be more charitable towards me, 'If you educate him, he'll be indebted to you. When he becomes an able person, he'll remain dutiful towards you. He'll support you in your old age. If you want to keep them coming to school together, by all means do so. However, only Sheoraj will be promoted to the next grade, not Roop Singh.'

After hearing this, the three brothers returned home in a state of despair, anxious about the future of Roop Singh. After that, Bhikarilal and Amma had frequent quarrels. Mutual compulsions constrained them to live together, but there was no affinity between their temperaments and values. Exercising his triple right as a man as well as the owner of the house and the breadwinner, Bhikarilal would beat up my mother. That day he kept on mumbling, 'So! The bastard is going to be a collector! The master says that he is sharp. It's I who feeds him and he is going to grow up to support his mother! Such a brat and that too brighter than my son!' It was usual for him to discriminate blatantly. All of us used to call him 'Dada', the term of reference for a father in the dialect of the village but in the modern, urban sense too he was a 'Dada', a bully! It was my mother whom he bullied the most. 'Enough!

From now on, there is no need for anyone to study. Get me their books, and you Dalla, their slates.'

The two brothers put their destructive plan into action. An enraged Bhikari broke the wooden frames of our slates with the pestle and just as he began to tear up my books, Amma sprang up to snatch them from his hands. Bhikarilal landed such a kick on my mother's chest that she fell on her back. He seemed like someone possessed by an evil spirit who went on to empty a can of kerosene on the books and lit a match to it. The books caught fire and soon the wooden frames, too, were aflame. The two brothers drew a breath of satisfaction on the conclusion of their task. They thought that they had managed to block my way to getting an education for all times to come. However, the fact remains that by burning my books, they had merely scorched the outward symbols of my quest for knowledge, but the spark of learning within me was not extinguished. Its flame in my soul remained safe, alive. No one from our neighbourhood came forward to stop him. And how could they? It was Bhikari's daily business to be violent and abusive. But my mother was screaming, 'This is a man with a black heart, whose own son has been flunking; lest my son learns to read and write, this scoundrel has burnt the books. May this man never forget that my Sauraj will surely receive an education. God will see to it that no matter how much you burn with envy or will it, your Roop Singh will never be able to study.'

My mother and Bhikarilal made dire predictions about the future of each other's offspring. Some of the neighbours did feel bad about the burning of the books but having reviled Bhikarilal as an evil man, they went back to their homes. For a day or two, I did not have access to anything in print. A few of my classmates lived in the neighbourhood so I would surreptitiously study the alphabet from their books. The numerals 1 to 100 were etched in my memory already. Yet even this was a source of annoyance to Bhikarilal. On learning about my endeavours, Bhikari's stepfatherly feelings would raise their head like a poisonous snake, waiting to strike at its prey. Like a predator, he hunted down my innocent curiosity.

Everyday I sought an opportunity to get hold of a few annas to procure a book and deposit it at some friend's house. Laturia was my bosom pal and I would often seek shelter with his mother to ward off being beaten up. They were Jatavs and, therefore, Bhikari could not enter their house at will. On several occasions I would spend the night at their house. I was afflicted with a tendency to wet my bed while sleeping and I would succumb to my ailment even while sharing the bed with my friends. But their mother was a very generous and warm-hearted lady, who neither took me to task for my lapse nor complained about it.

During those days, many gambling matches were held in our village around the festival of Diwali. Daalchand, the younger brother of Bhikarilal would boss over the villagers through his penchant for gambling, apart from his propensity towards petty thievery and muscle-flexing. In the joint family, it was Chhotelal who was the sole regular earner of wages. It was his destiny to slave like an ox. He was a wage-earner in the leather factory in the outskirts of the village, which was owned by the well-known Dalit leader B.P. Maurya, and sent money home from his monthly income of seventy-to-eighty rupees. Bhikarilal himself made a living out of scavenging and crafting shoes, stirrups, and whips which he made from processed leather. At harvest season he would trade in leather goods with the farmers and bring home wheat and maize. After I had been taken off the rolls of school, I too was engaged in removing the carcasses of dead animals or in gleaning the fields for remains from the crops harvested. At every harvest, my sister and my mother would also be out in the fields. Teams of Chamar women participated in the tasks of harvesting. But Daalchand shied away from any enterprise which involved stressful physical effort. He could not steal on a regular basis. In any case, he was just a petty thief. Sometimes, he would speak about killing cattle by feeding poisoned balls of atta to them. It was a risky job of a criminal kind. The villagers would be alerted to this only when the animals began to die at regular intervals. They would suspect it to be the work of skinners or pharaiyas. The owners of cattle were Jats, Brahmins, and Lodhs, who practised untouchability and would hardly ever touch the dead animal to ascertain the cause of death, however faithfully it might have served them. The Pharaiyas took great interest in such work since they earned a good amount from it. A greater quantity of meat would be carved out of the animal that was killed. The fat extracted from the corpses of the dead animals would be transported to the butchers of Atrauli. Everyone would be quietly advised to not eat the meat, as it was from a poisoned animal. Large chunks of meat would be heated in a big wok to melt the fat, whereupon it would shrink to small pieces of dark-coloured flesh. We would refer to them as *churriyan* and consume large amounts when they were still hot from the wok.

The preachers of Gandhianism would come to the bastis of Chamars and Bhangis and assure us that the benefits of Independence would soon be reaching us, even if it took some time. However, after Independence the condition of Dalits has worsened in direct proportion to the increase of the affluence of the savarnas as has the hostility between castes. Along with caste distinctions, economic faultlines have also grown deeper. Post Independence, it seems as if Gandhi has been proved wrong and that many of Dr Ambedkar's fears have come true, one of which was that once the British were gone, the Dalits would be ruled by the non-Dalits. Is it not true that Independence, without the implementation of the principle of participative governance, has proved to be a great disaster for the Dalits?

Daalchand had won some money in a gambling spree a day prior to Diwali and had got some sweets for home. I entered the house and espied Daalchand's kurta hanging from a peg. Casting my eyes around, I advanced towards it and surreptitiously started to frisk through the pockets. Deftly taking out the bundle of notes, I extracted a rupee and kept back the rest as before in the pocket. I quickly came out of the room after latching the door. Nobody had seen me slip in and out of the house in my act of theft. Hurriedly, I made my way through the weekly bazaar hoping that my uncle would never discover the loss of one rupee from the horde of rupees in his pocket.

On reaching Durga Bania's shop, I made impatient enquiries about the price of a textbook, a notebook, and a pencil, at which he grew irritated and asked, 'Are you going to buy something or only keep enquiring about prices? Let's see your money. A notebook is for two annas and a pencil for ten paise.' On seeing him lose his temper, I asked, 'So, will one rupee will suffice?' Lala was happy to hear this. I had kept the stolen note folded in an empty box of kajal discarded by my mother. As I was checking out the prices with

Lalaji, I saw my uncle Chottelal coming from the direction of our house which was at the other end of the weekly bazaar. I pointed towards him and said, 'Lalaji, look my uncle is coming this way, he will pay you.' Saying so, I hastily stepped out of Lalaji's shop and on my way, I dropped the box containing the note in the narrow drain in front of Srinivas's house, hoping to recover it later.

Chhotelal had a different disposition from that of his two brothers. He would never hit children and his rebukes were always verbal. He was sweet-tempered, generous, and extremely fond of children. I was never scared to go to him. Just as I reached him, he caught hold of me and searched my pockets as well as the waist bands of my pajamas and underpants, asking, 'Did you take the rupee from Dalla's pocket?' I lied to his face, 'Of course not.' 'Then why did you go the shop?' was his next question. 'To find out the price of a book,' I answered, trying to master my fear.

Not satisfied with this, he went to the shop, but Lalaji intercepted him before he could speak 'Chhotelal, why do you send children shopping without money right in the morning and make the day begin inauspiciously?' My uncle promptly gripped me by the hand and headed home. While walking, he said, 'Somebody has picked a rupee out of Dalla's pocket and he has raised a storm at home. Without cause, he suspects your mother. Ever since she has come to our house, the fortunes of the house have been transformed for the better but it is beyond the crazy Dalla's capacity to appreciate this.'

I returned with my uncle to find my mother hollering like a cow that was being slaughtered by a butcher's knife. Her howls were audible to me a long distance away from our house. I ran to her as she lay groaning with pain in the alley. To begin with, Bhikarilal, and afterwards Daalchand, had rained lathi blows on her body. Every part of her body had been struck except for the head. After screaming aloud and moaning, my mother had lost consciousness. Birbal Baba's wife tried to revive her by pouring water on her face. All the Chamars of the basti and the Jats, Banias, and Brahmins who were passing by had gathered at the spot and began reprimanding them. Bhikari, in a bid to display his manliness, spoke in a dramatic manner—'Arre saab, this woman does not lack food or clothes. The three of us work day and night to feed her and her children twice a day. And that too without any hope of returns. Even then this good-for-nothing has compromised her morals for a rupee. She could have asked for it if she needed it.' Bhikari spoke in a beastly manner while Dalla sat on a charpoy, wearing the look of a warrior who had returned victorious from the battlefield. 'This slut has started her game by pocketing a rupee. Little did she know while picking my pocket that I have picked the pockets of many a high-and-mighty.' 'Do not help the whore up,' he warned Chhotlelal whose heart was bleeding for my mother.

'Dalla, you will be damned for this. I would have given you ten rupees for your one. Instead, you have broken all the bones of the poor woman's body.' Chhotelal was indebted to my mother as at the time of his serious illness the previous year, she had saved his life by selling her bracelets to arrange for his blood transfusion. The medical treatment amounted to almost one hundred rupees and the bracelets fetched eighty rupees. She had also nursed him back to health on his return from the hospital.

That day, the hearth at home remained unlit. At night, still groaning, Amma instructed my sister to roast some grams for us to eat. I was tormented by guilt—I had stolen the rupee but the punishment had been borne by my innocent mother and that too so severe as to be remembered for a lifetime. It was not a punishment for theft but a male ego's violent backlash to my mother's constant protest against Dalla's misdeeds. Amma's face was bloated, her lips were swollen up, and she could barely speak. I kept wondering whether I should confess my guilt but I knew that if I were to do so, I would meet with the same fate as my mother—my fear made me decide that it would be better to remain silent.

Amma lamented tearfully, 'I have never taken even twenty-five paise of anybody's earnings, why would I take a rupee today?' She was seeking to exonerate herself from the charge of stealing in the eyes of her children because my sister, Maya, had asked, 'Amma, why on earth did you take the rupee? The whole village will call you a thief!' Expressing her faith in divine justice, Amma said, 'Let them think what they will, my child. God is my witness. I do not know who stole it, but whoever stole it, God will have their bodies preyed upon by worms.' And likewise, she went on cursing in her misery. As her pain aggravated, the people of the basti began to curse Bhikari. He began to feel somewhat guilty and instructed us to give her a glass of milk stirred with alum and to massage her body with turmeric paste.

As I daubed turmeric on her back, I felt as if the letters of the alphabet were imprinted on my mother's back and Amma herself became transformed into a text. Dalla had kicked her on her chest. The lower end of her breasts had turned blue. My sister and I continued to rub turmeric on her breasts, her waist, and her cheeks. I knew that her private parts had also been grievously injured. I went out of the room and my sister attended to them also with turmeric paste. I re-entered the room to find my mother on the charpoy, soaking in the warmth of the fire lit for her. She demanded of me, 'Child, you were throwing a tantrum about the books; have you done this deed?' For a moment I was struck dumb. I did not have the courage to tell the truth. Perhaps as a mother she knew it already. 'No Amma, I did not,' I lied without blinking an eyelid and followed it up by solicitously ministering to the marks on my mother's back with heat fomentation. In my imagination, I perceived a curious similitude between the scars on her body and the letters of the alphabet in the book I had tried to purchase with the ill-gotten money. The next day, I scanned the drain for the box discarded by me, but failed to locate it. Perhaps someone had picked it or it lay buried in the muck.

I meditated upon the turn of events that seemed to me as cataclysmic as an earthquake. Should I have told the truth to my mother? Would she have felt better? I was so utterly self-centred and obsessed with the idea of learning that even as I heard her painful cries, I could only think about the books I desired. That night, Dalla cooked for us and we got to eat a roti each.

What were the circumstances and the context which led Bhikari and Dalla to be so frustrated and abusive in speech? They belonged to a community that for generations had been deprived of resources for survival, education, and culture. However, it must be borne in mind that these uncouth, uncultured brothers had supported us in those terrible years of 1962–4, when the country was facing an acute shortage of grains because of the famine. Our home was also reeling under the effects of inflation. When we had no one to support us, these brothers had arranged a meal for us, albeit, one that only partially satiated our hunger.

Even though I had been out of school for a month, it continued to hold its charm for me. One day I saw a long row of school children dressed in clean white uniforms, holding small flags in their hands, passing along the road. Badshah signalled at me to join the ranks and handed me a small flag from his pocket. I had barely walked a short distance with the children than I stood out amongst them on account of my dirty attire—like the demon Ketu mentioned in the mythological texts, who sat with the gods at time of the distribution of *amrit* after the churning of oceans. At the moment when I was chanting loudly—'*the beloved tricolor world victorious/ May it fly high ever glorious*'—Masterji indicated with his stick that I step out of the row and Bhikari Dada pounced on me. It was a foregone conclusion that I would be thrashed for my defiance. Kicks, punches, slaps, abuses followed, and my back was whipped with leather straps. I let out screams but he demanded, 'When you have left school, what have you to do with it?' Armed with a volley of questions, I was dragged to Amma, my ears being twisted all the while. My crime was declared to be the inability to give up the love of learning. Amma scolded me, 'Put aside the flag and hold your ears to swear that you will not hang around with schoolgoing children anymore. You will shun their company.' I was made to sit at home but I got away as soon as I got the chance. Bhikari found me out but when I escaped again, then I decided to stay away from home the entire day. Bhimsen's mother hid me at her home for the night and also fed me with some with leftovers from lunch. I went off to sleep in tears and full of trepidition until Amma discovered me late in the night after finding out about my whereabouts. She woke me up by shaking my head and put aside the flag that had shrunk to the size of a kerchief, wet with my tears.

For more or less a dozen years following this episode, I did not cross the gates of any school as a student. Indeed, my sister and I were parted from our mother very soon and brought back to our native village in Nadrauli. Neither of us was older than seven or eight years of age, and yet we sustained ourselves through daily labour, sometimes paid in regular wages and sometimes not.

My mother had been reduced to chronic ill-health, burdened as she had had been with the weight of dire poverty, along with my own lack of means and malnourishment. Amma had left Pali in the hope that her sons would fend for her. It was another matter that she kept going back to Pali as three of her other children were there. They had held back the sons and packed the daughter Rajmala (Manorama) off with Amma. Tuberculosis had taken a toll of her health. I would always be filled with a sense of guilt towards Amma. I felt so helpless that I could do nothing for her but I wanted that she should, prior to her death, be told the truth about the episode long forgotten, that she empathize with my quest for knowledge and pardon me for my sins—one of which was to give up the work in the village in order to pursue my studies. Deprived of nutrition and of medical aid, my mother died before I could get a job. Despite knowing that she was dying of want for food, I had run away from the village in quest of an education. She would always wonder why I did not take up a job after clearing my Tenth-Class exam. My Mausi's son had joined the P.A.C. the moment he passed his Ninth-Class exam. She wanted me to become a soldier like him but I had bigger dreams and very poor sources of sustenance. As it turned out, I could not even catch a last glimpse of her corpse. By the time I reached, her ashes had turned cold. For many days, I would go and sit near her ashes. Amma was no more but I was grateful for her memories that remained with me.

I wonder that if I had felt so responsible and was conscious of my duty towards her, then I should have taken care of her and got her treated. What was the point of shedding tears now? Only I know how helpless I was! Perhaps she would have lived longer if I had stayed on in the village and continued to work there. But then I would have died a little by little and she would not have been able to bear that. She was obviously mistaken in the belief that I was not earning even after having studied. The fact was that I was trying to get any sort of job—from a security guard's to that of a clerk.

The other memory I have of Amma is that of a respectable woman of the community, when my father was alive. However, later she suffered such atrocities that would not be directed at an animal and yet she remained as mute. Like a slaughtered cow, she could only let out screams. She had no other language and no one to understand her. She did not know the law and the concept of divorce was unknown to her. She was dependent on a man, a cruel person who was supposed to be like a god for her, whom she had been compelled to accept. And then there was me. Was I any different from her? I just wanted to be free of these circumstances. My life lay like a huge mountain before me and I had to make a passage through it. Even after stumbling through a journey filled with insults and indignity, impoverishment and barbs, when I managed to strike a plainer ground, was I any different from Amma? We were both victims of circumstances in our own ways but even then I continue to reproach myself. On what grounds could I keep my morale high? Should I reason that had I not given up wage labour, there would have been no beginning to literacy in our family? Or should I say that had I not done what I did, neither I nor Amma would have survived? Whatever I could make of myself after I left Amma to die, and have been able to speak on behalf of the Chamar community in the form of this narrative, should I be proud of it? Or should I believe that my life narrative poses a question about the entire Chamar community to which there is no answer in this century?

Hard work cannot dispel poverty. Till date, the unorganized workers of the village have not seen the implementation of the government's wage policy. Therefore, there is neither any provision for their health and sickness nor schools for their children. Their basic needs are not met with. Land belongs to the savarna and they pay five rupees for a work that should fetch fifty. Like Phupha, there are crores of Dalits whose blood is being sucked in independent India. I began to revolt the moment I understood the extent of our social slavery that had been carrying on for centuries and I feel it all the more intensely now. I have yet to see a Brahmin or a Bania working in brick kilns, and it is unimaginable to think that they will take the task of cleaning from Bhangis into their own hands. I have never found a Bhangi or a Chamar as the priest of a temple or a monastery. It is easy to make out from their language and behaviour, the extreme hostility the savarnas have to our taking up more respectable jobs.

Most of the Dalits of Pali (Aligarh) would work for eight months in brick kilns and survive on an advance taken for the remaining four months. The majority of the brick-moulders were Chamars and that is true even today. I had been invited to a function organized by the Ford Foundation in honour of the Dalit activist A.K. Akela in November 2007 in Aligarh. I was then at the Shimla Institute of Advanced Study. I had conducted a survey of Pali and compiled a list of workers in kilns, of which 104 were members of the Jatav community. As I am writing this, Uttar Pradesh has seen the election of a backward-caste government, but even this government has not given them sustainable livelihood. All the workers in these kilns are landless proletariat Jatavs.

The Painful Reprieve

Bhikari had, without consulting Amma, taken an advance from a contractor and decided to send Maya and me to the kilns when we were barely seven to nine years old. Amma was upset about this decision, as she wanted that either the entire family should go to the kilns or that the children remain with the family. Bhikari, on the other hand, wanted his own children to remain at home while we, his stepchildren, would go to the kilns and earn for him. Children proved very handy in the entire process of making of bricks—from forming moulds to cutting them and drying them to finally arranging them one upon the other. The contractors benefitted by paying them half the wages. However, it was very harmful to the health of the children, who would be extremely fatigued by this hard labour and all the running around. Many guardians exploited the labour of children for their earnings and Bhikari was no exception. Amma could clearly see that the very man she had chosen to secure our futures was hell bent on destroying them but she had no alternative arrangement for us if he refused to feed us.

The amount of advance that Bhikari had taken was not known but it was to be spent in the monsoon months and we were to set out with the other brick-moulders for the kilns in winter. Amma and Bua grew very anxious at the prospect of us going off alone. They were more concerned about Maya, as there was hardly any safety for girls in the kilns. They confronted Bhikari with these doubts and questions but he wanted us to be apprenticed early. On the other hand, just after I left school, Roop Singh was readmitted to it but he continued to fail. Bhikari was completely dictatorial and his word remained final. His weekly bath at the Ganges did nothing to repair his cruel conduct and this would provoke Amma to comment ironically, 'Ganga Ma will certainly pave the way to heaven for a crocodile like you.'

Thus, in such a situation it was only Mano Bua who proved to be of some help. Amma and she met in secret to discuss our impending departure to the kilns and devised plans for our deliverance. Bua somehow managed to put together some money for the fare and sent Phupha to Nadrauli to get Tau and Babba to come immediately to prevent us from being sent to the kilns. The blind Gangi Babba and Baburam Tau realized that if they did not fetch us now, they would never be able to get us back to the village. They also knew that the greedy Bhikari would not allow the children to go back with them easily. Thinking thus, they contacted all our other relatives and called them together and reached Pali in a day or two. There was still a week to go before our being sent off to the kilns. Tau confronted Bhikari but he shot back, 'Now these kids are mine. Whether they are butchered or made to sit at home, I, their owner will decide that. Who are you? I have fed them and reared them. If you thought they were your nephew and niece, why didn't you hold them back in the village in the first place? Go back to your homes, you blind men. You can hardly fill your own stomachs, how are you going to fend for them?'

Tau acted wisely by calling for a panchayat, which decreed that instead of letting these small children go alone, Bhikari should take his entire family to the kilns or if he did want not to look after these two children, then he should allow them to go with their Tau and Babba. It was finally decided that we go back to Nadrauli with our paternal relations, a decision that Bhikari agreed to after much exhortations and on the condition that we never return again to meet our Amma.

For Amma, this came as a relief but even she knew that there was no provision for food for us in Nadrauli. It was enough for her that we had been saved from going to the kilns and she knew that we could always work for food. She found a way to console herself. The scene of our separation from our mother after the panchayat's decision is still stamped on my memory. The distance between Pali and Nadrauli was about eight to ten kilometres and Bhikari had followed us for quite a distance, arguing all the time. 'Now that you are taking them, at least give me back the money I spent on feeding them. I have taken an advance from the contractors. How will I return that?' I am certain he tortured Amma for this. The truth was that Amma did not wish to be separated from her children even for a moment but she had no option, given the fact that she had an infant Tej Singh, Bhikari's son, and my youngest brother Rambharose to look after. She would keep coming over to Nadrauli every six months in a year or so.

In Nadruali too we were worse off. Tau had got us from Pali but he did not have the resources to give us even one meal. We had escaped the kilns but it was not as if we had passed from the season of autumn into spring. It was more like from the frying pan into the fire. From the very next day, we had to start working for our meals. Maya dug grass and I would carry it to the city to sell it. We were relieved that we were among our relations but were pained by the separation from our mother.

◆

Custodians of Community

In the year 1967–8, Amma had brought us from the village to Chandausi to stay in my Mausa and Mausi's house. In lieu of the rent, we were required to look after the maintenance of the house. Since any kind of hard labour was out of question, another boy, Phool Singh, and I learnt to polish boots. Even today in Chandausi this work is done by Dalit children. We would polish boots on trains and in the city for shopkeepers and agents—a pair for ten paise and two pairs for fifteen. We would be instructed to sit with the labourers at Gandhi Chowk but Phool Singh would pick me up from there and we would roam through the city's cinema houses, stations, and hotels, gazing at glossy posters, to return home in the evening. Phool Singh's father was a mason by profession but had taken up shoemaking due to lack of work. He was, therefore, always on the lookout for a better job. In any case, even if Phool Singh did not earn anything, his meals were taken care of. On the other hand, at my home there were many mouths to feed and only two earning members—my mother and I, a child labourer. If I didn't earn, we would not be able to provide for our next meal.

Around that time, a resident of Chunni mohalla, Harishchandra's father Shri Deepchand, got a contract for building mansions for which he needed women and children as labourers. Amma was running a fever and so I was enlisted. We were working on the construction site of the Allahabad Bank. My job was to carry gravel stones and cement to the mixer and for that I received a rupee a day. Since no cloth had been provided, I would carry the heavy load on my bare head, having to walk over sand, stones, and iron rods. One day, my hand got deeply cut from a broken metal basin. It was a severe gash and I had to stop working. The palm was bandaged and I was sent home. For many days, I could not use my hand and had to dress it for a week. Amma went to the contractor's home to ask for my wages but was sent away on the assurance that once I resumed duty, the account would be settled. On Amma's persistent demands, the contractor deducted eight annas for the loss of an hour's work and handed over the remaining eight annas to her. Amma argued that a just deduction should not have been more than four annas and that he should be giving her twelve annas instead. For fourteen days she kept pleading for four annas and to this day I have not received my fair share.

About twenty years later, I had to go to the same Allahabad Bank to open an account for a scholarship. There I was informed that the same Harishchandra, who was now the local MLA, had sent me a dinner invitation. He was a social worker but was facing competition from the new Dalit leadership.

Meanwhile, I had gained fame as a Dalit spokesperson and reporter. The politician wanted to use my popularity to his own advantage. He seemed like a gentleman but what does one do with reminiscences? The memory of the childhood incident caught up with me and I left my dinner half eaten.

Ancestors

Ever since childhood, I had observed that for several generations now, newlywed brides of the mohalla would be first brought to Dayaram's courtyard and only after that, proceed to their marital home. I would often wonder at this tradition and enquire of Dayaram, 'Did our ancestors have a history of their own?' I, for one, did not even know my grandfather's name, whereas most educated people could trace their lineage right back to several generations. I could, of course, recall the past in patches that had been related to me as piecemeal events by Tau and Babba. Surely, ordinary people like us must also possess some knowledge of our past! Dayaram assured me that he could recall everything and on my insistence began his narration to which Dori, Chhote, as well as the others, kept nodding in agreement.

In Bulandshahar district, Bhopur village falls between Anoopshahar and Jahangirabad (I could recall its mention in a puja called Bhopur's Chamunda Devi). A Chamar named Javhar (Jawahar) lived there with his five sons—Bakhshi, Nanhe, Chitai, Sanehi, and ... I cannot recall the fifth son's name, and a daughter. Bhopur was owned by a zamindar and all our ancestors served as slaves on this estate. They had nothing to sustain themselves except for their own labour. One of Jawahar's sons had married and settled in Nadrauli.

One day, the zamindar's agent turned up at Jawahar's home to summon him for unpaid labour (*begaar*). At that time, Jawahar was having his meal. 'I will come as soon as I finish eating' was his reply, whereupon the agent began beating him up.

The sons got to know about it when they returned home in the evening. Even though Jawahar was reconciled to bearing the humiliation, the sons considered it as gross insult. They conspired to seek revenge. Of the five, Bakhshi possessed Bheem-like strength and Nanhe, though weak of body, had a sharp mind. Sanehi and Chitai were willing to go along with whatever the others decided. Bakhshi suggested that they kill the agent, whereas Chitai and Sanehi felt that a complaint should be lodged with the zamindar and a request be made that such incidents should not recur. However, Nanhe was of the opinion that, 'We should take revenge in our own way.'

They planned to first approach the agent quietly and, after greeting him politely, seek an explanation for his actions. If his answer did not satisfy them, they planned to kill and bury him there and then. The brothers went to the agent's home according to their plan but instead of admitting his mistake, he began to behave in the same abusive manner with them. Bakhshi lost his temper and broke the man's skull with his staff. He fell in one swoop. The other brothers did not even have to stir; the man was dead. They left him there and returned home. The British ruled then and the zamindars were hand in glove with them. Fearing punishment, the five brothers took their sister along with them and went into hiding. After several months of wandering here and there, in course of time they went to the home of their brother's in-laws in Nadrauli. They had initially decided to stay there on a temporary basis in order to bide time. Later, a truce was affected between the zamindar and Jawahar through the intervention of the British. However, the brothers and sister finally settled in Nadrauli itself. Among them, Bakhshi had two sons, one of them was Bihari. Bihari had three sons—Durjan, Tundi, and

Lauki. Durjan's three sons were Ganga Sahay, Dori, and Pyare. Nanhe also had three sons—Bhagirath, Vidharam, and Gangaram. Chitai had two sons—Lachhman and Kallu. Lachchman had two sons—Sahay and Bhajani, while Kallu remained childless. Sanehi had four sons—Khamani, Khargi, Kalu, and Uttam. Khamani had a son, Dayaram, and a daughter, Khushalo. Khargi had one son Chhabi, who did not have children. Kaalu had three children—Tussi, Khubi, and Pitambar. Among these, Tussi had one child, Champa, and Khubi had four children—Ramchandar, Munshi, Leelawati, and Chandravati. Tikaram had a son, Narayan, and a daughter, Harpyari. Pitambar had one child, Naikasia, and Uttam had Paimi who remained childless.

Thus, our original home is Bhopur village, the proof of which can be found even today in the prayer rituals associated with the invocation of spirits. When Chhote, Makkhan, or Khacheri are possessed by a devi and a rival spirit threatens to overpower them, ultimately the 'Chamunda of Bhopur' is called upon to intervene. She descends and overthrows her competitor, claiming credit for the successful exorcism of the spirit.

The significance of the newlywed brides being brought first to the house of Todi and Janaki now became clear to me. In any case, we were never part of this tradition, as we had been excommunicated by our own community. Since Todi was a respected member of the community, the brides' arrival into his home first was considered an auspicious beginning. Todi and Janaki belonged to an honoured lineage because our ancestors had sought refuge with their relatives on the daughter's side.

There is no historical record that testifies to the lives of these five or six generations that spanned a period of two- to four-hundred years. It is in recognition of the necessity to belong to a context and the need to be rooted to one's past that I have brought this record into the public domain. I may have got a few names or time sequences mixed up but nothing has been added on. The generations descending from Jawahar shared his fate—deprived of any means of livelihood, they were forced into working for others—on fields, in homes, and other places. No one can comprehend the import of my struggle for existence without knowing this generational pattern.

Even before Independence, my ancestors lacked the means of eking out a living, so also my great grandfather's family (his middle son Vidharam's sons—Baburam and Radheshyam and their three sisters—Kalavati, Mano, and Chhoti) had neither fertile land nor resources for trade. They were Dalit proletariats. In comparison to the savarnas, they are far from attaining full human dignity even today.

In Chunni mohalla of Chandausi, the homes of the in-laws of my father and Tau are located at a short distance from each other. Even Durjan's son Dorilal had married there. In that context, my mother and Tai would be related to Dorilal's wife as aunts but they were all contemporaries and lived as friends, calling each other by their first names.

We were basically meat eaters but before my father's death I had never tasted the flesh of dead animals. In those days, we would eat the head and hooves of the goat. This much I can recall and the rest of the information has been provided by my mother: The mohalla of the Chamars was divided into two blocks that were separated by a road and their backyards fell on either side. It seemed as if they had turned their backs to each other. Even their gods had been partitioned. From either mohalla, many people had passed away, but their gods were not dead yet.

On the other side of the road, Ramsaay, Happu, Hoti's son, Kedari, and Ramcharan Master considered 'Jaharveer' as their main god. On our side, 'Sayyed Baba', 'Bangali Baba' along with 'Bhopur's Chamunda', 'Karanvaswali', and 'Belonwali' goddesses were worshipped.

During skirmishes between the two mohallas, the gods and goddesses would often be invoked in a show of strength. Since we were more in number, our gods or spirits would also prove to be stronger. Every third or fourth day, Makkhan, Khacheru, and Dori Tau's father, Durjan, would set the arena for a tussle between the rival spirits. Sometimes steel plates would jangle on earthen pots and other times Sayyed Baba would establish his superiority by getting the person in the trance to dig his elbows into the ground. The ustad would chant while placing his hand over the *shaagird*'s head and then the spirit would possess his body. This was considered a guaranteed cure for all diseases. The entire prayer-ritual would be as entertaining as a musical. A collective singing would ensue to rouse the spirits. Sample this:

Your arrival is awaited, O Warrior!
You had promised to return in a year.
Your mother, your sister, bewail and fear.
Do not go to the battlefield, O Peer!
You belong neither to the earth nor the sky,
You belong to the space that between them doth lie.
As the clouds of war gather overhead,
Your brave deeds are hailed from the west,
O Bangali Baba, show the power that people dread,
From the jaws of defeat, victory wrest.

If the verses broke off at some point or a singer forgot some part, my Tau, Baburam, would fill in the missing bits. Though he was blind, he had memorized dozens of ballads by heart. I would sit beside him, listening and learning.

Even our gods and goddesses were voracious meat eaters but they preferred fresh meat and would not touch the flesh of dead animals. Sayyed Baba preferred chicken and Bangali Baba demanded a ram. Once a person was cured, a goat or lamb would have to be offered on an appointed day. The meat would be set to cook as the spirits battled with each other. The cooked meat would first be offered to the spirit and the rest would be distributed to every home.

In those days, there was no Chamar family in both the mohallas that did not go fishing. The village was surrounded on all three sides by lakes and a seasonal river, Karakvai, in the south. In summers, the Chamars, Bhangis, and Muslims (Fakirs and Telis) collectively fished in one or the other lake. Apart from two pucca homes, all other Chamar homes were made of unbaked mud. The roofs of the Chamar and Bhangi homes were joined on both sides. We could easily climb one to pass on to others. A *khonch* or a fishing contraption made of reed, which was broad at the bottom and narrow at the top, could be found on every roof. One could easily pass a hand or even a big fish's mouth through this khonch. A fish-catching competition to ascertain the best among them would often start off. Dori, my 'Chacha' Radheyshyam, Khacheru, and Makkhan were experts at catching fish. The Yadavs would not permit fishing during the day, as they had captured the lakes. They were habitually violent and abusive; therefore, when the entire village would fall asleep, we would all gather like thieves and raid the lakes. In the night, the women would cook pots full of fish and in summers this would turn into a feast-like celebration.

At the time of my birth, all three brothers—Babba, Tau, and my father—would collect the dead animals from the village, skin and tan them in the hut on the outskirts. The entire process was an arduous one. The animal would be turned on its back and its four feet would be tied. A couple of bamboo rods would be passed through the tied limbs and four men would be required to lift the dead animal on their shoulders. The only thing that has changed in the twenty-first century is that this work is now done by Muslims in Senjna, near my village. On account of the monopoly the Chamars enjoyed over the resources of production, the Banias, Telis, and Yadavs would denigrate their profession. Muslims are now running a lucrative business in dead animals. However, the basic work is still done by Chamars. At Zarifnagar and Pali, several of my maternal relations, Kaumal Singh's brother and Nek Singh, are working as contractual labourers at a minimal wage for lifting and skinning dead animals. It is for this reason that there has been no change or improvement in the quality of their lives. Even today, none of them is literate. Ignorant of the letter, they do not even vote according to choice and, therefore, their judgement has no role to play in the making of governments.

Till the first generation, the entire mohalla, along with my father and his brothers, was engaged in this work. However, by the time I was born, there were very few homes carrying on with this work. The three brothers, Dorilal, Gangsaay, Pyare, as well as my Tau and Babba continued to work with dead animals. The tanners made more money as compared to those Chamars involved in other kinds of labour. Even those who had lands were not better off, as their techniques of agricultural production were outdated. Since the tanners earned more, they could afford a relatively better quality of food. They also preferred to marry among themselves. If they had to choose between a man possessing four bighas of land and a tanner, they would prefer the tanner. The tanners had an edge over those who merely skinned animals.

My Nana's family also depended on the money procured from selling animal skins. My Nana had neither the means for tanning nor an assigned village from which to pick dead animals and thereby ensure a fixed source of income for himself. Nevertheless, he did manage a decent amount from dealing with animal skins and so his family got on well.

If one were to set aside the compulsion of love as the basis for marriage, it is still contracted largely between people of the same caste and class. My maternal and paternal grandparents also approached each other for the marriage of their children for this reason. Moreover, my Nana had spotted another quality in my father—the talent of an accomplished worker.

People of that generation recount that in the early 1960s, when the movement led by the Republican Party in Agra and Aligarh was at its peak, several villages had come under the influence of its reformist appeal. Many had begun to regard the work related with dead animals as reprehensible. Once the Chamars themselves began to consider their work as demeaning, matters deteriorated rapidly. Our families had been doing this work for generations and since we had given up tanning, selling animal skins was the primary means of livelihood for the entire basti. To be fettered to one's hereditary work did not seem to be a wise thing to do but we had no opportunity to do anything better. We could have settled for some odd job if nothing better came our way but to not find an alternative was a sure case for self-destruction.

Every market day would be celebrated like a festival. The tanners would use the dyed leather to make shoes and other agricultural items, which would fetch a good income. Chamars would be quite happy to marry their daughters into the homes of the tanners. Not only would the girl be well provided for, she would also not have to work outside the home. Even though he was four years older, Tau got married after his younger brother. It was partly because he could only skin dead animals and tan them but had no aptitude for shoemaking or it was that he simply did not possess the skill. The gradual dimming of his vision took away from him the possibility of becoming a skilled worker. One can still find Tai's brothers and nephews polishing shoes on the streets of Chandausi. There has been no improvement in their economic condition. However, on the basis of the images that flash upon the mind's eye, I can say that since we engaged in the same sort of work collectively and were constantly interdependent in an exchange with each other, there was a great sense of brotherhood, camaraderie, and love amongst us. Even though the standard of living was low in comparison with the touchables, our people always shared each other's sorrow and happiness.

Since I was too small, and unlike these days, there was no impatience to enroll the child in a school, I was not sent to one. The other boys of the basti—Ulfat, Ramsingh, and Shyamlal—had already got admission. Among the Yadavs in the village, there were a few enlightened teachers, mostly freedom fighters and those from the Arya Samaj, who were personally in favour of sending untouchable children to school. They would come into the Chamar basti to enroll students and drag back those who had run away from school. Phool Singh was six months my junior and even he did not go to school. That made the two of us into playmates. However, even though I was not on the rolls, I would, every now and then, follow the other children to school. The teachers would turn me out saying that I had to be admitted first but I would keep playing outside and wait for the school to close in the hope of joining my friends. Till then, this was my only association with school. Nevertheless, I once managed to filch a pen from school and upon discovering it my mother had caught me by the ears and dragged me straight to the teacher's home.

Our Neem Tree

Though Babba was very old, our neem tree was older than him. He would always maintain that the tree looked exactly as it did since the time of his birth. The hoary, enormously tall neem tree, with its huge circumference of roots, was a mark of identification for our caste. Since we travelled mostly on foot, a glimpse of the neem tree from afar would fortify us. I wonder why it was that we were so proud that no other caste could boast of a neem tree as grand as ours. It stood close to the backyard of our ancestral home that Babba had built. In my entire life, I have not seen such an ancient and gigantic neem tree. Since all living things must die, the neem too was struck by a disease and started drying up. Its dry branches would sometimes fall in the courtyards of the Chamars and Bhangis or that of the Muslims. Unknown to us, we shared a deep bond with the tree. It was the legacy of our ancestors. Its branches extended to our courtyards.

Matru Bhangi, whom I called Tau, who worked as a sweeper in Bombay, wore a uniform which I found attractive. I would often ask him to find a job for me. His reply would be, 'I can take you to Bombay, but will you sweep its streets? Will you be able to wrench yourself from the gentle winds that blow through your neem tree? Not only you, no Chamar will take up a sweeper's job.' I wonder why the Chamars considered themselves superior to the Bhangis! Whenever people gathered under the shade of the neem tree to relate long stories, caste distinctions would be immediately visible in the manner in which the Chamars would occupy the higher parts of the hill and the Bhangis, the lower. If a Yadav or a Muslim turned up, then both Bhangis and Chamars would vacate their cots and sit on the ground. Before being associated with the Arya Samaj even I was deluded into believing that Chamars were superior to Bhangis, whereas economically we were weaker than them.

It is difficult to say for how many generations the neem tree had been a part of our legacy. We did not pay attention to its withering away, as we had been unmindful of our heritage. All we wanted was for it to remain there for us forever. However, once stormy winds struck the tree and a part of its branch broke and fell over our roof. It elbowed its way into the house by breaking through the beams and the joints of the corners of the walls. That night, I had gone for a wedding feast, and on hearing about the neem tree, I left immediately. On approaching the village, I found that the neem tree was no longer visible. It struck me that Gangi Babba was blind and if the tree had fallen when he was asleep, what then? The scene that greeted me at home stupefied me. The elbow of the neem branch had broken through the roof and had fallen right between Babba's legs to rest on the ground. Babba had escaped without a scratch.

Later, its leaves began to dry and fall off. Its green foliage changed to dry barrenness. The people of the community got its branches chopped and bullock-cart-loads worth fuel was packed off to the city. A good amount of money was also procured but not only was our house left unrepaired, we were also not given our share of money. It was said that the neem had been planted by a common ancestor and since its shade had benefited Gangi and Radhey the most, any further claim was out of question. Moreover, the other rationale for excluding us was that the money would go towards calling the panchayat. Soon the entire land of the Chamars went up for sale and we were still deprived of our share of money. This time it was said that since we were always going off to the city, we could not claim anything from the village. Paiju Tau's son, Ramcharan, had managed to capture the area surrounding its roots. However, the place had lost its initial spring-like bloom and the entire basti became deserted. The Bhangis and Chamars sold off their homes to the Yadavs and went off to settle elsewhere. The rest had already migrated to the city.

The neem had stood there since Babba's childhood and must have been older than a hundred years. This family of disabled people could hardly put together the remnants of their sundered home. When the inhabitants themselves were shattered, how could they repair its roof? The walls were cracked to the very foundations and till date they remain shaky. Tau divided the wooden beams of the roof amongst us and I managed to build a makeshift home. Since there was no cement to plaster the walls, the rainwater could not be prevented from seeping in and the treasure of memories—my papers and photographs—were ruined. Even today, the very thought of it fills me with remorse.

Punished for His Skill

As I had mentioned earlier, my father was an extremely skilled shoemaker. Those days, Todi had provided his courtyard as a place for all shoemakers to work collectively. One day, a troubled customer came to him with a peculiar problem. He could not find the right size of *jootiyans* for his feet. In order to fit into one, he had to cut out the big toe part of the jooti but that was a source of discomfort. Todi felt confident that my father could meet this challenge and fit this man with a special shoe. He took an advance and handed him back a customized shoe. This established my father's reputation as a skilled shoemaker. My father, though illiterate, was a man of sharp intelligence and this incident had only gone on to prove it. I am sure had he got the opportunity to learn, he would have proved to be a very talented student.

However, this expertise got him into trouble with the police once. He had accepted the challenge of making a shoe for a man with two big toes and crooked feet. All the other shoemakers had turned it down but he managed with his characteristic skill. The shoes made by him were marked by his signature style but it was precisely this outstanding quality that often landed him in trouble. My mother related this incident to me: There had been a dacoity in Raipur village during the night, and when the villagers woke up, the dacoits ran away. But one of them had left a shoe behind. During investigation, the police found the shoe and started enquiring about the matter in the entire district. The clues led them to our village in Nadrauli and Chacha was summoned. The inspector wanted to know whom he had sold the shoe to. As he kept no record, my father expressed his inability to furnish a reply but the inspector grew angry and as if that was a signal, the sepoy began rewarding my father for his skill. As the blows of the rod fell on his body, he groaned with pain. When they rained kicks and pounded him, he cried for help but to no avail. Finally, Chacha had to pay a fine of one rupee and fifty paise in addition to being beaten up.

The women in our homes did a great amount of work but the house would be run in accordance to the ways of men. They were under no obligation but the men would be quick to volunteer and take up responsibility. When my father was alive, we would keep a cow or a buffalo for milk. Since we had a small plot of land, we would dig it up and scatter the seeds or hire someone for sowing. The bucket would be ours but the water had to be rented and the small patches of land were clearly demarcated. For tanning, we used a smaller well and for the rest we had no water resources. Therefore, this minimal agriculture took up more effort and yielded very little produce. Owing to the very small area of land, we could never keep a bullock. Even the ploughing was done by hiring someone. Right from cutting the grass for the cattle, feeding them, and milking as well as dispensing with the dung were tasks which were primarily done by women. We would dump our garbage at the back and after eight or ten days, fill it up in large baskets, and dispose it.

Gangi was a very strong person and when my father was alive he too would volunteer to work according to his own ability. Since he was blind, he was put to use like a mute animal. Thousands of years of illiteracy, indignity, and contempt had left people like him no different from animals—*a person without literature, art, and music is comparable to an animal without a tusk or tail.* This proverb proved true in his case. He was employed primarily to lift heavy loads. My father's untimely death not only affected me directly but also threw the three brothers into a crisis. My father's physical fitness and good vision had helped to compensate for the disabilities of his brother and uncle. Babba and I would assist them in the task of lifting dead animals. After skinning it, we would cut out about ten kilos of meat from it. Compared to *jhatka* meat, the flesh of dead animals was tasteless, but hunger had to be appeased and thus even this became food for us. At Dorilal's, pots full of dead meat would be cooked.

In those days, there were no mills to ground grain. This work was done at home by women in almost all castes, including Dalits, Muslims, and other backward castes. Gangi Babba would also engage in this work but only for his own consumption. My mother and Tai would grind grain not only for our household but for the entire village. Their kitchens were separate since the two of them often fought with each other, even though they came from the same mohalla, and in the basti they were called cousins. Early in the morning, when at dawn the grain would be set to grind, I would sit with my brother or sister in my lap and watch my mother grind and sing. Other women would also sing a variety of songs while grinding the flour. Babba would grind the flour for many homes but for Ram Singh Pradhan he did it on a permanent basis. The pradhan's mother was someone whom Babba trusted completely. He would deposit his wages with her. She was his most trusted bank—her word for him, was his account and his trust in her, the passbook. But our story was different—should I not call it a lifelong incarceration?

The women would look after the home and children, in addition to digging up the grass, sifting pebbles, weeding, and cutting. Before my father's death, my mother and Tai would not work on other people's fields, as the tanning and shoemaking brought in sufficient money. The women would cut the bark of the babool tree to prepare an extract for the tanning of the animal skin. On their front, they contributed wholeheartedly to men's work.

As far as the religious traditions were concerned, we worshipped our own gods and goddesses. Kabir and Raidas coexisted alongside our supernatural beliefs. There were several myths and legends prevalent about them—like the ones in which Raidas cuts open his chest to display the sacred thread or that he had produced a bracelet from his wooden bowl or that he had converted a queen into becoming his follower. The stories of these miracles made us forget the material and lived reality of these saints. Several other religious strains, like those of Tulsi, Surdas, and sometimes even contrary schools of thought, had got jumbled up in our cultural context.

Unpaid Labour

After my father's death, tanning ceased to be our family's occupation. His untimely death, the gradual dimming of Babba's vision, and the impairing of Tau resulted in the collapse of the entire household. We had neither the information about nor the money for medical treatment. In fact, there was a rampant belief that eye surgeons gouged out the eyes of their patients.

We would pick neem fruits and dig a hole in the ground to wash and clean them. In the monsoons, we would fill neem seeds in sacks and take them to Chandausi. Dori's son, Phool Singh, and I would skin a buffalo calf and travel three miles to sell it to Udhon, the leather contractor at Gunnaur. He was an old customer and his tannery was located in a jungle outside Gunnaur. He had managed to improve his economic status by continuing with his hereditary profession. Later, he became an elected member of the municipal corporation.

A lavish ceremonial feast would be held whenever an elderly Yadav passed away, exactly along the lines of the competitive spending witnessed in weddings. Hundreds of guests would arrive in bullock carts and carriages, and dowry-laden vehicles would take off to the groom's home. However, the Yadavs never showed any interest in educating their daughters.

We would be summoned in the middle of the night for unpaid work. People of the Valmiki community would wait at a distance and later ask for the shroud and charity. The close relatives of the deceased would be the last to leave and a ceremonial meal would customarily follow. This was an opportunity to eat to one's heart's content. I would latch on to Babba's stick and accompany him on such occasions. We would sit near the Valmikis who would carry away the leftovers. The mat would not be spread out in this space and the dogs would also scramble for food among the leftovers. However, Chamars never accepted leftovers, as this had never been part of their culture. I never ate leftover food; the very thought of it would make me want to throw up. Nevertheless, people would always scorn at us. 'You call one blind man and two people turn up! Gangi, why have you got your grandson?' He would reply in a whining tone, 'Lambardar, I got him along to hold my stick. I'll eat a little less and he could have some of my share. You have so much in abundance and he has a very small appetite.' Babba would very often employ a piteously entreating tone but once I led his hand to the food, he would eat heartily. In order to partake of the feast, it was expected that one should appear pitiable. Once at Master Mohkam Singh Yadav's feast, I went all dressed up. I had washed my shirt with *reh* (a salty, snow-white weed used as a natural detergent), oiled my hair, and polished my shoes to a brilliant shine. On seeing me, the Master commented, 'You hardly look like a Chamar! All dressed up like a Nawab, did you hope to gain entry into our courtyard? Out you go!' I left immediately. It was then that I felt the first stirrings of my sense of self-respect.

Some well-to-do Chamars and Muslims would be formally invited to Yadav feasts. Even the Valmikis would be called to clean up the place but Dori's and our home would be left out. Only if we were assigned the task of plastering and whitewashing, would we get to eat at the feast. Likewise, when the Jatavs and Telis held a feast, they would return the gesture by going to the homes of the Yadavs with rice grains and raw sugar. Obviously, we were in no position to do the same. At wedding feasts, I would run errands, feed the bullocks or pick their dung in the hope of getting to eat some food. Once that was clinched, I was sure our turn would come when everyone had eaten.

There are several memories associated with such feasts. On the first day and thirteenth day of the ceremonial feast, we were sure of getting something to eat. On these days, we would fast from morning onwards and eagerly await the call for our turn. We would climb the roof and find out if the others had eaten. It would then be the turn of the Telis, after which the Chamars and Bhangis would be called together.

In the beginning, the Chamars and Bhangis lived outside the village. However, when the Yadavs and Telis bought land and constructed their homes on the outskirts, the Chamar and Bhangis came to occupy the centre. The Yadavs considered the Chamars, and more so the Valmikis, to be untouchables and were, therefore, unhappy about their location at the centre. The pigs of the Valmikis could not move freely and they found it difficult to rear their animals in such a congested area. Therefore, the Bhangis and Chamars sold off their homes to the Yadavs and were once again back to living outside the margins of the village. They were landless then and they remain so. The leases given out by the government existed merely on paper. Even though under the particular influence of Arya Samaj teachings, the horrific practice of untouchability had declined, inter-dining caste codes were still in place—to the extent that the Telis would discriminate against the Chamars and the Jatavs against the Bhangis.

Like a greedy child, I would hop over from Rukmini's and Todi's roof to Matru's home whenever he came from Bombay. Meat and fish would be cooked at his home at least for the first two days. I ate pork at his place but the thought of the muck-eating pigs would put me off. The Jatavs avoided working as masons for Matru when he was getting his house built, even though he was willing to pay more than the Yadavs. Therefore, Munshi, a simple, poor Chamar, and I worked together to construct his home. My job was to hand over the bricks to him. It was indeed a strange situation that we would have to hide the fact that we drank the tea provided by Matru. Some well-fed Jatavs amongst us turned out be more fanatical than the Yadavs. The irony was that the other villagers called them Chamars, whereas they called themselves Jatavs.

Since I was very young, no mason wanted to employ me but Matru paid handsome wages for my labour from the money he got in Bombay. He also suggested that I get a shiny bright shirt made for myself. However, at dawn, when every other child would be sleeping, I would be woken by some claimant or the other, for some work or the other. Even contractors would be wary of employing someone as young as me. On the first day when I had gone with Khacheru to supply some bricks, everyone had teased me about being such a 'little mouse'. Nevertheless, they had especially monitored me to check if I was doing their money's worth of work. I would do my utmost in order to prove myself and not be rejected by any prospective employer. That would often mean that I ended up doing more work than an adult since I would hardly be able to survive without work. The hours were not fixed and the endless cycle of work would go on from dawn to dusk.

At Udaybhanpur, a Valmiki family had to come to Nadrauli to hire masons from our village. Munshi and I had got an assignment there. He was the chief mason, and I his digger. I would always seek those jobs where food was provided. It did not matter if I got a little less money but food was crucial. The butter milk that the Yadavs provided was a most satiating drink but they cooked a particularly bland and watery dal with very little salt and spice.

Once I was not carrying any food and an old Valmiki woman offered to make some rotis for me. That day, Munshi Chacha was carrying his food and I had brought nothing. I looked in Munshi's direction. He nodded, 'Go ahead, I won't tell anyone. In any case, your family has been excommunicated and an outcasted Chamar is as good as a Bhangi.' Just as I began to eat, Chacha told me that the Valmikis were manual scavengers and the images that my imagination conjured filled me with distaste. But I was hungry and managed to finish my food. In the evening when everybody gathered to recount the day's experience in Todi's courtyard, Munshi announced, 'Today Sauraj has eaten a roti made by a Bhangi.' This caused a sensation in the courtyard. There were at least twenty people present there and not one of them said that it was no sin to eat at a Bhangi's home or that it was wrong to have ostracized Sauraj's family.

They could hardly pronounce any punishment for me because in any case they had always treated my grandfathers and father as Bhangis. These were my own people and would always remain so.

From the point of view of tradition, even today I stand cxpelled from my caste. No Chamar will share his hukkah with any of my relatives and since I never took to it, there was no question of excluding me. Of course, on the pretext of smoking a *beedi*, I would often seek rest but when it was said that work must not stop due to smoking, I gave it up. It never developed into a habit with me. Since the community well had been dug up by my Babba and Shyamlal's Babba, we insisted that those who had objections could dig their own wells. That is why this never developed into a controversial issue.

Ancestral Home

My Hindi publisher, Shri Arun Maheshwari, had suggested that my autobiography must have a picture of my ancestral home and therefore I am sketching one with words. If the reader travels to Nadrauli, a whitewashed house would be visible from afar. Ramsingh Lekhpal is the present owner of the house. He bought it from Dorilal, which at one time belonged to Babba Bhagirath. The details related to the possession of the house do not end here. How did Dorilal come to possess the house? I would like to furnish the complete story about how he procured the house.

My elder grandmother was from Rudayan and came from a relatively well-to-do family. More significantly, her family was very supportive of her. Despite her advanced years, there was always a place for her in her parental home. Therefore, Dadi would visit her home once a month and always return with enough provisions to last for at least ten to twenty days. She would always press upon Babba to move in with her family. Babba, however, was determined to fight the battle of life on his own home ground. Moreover, his self-respect prevented him from giving in to this proposition. Everything was acceptable to him except to leave his birthplace.

Once, when Dadi was away to Rudayan, Dorilal approached Babba, 'Look Tau, you don't have any children, even your nephew is dead, and the rest of the children will not live in the village. Babua stays here but one house is enough for him. I suggest that you sell your home to me. You could spend the money you get from me and continue to live with me all your life. I will never throw you out but you must legally hand it over to me.' Babba gave it a thought and decided to wait until Dadi got back but Dori was impatient to execute his plan. He cut out three papers into the size of a hundred-rupee note and handed them over to Bhagirath (Babba), saying, 'Put these hundred-rupee notes away safely, Tau, so that no one comes to know where you've hidden them. Let's quickly go to the sub-district office and get over with the paperwork. Tai will be delighted to see the money when she returns …" and so on.

Babba was completely taken in and he put away the pieces of paper in some safe place. He wanted to take them to show the registrar but Dori dissuaded him, 'What will you do if someone snatches the money or if you lose it?' The blind man with a true heart trusted Dori and left the pieces of paper back in the house. He did not realize that on return from the sub-district office the house would no longer belong to him. At the time of registration, it was enquired, 'Did you receive the full payment for your house?' 'Yes Sir, I have received three-hundred rupees.' After returning to the village, Babba went straight to his home, as was his wont. 'Tau, you've just sold the house to me and today itself you are getting back into it? I suggest, you move into Gangi Chacha's hut. This house has been purchased for my children.' Babba was shocked to hear Dori's words. Here was a man who had assured him a home for a lifetime and now he was throwing him out on the very first day. The next day when Dadi returned, she found Babba sitting outside and Dori's family occupying the house. She wanted to know, 'What happened? Why are you sitting outside?' to which he replied, 'I've sold the house.' 'Sold it!' 'Yes, sold it.' 'Why did you sell it?' 'What could I do? You keep going off to your home and I can hardly earn any money. At least now I have some money.' 'And if you've sold your house, where will you live? Where will I live? And where is the money?' 'I have it safe with me,' he assured her patting his pouch. 'Then let me see those three-hundred rupees.' Babba got the pieces of paper out of his pouch and passed them to her. Dadi was struck as if by a bolt of lightning but she regained her composure and asked, 'Are these rupees or pieces of paper? Dori has made a fool of you. You've been cheated.' She took Babba to Dori but he made it clear, 'The registration was done only after the full payment and he affirmed that to the registrar. How would

I know what he did with the money or who stole it or from where these pieces of paper turned up?' Dadi raved and ranted and called the panchayat but among the disunited Chamars, there was no one to take the blind man's part. At the most, they took pity and gave him food for a few days. The Yadavs intervened merely to placate and reinstate the status quo.

Babba repented his gullibility but it was a severe blow that broke him from within. He collapsed in Gangi Babba's hut. After Chacha's death, Gangi Babba had moved into the house in which Amma used to live. Babba hardly survived the shock and died soon after. Since Dadi had no one to look after her, she immediately left for her home. The day she left she told Dori, 'You'll never prosper in this house.' One may not believe in irrational and illogical things like curses but the fact remains that Dori's family does not occupy that house anymore. Ramsingh may have fixed his lock on its door but even his family did not stay there for long. For those who believe in such things, it was an accursed house in which no one would flourish. For five generations now, the story of Babba's betrayal lives on.

Gangi Babba's Hut

Gangi Babba had grown old and had taken loans from the Yadavs in the village. He had wanted to contribute towards my education, but where was the money? One day on returning from school I found out that Gangi Babba had taken along Chhote with him to the sub-district Revenue Office. I went there immediately. On wanting to know why Babba had gone there, Chhote replied, 'You'd better not say anything. Gangi Chacha is selling his hut for six-hundred rupees.' Dorilal brought Urman Singh Yadav along with him just when the papers were being prepared. Urman Singh was a very influential man and people would also refer to him as the sarpanch. He said, 'I have been brought here by Dori who has told me that Gangi is selling his hut. You must pay up fifty per cent to me. The wall at the back of Gangi's hut is joined to the wall at the back of my house. I will not let him sell it and if he does, then he has to pay three-hundred rupees from the six hundred he gets for it.' He was asking for half the amount only because the hut was at the back of his house. These were typical strong-arm tactics of a Yadav. If we did not pay up, he would not permit its sale. I tried to look for help and spotted Master Khushiram Yadav. He was a prominent man as well as the school headmaster, and was known for his sense of fair play. I approached him, 'Sir, you must tell the sarpanch that he should have nothing to do with the hut.' But I could see that he was completely helpless. He explained, 'Look, I know that Urman is completely in the wrong. He has no right to claim half the share but I think you will have to give in. Give him the money. What is the point in fighting? After all, it was Dori who got him. I guess he will also make a few rupees from this.' Thus, sightless Gangi's hut was sold. Urman had made away with half the price and I could do nothing about it.

◆

Maya's Marriage

During her stay at Pali, Amma was constantly anxious about securing Maya's future. As soon as she turned eleven, her marriage was fixed. In my village, child marriage is the norm among the people of my community. It is practised even to this day. In this case, the boy Gangawasi was about ten to fifteen years older than my sister. There were three reasons as to why he still remained unmarried. First, after the amputation of his father's leg, a Jat, Chaudhary Ramsahay, had kept his mother, Phoolwati, as his mistress in his home. The worldly-wise people of the village knew about this illicit relationship, which was being carried on openly. Even though he was agonized within, the boy's father, Matrulal, seemed to have accepted it as the inevitable consequence of his impairment. The village was dominated by Jats and Brahmins and the tacit support offered by them to the Jat led to this Chamar family's ruin. This was the main reason why a match could not be found for the boy.

My Jeeja's, that is, brother-in-law's, father, would make shoes and sell them in the market. He did not possess the mental strength to overcome his physical impairment but imagined that it could be countered by getting Gangawasi married. About eight years ago, his wife had given birth to a son in Chaudhary Ramsahay's home and this had angered the entire Jat community. They disapproved of the open manner in which he was keeping a Chamar woman in his home in which his wife was already present, but from whom he had no children. Sometime later, the Dalit mistress died suddenly, after which Ramsahay Jat and Matru Chamar jointly brought up the baby with great love and care. The Jat was the real father but publicly the Chamar's name was declared. This secret was well-known not only in our village but in the neighbouring villages as well.

An additional reason was that Matrulal's elder son, Gangawasi, was not considered good-looking. However, I must add that this was strictly an assessment of his physical appearance. At heart, he seemed a good man and about this both my sister and I concurred. I have had to mention his unattractive appearance as the second impediment in the context of which he had remained unmarried at that age. The third reason was something that was common to all Chamars of Mirzapur— almost all the homes sent their young men and children to the markets for shoe-repairing work and that has not changed till this day.

Gangawasi's father possessed about twenty-five bighas of sandy land. No Chamar had so much land in his name. It was only because of the above-mentioned drawbacks that an alliance with an extremely poor family such as ours was made. My sister was very beautiful but completely illiterate, whereas he had studied up to a couple of levels. The formalities got over late at night and the next morning, the baraat left without being given any refreshment. Many grumbled over this while others expressed sympathy, 'After all, she is a widow's daughter. Where will the poor woman get money to feed a baraat?' Jeejaji's father offered, 'Come on, I'll arrange for some breakfast at Babrala.'

Bhikari had not come for my sister's wedding and had sent Chhotelal with a few rupees instead. That money was offered as *kanyadaan* (the ceremony of giving away the bride). My mother had been hoping that from Pali, Bhikari would extend a little more help. Among our other relatives, three of my paternal aunts were present. I knew that after the wedding was over, Amma would return to Pali and the other relatives to their respective homes. I would be left alone with Babba in the village.

Who would be my companion here? My heart was filled with the dread of loneliness. The going away of my sister was especially painful for me. In our family, it was not customary for the bride to leave for her marital home immediately after marriage but the groom's relatives had already fixed with Tau to take her away. Therefore, the next morning when the baraat prepared to leave, my eyes filled up with tears.

There were a few carriages owned by the Jatavs in the basti but no one was willing to give it for an hour or two. Since we were outcasted, no one would take the fare from us nor be willing to give it for free. Finally, Babba succeeded in hiring a bullock-cart and the Lambardar agreed to take my sister in the cart but refused to let my brother-in-law travel in it. My Jeeja went on foot with the rest of the wedding procession. Even though the fare was paid, it was stressed that in ferrying her to the main road a great favour had been done to us. Everyone went back home but I insisted that I would accompany her till Senjana and so I kept sitting in the cart. Somehow, I could not tear myself away from her. The moment she got into the bus, I felt a lump in my throat and I too climbed into it. It was only when we reached Babrala station that everybody noticed me.

The wedding procession reached its destination late at night. Since no meal had been provided, the groom's party had managed with some melons that were eaten on the way and by the time it reached the village, everyone was very hungry and thirsty. Some people began to say, 'What kind of an abject poverty is this that they could not even afford to provide one meal?' Others pointed out, 'At least Gangawasi has got married and that is no mean feat.'

A few days back, the homes of the Chamars in this village had been set on fire. It was said that the Chamars had refused to work for the Jat-Brahmins for low wages and had stopped working on their fields. Therefore, it was alleged that the 'upper' castes had set fire to their homes but there was such an atmosphere of fear that these views were voiced in hushed tones. It was a small village with only one Bhangi, four Chamar, four Brahmin, and five Jat homes. At the time of my sister's wedding, most of the Chamar and Bhangi homes had been burnt down. Balle Singh's home was the only one to survive the fire, as it was a pucca house. The Chamars managed to cover their roofs with thatches before the onset of monsoon and it was to one such newly thatched-roof home that my sister arrived as a bride. The main road ran close to a well near Maya's home. Due to a heavy downpour, the water from the road filled into the well, as it did not have a plinth cemented around it. The elders of our community gathered together to approach the Brahmins and Jats to ask for water from their cemented, secure wells. Like suppliants, they pleaded their case with folded hands but untouchability was so strictly observed that that the Jats and Brahmins did not provide a drop of water. The one Valmiki home as well as all the Chamars were forced to drink the contaminated water. The consequence of this was that in every home children fell sick with some throwing up and running high fever. Within a few hours, several died. Even my face, hands, and feet developed a swelling which was to become the cause of my chronic rheumatic condition. Jeejaji caught a throat infection that resulted in his death later.

The Relish and the Agony

On my arrival at Maya's marital home, I was received with a lot of warmth. Each time I returned from my wanderings, Chandro or Mandro, Maya's sisters-in-law, would hand me a laddoo or some such sweetmeat. For me, sweets or good meals were hard to come by and perhaps, it was for the first time since my father's death that I was getting to eat without having to work for it. My spare time would be spent in playing and jumping around but food was always topmost on my mind.

At my sister's marital home, I came down with a terrible case of gripes on consuming a large amount of unripe mangoes. My sister began to cry on seeing me writhe with agony and there was no medicine man to be found in the village. It was suggested that I be taken to Sakatpur and my Jeeja's brother-in-law, Chhiddalal, carried me on his shoulders all the way. The doctor at Sakatpur turned out to be a quack but the medicine he gave worked. I stayed there for a couple of hours and was taken back in the evening when the afternoon heat abated. My eleven-year-old sister, who had come as a bride to this village only a few days ago, was weeping bitterly for me. She kept coming to enquire about me all the while she was being taught the customs and observance of the veil. However, I was feeling much better and had there been any delay in taking me to a doctor, matters would have taken a completely different turn. It would have been assumed that I was in the grip of some evil powers and like my father I too would have been subjected to the same exorcism which led to his death. Since my Jeeja's brother-in-law was a dweller of Amroha town, he had insisted on medical treatment instead of superstitious cures.

At My Sister's Marital Home

My sister had been sent off to her marital home at the time of the wedding itself, instead of having been given a separate farewell or *vidaai*. Today, when I reflect upon the heart-rending songs that my Tais and Chachis sang at the time of her departure, I am compelled to ponder over their core meaning:

O dear father! You gave my brother,
A palatial home to live in style,
And I have been sent into exile.
O dear father! I am the garbage pile,
In your courtyard, disposed of the very next day.
O dear father! I am the bird of this house,
That will fly away abroad one day.

The irony in our case was all the more tragic. Neither was the father alive nor did the brother occupy a palatial house. Even two square meals could barely be managed. In my sister's case, we had gone against the conventional practice of bidding farewell to the bride after she had spent a couple of years at her parents' home. The girl was expected to stay till her *gauna* (farewell ceremony) was performed. Maya had been sent off with the bridegroom's party because there was no one in her parental home to take responsibility for her.

My Jeeja did not have bullocks and would need to hire or borrow them from his aunt in Nagri. These too he got only if they could be spared. Often, his crops would dry up completely due to lack of water. I would help him out in the tasks of irrigating, sowing, and harvesting.

Rheumatism: At the Mercy of the Wise Men

In due course of time, I was struck with rheumatic pain and Jeejaji lost his voice. There was no source of income and though Amma had called Jeeja over to Nadrauli, there was little she could do. She came over the moment she heard about my joint pains and Jeeja's disease. She was so anxious to have us cured as though something had been ailing her own heart. Jeejaji had mortgaged his fields and arranged for about two hundred rupees for his treatment. In his village, the Jats and Brahmins would lend money to Chamars at an interest rate that would be fixed arbitrarily. Amma decided to go to her elder sister, Sukhdei, and seek her son Nathulal's help, who was pursuing higher studies in medicine in Delhi. At that very moment, Makkhan, Khacheru, and Paiju came into the courtyard and began to say, 'Radhe's wife! Why are you speaking of going to Delhi and Calcutta when in our own village we have such well-known wise men? Don't you think it will be a matter of very great shame for us? Patients come to us from such far-flung areas and you are talking of taking your son-in-law elsewhere! If you want, this very evening we can arrange for a meeting at Khacheru's house. Bangali Baba, Sayyed Baba, and Bhopur's Chamunda will descend. Gangawasi's disease can be described and the Gods will bring about a cure.'

'Then do whatever you elders think is best, otherwise I am willing to go any distance for their cure. My Sauraj's limbs have become inflamed now but had he been well enough, he would have earned some money and spent it on the treatment. Now I have to wait for him to get better or else I would've left for Delhi tomorrow itself,' Amma answered.

That night, the wise men met and a musical invocation of the Gods began. All our Gods were non-vegetarians and would also demand alcohol the moment they descended. Sayyed had possessed Makkhan, 'Sayyed Baba is here! Sing on the verses! Babua, you must begin ...' Tau would immediately sing, *Your victory is hailed from Bengal and the west! You've defeated many a warrior and emerged the best!* In a flurry, Khacheru called for my mother but she asked Tau to speak on her behalf. Tau felt his way along the wall and addressed Sayyed Baba, who was riding on Makkhan's head, 'Yes, Maharaj! Our son-in-law's voice has disappeared. Has some evil power grasped his vocal cord? Is there a bigger power than you in this world?'

On hearing his praise, Makkhan drummed a beat and dug his elbows into the loose soil with full force. 'Can anyone dare to be more powerful than me? Come on, hail my power!' Everyone said, 'Jai Maharaj!' Once again, Makkhan dug in his elbows and began on his own, 'I know everything. Radhe's wife's son has been overpowered by a witch and Gangawasi is in the grip of a wind from Bengal.'

'And what is wrong with Sauraj?'

'What do you mean? Sauraj must give up reading books and newspapers....'

Everyone was struck with terror having heard this. 'But Maharaj, Gangawasi has not been to Bengal even in his dreams...!' 'Has anyone been able to check the wind?' another intoned. 'But what is the cure?'

'The cure will commence right away. Now that Sayyed Baba is here, you have nothing to worry,' Paiju assured us, acting as his medium.

The descending of spirits on Makkhan, Chhote, and Khacheru, had begun to appear somewhat suspicious and pretentious role-playing to me but Amma had faith in them and I was unable to raise my voice of protest. I did not have a satisfactory answer to this logical question: 'If there are no evil powers at work, then why can't I stand on my feet?'

Meanwhile, the entire programme was being conducted as if some festivities were under way. Maharaj spoke, 'Hurry up with the offerings! The sooner you arrange for the prasad, the earlier you will be cured.' A rooster was the ordained offering for Sayyed Baba. Therefore, Khacheru said, 'We'll arrange for the fowl right away.'

'Not one, at least two!' Makkhan announced in a loud tone with a shake of his head. 'Radhe's wife! Hurry up! Arrange for a lamb, get hold of some fowls and all will be well!'

It was the rainy season and neither a rooster nor a lamb was available in the village. Amma began to despair and I ended up volunteering to fetch them from Rewada. Shyamlal also offered to accompany me, as he considered it to be something of an adventure. In the darkened hour of an eerie night, we set out with our spirits high, since we believed that the gods themselves had entered our beings. I could barely walk due to my inflamed knee but we crossed the river Karakvay, which was in full spate, to buy a weighty, country-bred rooster at a dear price. We also bought a lamb that we carried on our shoulder. It began to rain heavily as we started back and had to swim across the now flooded river to reach home before midnight.

The spices had been readied and the wise men were at their vigil. Pure ghee was taken on loan from Todi and a small fire of dung cakes had been lit. The moment Khacheru applied the knife to the rooster's neck, a stream of blood poured down to the ground. Makkhan, possessed by Sayyed Baba, accepted the offering by drinking two sips of the blood. The instructions were given to prepare the dish and Makkhan walked away. For every God, there was a separate offering. In our basti, no one believed in or worshipped Ram, Krishna, or Shiva as compared to these spirits. In fact, many childless, savarna couples would throng to the homes of these Chamar exorcists.

The meat was cooked at Khacheru Tau's home under the supervision of Paiju Tau. Not a single vessel from our home was used. This was the untouchability that was practised amongst us untouchables, of which all members of my family were victims. As was the custom, Paiju Tau was entrusted with the task of distributing the meat and curry. That day he distributed in such a partial manner that he ended up giving more to both his daughters. As a headman, he was given to favouritism without caring the least for Radhe's wife's two homes or that one of the patients happened to be the son-in-law, whose money had been spent in getting the offering. There was only some curry left for us in the platter. Anyway, we kept watching on to see if Jeeja's voice came back. Even after two to three weeks, there wasn't an iota of difference in his condition. Instead, the inflammation in my knees had increased all the more due to excessive walking, swimming, and getting wet in the rain.

All kinds of treatment were being tried on me. From my sister's village, ashes were brought and exorcisms were undertaken. I began to take some regular medicine from a doctor. I found some relief after consuming it for ten–fifteen days but it did not prove to be a cure. For two to four months, I could not walk without the aid of a stick.

On the Verge of Widowhood

It had been barely three to four years that Maya had been married and Jeejaji's condition had steadily deteriorated. Amma was waiting for Sayyed Baba's cure to come about while some sensible people in the village advised us to go to a proper doctor. Amma had begun to see sense and by then my maternal cousin Dr Nathulal's letter had also arrived. He had completed his MBBS from Maulana Azad Medical College and was interned for a house job at Irvin Hospital (LNJP). This was probably the last year of the course. In his letter to Amma, he had asked her to come over to Delhi and also to make her own arrangements for the stay.

Amma took a loan of three hundred rupees at the monthly interest rate of five rupees per hundred and with that we arrived in Delhi. Amma took us to a jhuggi in Rajouri Garden, where she had worked in a flour mill. Fortunately, we found a room, which was vacant and, therefore, temporarily available. The kind-hearted people of these jhuggis had offered it to us without payment of rent. Dr Nathulal came over as soon as he received our letter and the moment she saw him, Amma's face kindled with the hope of finding a cure for Jeejaji's illness.

Jeejaji in Hospital

A few days later, Jeejaji was admitted to the hospital for an operation. On the day when Amma went to visit him, his eyes filled with tears. He keenly desired to return home a cured man and though he was hopeful of the treatment, he was also full of apprehensions. Amma tried to reassure him but he kept looking on, helpless and speechless. Amma was also willing to donate blood if it was required during the operation.

Upon admission, Jeejaji was made to inhale into a pipe-like contraption and after a few days a date for his operation was fixed. I stayed with him as an attendant. The operation was done on the appointed day and he was shifted to a ward with a pipe fitted to an opening in his throat. This was a procedure through which fluids such as tea or milk could pass through the pipe to his stomach and through the same mechanical method, phlegm would be extracted. In that ward, there were several other patients who had undergone a similar operation. A whistle had been fitted inside their throats but I could not see anyone being able to speak. My heart was filled with fear and doubts about his full recovery. I was now permitted to stay with him all the time and we kept waiting for the cut in his throat to dry up so that the whistle could be removed and his treatment quickly reach its end. It was expected that he would be able to speak then.

I had been staying at the hospital for about a fortnight now. Once, in the middle of the night, Jeejaji began to cough and it would not stop. I panicked when I saw a stream of blood shooting from his throat. His chest was completely soaked in blood. I rushed to the nurse but could not find a single doctor on duty. The nurse ran off to call a doctor and I hurriedly returned to Jeejaji. His death began to seem imminent due to the heavy blood loss. His throat was producing a wind-like sound and he indicated to me in sign language that he would live no more. I thought that he was trying to say something about his wife and newborn. He shook his head and spoke in a hoarse whisper, 'I am not going to survive.' I can never forget the helpless expression I saw in his eyes as he confronted his death. Watching him in the throes of death, I began to see in his image, the scenes of my father's untimely demise. Their faces seemed to blur into each other. His speechless communication was that I must look after my sister. I hurriedly ran off to look for the doctor. The day he got admitted to the hospital, my sister had given birth to her first child, Vinod. Even though I tried to reassure him, I began to lose hope. At the age of five or six, I had seen my father die before his time in a similarly agonizing manner. In his case, he had died due to lack of medical help and at the hands of exorcists, whereas my Jeejaji was dying in a big hospital in the capital city of the country, in the presence of doctors and nurses. I had suffered the consequences of my mother's widowhood and I could see my sister's life falling into a similar ruin.

I ran to the doctor's room and informed the nurse but the doctor on duty, Dr Narrotam Puri, came very late and that too without any life-saving equipment. This delay and negligence resulted in a further loss of blood. I was sent out of the room. No oxygen cylinder was available and they could also not arrange one from another room. Jeejaji breathed his last. Ten or fifteen minutes later, the team of doctors emerged from the ward. Several doctors came one after the other and no one said anything. Subsequently, the doctor on duty called me to him and said, 'Very sorry, son! We could not save your Jeeja's life. You must take hold of yourself.' Not a single drop of tear rolled down my cheek to see my Jeeja, now turned into a corpse. Somehow, I couldn't believe he was dead. The shock of his death had rendered me numb. Perhaps out of professional solidarity, they sent a helper to accompany me to the hostel. Nathulal used to stay up late at night and I met him outside the hostel itself. He was stunned by the unexpected news of Jeejaji's death. He asked, 'What are you saying, Sheoraj? It was only last evening that he was operated upon! How can this be? He had managed to survive the more critical junctures.' I repeated, 'Yes, he is no more.'

He immediately rushed back with me to the hospital and kept exclaiming, 'Really, this is terrible! I have not even completed my house job as a trainee and to witness the death of my cousin's husband at my very entry into the profession! It is a blot on my career! What will my sister, Maya, say? You came to me in Delhi with such hopes!' Thus, despite the fact that he had done his best to help us, he kept blaming himself. I said to him, 'The doctors' negligence has caused his death. He died because he kept bleeding. He was given neither blood nor oxygen on time but you are not to blame.'

Nathulal Bhai was saddened at the sight of Jeejaji's dead body which was immediately taken away. Wiping his eyes with a handkerchief, he marched into the doctor's room and said, 'Sir, you did not take care of the patient. He died because you could provide him no aid. It's a clear case of medical negligence. I am going to lodge a complaint and get a post-mortem done.' A long argument ensued and the team of doctors displayed their blood-stained clothes to prove that they had left no stone unturned in performing their duty. They explained in English and pointed out to Nathulal that he too would be a doctor some day and must consider why any doctor would want to kill a patient. They emphasized that this was against the principles of their profession, 'When a patient dies, we are saddened. Look at our shirts, the blood spots everywhere. We tried our best but he had bled excessively. How could we save him? There was also the lack of resources to consider.' The matter was allowed to rest.

Maya: Child Bride to a Young Widow

Bhai Saab instructed his friends to send telegrams to my sister and other relatives to inform those who desired to see Gangawasi before the cremation. The moment I got back to Bhai's hostel room, I broke down. That night I did not get any sleep at all. I was neither weeping nor entirely normal. I felt somewhat detached from the whole thing. I could not figure out what was happening. I was not at all mentally prepared to cope with this heart-rending tragedy. At the most, we had thought that if the doctors would not be able to cure him, at least he would live and manage to survive a few years. We had anticipated our defeat till only this eventuality. What will happen to sister Maya and her barely month-old infant? Amma had entertained such high hopes. She would tell me, 'Your Jeeja will get books for you and then if you want to study, you can do it at home. One day, your Jeeja will also shoulder the responsibility of your marriage. So what if you don't have a father, you have the support of your Jeeja.'

The next day as we took the DTC bus to Rajouri Garden, Bhai Sahab advised me not to blurt out the news of Jeejaji's death but to reveal it only gradually to Amma. Amma was constantly praying for Gangawasi's recovery. Her thoughts were chiefly taken up with the idea of his treatment and our return to the village. She had not found any work in Delhi yet. We had thought that if the treatment provided some relief, we could go back to the village to arrange for more money, even if it meant selling off the house. However, Amma was fearful on account of the rumours she had heard about doctors in the city and their treatment of the poor. It was said that the doctors operated upon the poor to take away their organs and fitted them into the bodies of the rich. She had heard that they experimented on the bodies of the poor like they would on a frog or a bigger animal. They tested their methods on the poor in order to gain experience and expertise so that they could serve the well-to-do people better. She had concluded that everyone did not have equal access to accomplished doctors.

It is difficult to say whether there was any truth in the perceptions that the villagers held about doctors in the city but who could prevent Amma from believing that her fears had proved right in the case of my Jeeja's tragic death? The ideal conception of a doctor for whom rich or poor, high or low castes do not matter and for whom a patient is only a patient—that notion had received a blow.

Our faces wore a sad look and Amma immediately sensed that something was wrong. However, we informed her calmly enough that his condition was very critical. Amma panicked and I could no longer hold back my pent up emotions, I burst into tears, 'Amma, Jeeja is no more! He is dead! He bled excessively from the cut in his throat and the doctors couldn't reach on time. Their delay caused his death.' I told her sobbingly. Amma collapsed and began to wail loudly. Several people gathered to enquire and Amma would stop crying only to recount her past sorrows and her fears about those that lay ahead. Nathulal sat in grief for a long time.

Late in the evening, Dr Lal left and the body remained in the mortuary for four days. It was futile to wait for anyone to arrive from the village. Keeping the body in the mortuary was going to cost us some money and furthermore, the cremation was in an electric crematorium. We would have to arrange for at least a hundred-and-fifty rupees. The next day, a friend of Dr Lal's came over to say, 'If you donate the body for further medical research, you will not be charged the fees for the mortuary. On the other hand, you may receive some money from the hospital.' Amma was not in favour of it. To hand over the body for experimentation and examination was against our cultural practice. Even the doctor knew it. However, when I think of it today, I feel it would have been better to have given the body for medical research. At least the doctors could have understood the disease and other lives could have been saved. In any case, the fact remained that he died due to delay and perhaps negligence. Somehow, I have not been able to drive away this thought from my head.

After the doctor went away, we waited for two more days for our relatives to turn up from Mirzapur or Nadrauli. Even though Gangawasi was sleeping his last slumber in the mortuary, the sorrow of his not waking up was still alive in our hearts. Our sense of mourning was so intense that it seemed as if his body lay right in front of us. We came to regret our decision of getting him to the hospital. If not for long, at least he would have survived for a few years. If he had died among his own people, at least no one would have blamed us for his death.

Donations for a Shroud

Now we needed money for our fare back to the village and for Gangawasi's cremation. We kept expecting that someone would arrive from somewhere. Like the body in the mortuary, we had also turned numb with grief. Our neighbours in the jhuggi provided food to us but what consolation could be offered in such a grief-stricken time? Our penury dogged us at every step and added to our sorrows. In our desperation, we thought of asking Dr Lal for some money but we knew well enough that he was completing his course in medicine with some money on loan or a scholarship. His parents were not well-off and we could burden him no further. If we didn't have the fare, we could always travel without a ticket. We could get by with explaining our situation. But how was one to cremate a body without money in a huge city like Delhi?

Ultimately, the people in the neighbourhood came to our help. An emaciated and dark-complexioned man called Bande came up close to us and, upon knowing our problem, spread the word. The people of the jhuggi dealt with the problem as if it was a collective responsibility. They had seen the doctor come and go. Since everyone knew that he was related to us, for many it was a matter of surprise that the nephew was studying medicine and the aunt did not have money even for a shroud. There were some though who knew our real circumstances. Our impoverished condition gave away the truth. Why would we be staying in a jhuggi if we had money? The poor have more compassion and thus they immediately understood our plight. They felt duty-bound to help us and many came forward genuinely to do so. Just like beggars who spread out a sheet for alms, we were begging for help. Some contributed a rupee, some two, and some even fifty- and twenty-five paise coins. They added, 'Don't worry! If more money is needed, we'll arrange for more donations. Your son-in-law's body must be given a dignified cremation.'

Overcome with gratitude towards them, I began to wonder if I would ever be able to repay their kindness. After all, I too was poor like them. How would I ever get an opportunity to help them? How affable these people were! The women had tears in their eyes when we left. These jhuggis were inhabited by Dalits who were rich in the emotion of love. Even today, I wonder if I have been able to do anything constructive towards the eradication of poverty of all those Dalits to whom I am so indebted.

Dr Nathulal took us inside the mortuary for a last glimpse of Jeejaji. Even after being in the deep freeze for four days, Jeeja looked as though he would just rise, speak in his hoarse whispers, and walk out with us. Finally, the body was covered with a shroud. Amma caressed his face after uncovering it. She also saw the cut in his throat from which the blood had been wiped clean and began to cry bitterly, 'You are dead, son! And we could do nothing about it! You must forgive us. You must convey our helplessness to God in Heaven. We are praying for you with our heart and soul that in your next birth you are born in a more fortunate home.' As she said this, Amma collapsed on the ground and Dr Lal had to help her to get on her feet.

Amma handed over the fees of the mortuary to Dr Lal, and at the crematorium we paid for the cremation. I sat next to Amma in the Waiting Room for our turn. Just as a paper is inserted in a photostat machine, the body would enter the incinerator on a stretcher and with the press of a button be reduced to ashes. Bodies arrived in the crematorium accompanied by large numbers of people. Our turn was about to come when I saw that a body was brought in an expensive woodworked, large coffin. It was decorated with flowers and accompanied by a huge retinue of people in cars, who seemed dressed up as if for a wedding. One glimpse and one could tell that they were very affluent people. The memsahibs had their hair cut short like men and wore expensive clothes. They were speaking English and when they came into the Waiting Room, they turned to my shabbily dressed mother with contempt and spoke in a condescending manner to order us out. Amma got up to go, whereas I felt that since it was our turn, we were in our rights to stay on.

By that time Dr Lal had also arrived and was surprised to find us still waiting outside. Amma said, 'We've been thrown out because of our ragged appearance.' On hearing of their behaviour, the doctor spoke in English with these upper-class, urban dwellers in a bold and emphatic manner. His face had turned red with anger and ultimately they had to apologise.

Subsequently, the officials carried Jeeja's body on the stretcher and with the press of just a button it was converted to ashes within seconds. They wanted to know if we wanted to take away the ashes and bones with us, which they referred to as 'flowers'. We wondered whose ashes we would be carrying away, as one after the other, bodies were being consigned to the machine. We refused the offer and walked away.

We took a train at night from Delhi and the doctor came to see us off at the station.We had come to the city, reposing faith in doctors and hopeful of recovering Gangawasi's voice but far from getting him cured, we had lost him completely. All through the way, Amma and I could only speak of our sorrows—what would Maya, the people at Mirzapur and Jeeja's sisters say? How will the newborn infant be raised? Entangled in this web of issues, we reached Mirzapur the next day. Not just our clothes, our hearts, too, were in a state of disrepair. Our feet moved ahead but it seemed that we were receding backwards. Maya's first question was, 'Have you got him admitted in the hospital?' Amma embraced my sister, and in the outburst of grief that followed, she recounted our entire tale to the basti.

The telegram carrying the information of Jeeja's death arrived on the day Amma and I were setting out from Mirzapur for Nadrauli. That day, I cursed the postal department. The rest of the telegrams also reached late. I learnt much later from the doctor that his 'upper'-caste colleagues had, in fact, not sent the telegrams that night. They were dispatched much later and, therefore, they reached very late.

Sillu

My sister's son, Sillu, by her second husband, Bhajjan, went on to marry Rani Sharma. Theirs was a love marriage. One day, I received a complaint from Rani that Sillu had lied to her about his caste and had deceived her into marrying him. Sillu had told her that he was a Jat but when she came to Delhi, Rambharose's daughter had unwittingly revealed to her that we were Chamars. Being a Brahmin herself, Rani had spoken in a shocked tone, 'Chamars! Chamars! In our community we don't allow Chamars to even sit with us! Why did Sillu lie to me?'

Before Sillu's wife could leave him for being a Jatav, I decided to intervene and inform her that he was not lying to her. This was indeed a tragic truth and one would have to go back to its very root. I had to tell Rani Sharma that my sister had been married to her step brother-in-law, Bhajjan, whose father was the same elderly and prosperous Jat of our village, Chaudhary Ramsahay, who had kept Jeeja's mother as his mistress. He owned about hundred-and-fifty acres of land. After Gangawasi's death, he had declared that Bhajjan would look after his stepbrother's child and also promised protection to Maya for as long as he lived. And he proved true to his word. In illness and adversity, he helped this family openly. He lived up to the role of a father-in-law for my sister. The Jat community was critical of him but even in his old age, he remained very influential. He had no other child and Bhajjan was known to have several vices. However, in accepting Bhajjan, my sister had consoled herself with the thought that it is better to have a bull that butts than to have an empty cowshed.

Ramsahay Jat had kept Jeeja's mother at his home even though his father was still alive. The child born at the Jat's home was called Harijan. Later, this was changed to Haribhajan, and now it had become Bhajjan. However, due to societal pressures and the harassment of savarnas, he had abandoned this child. Neither could he accord to his mistress the status of a wife. After Bhajjan's mother, Phoolwati's, untimely death, this adulterous relationship came to an end. But, do blood ties ever end?

It was a fact well known, far and wide that Bhajjan was not Matru Chamar's but Ramsahay Jat's son. In an attempt to give this bond its due, Ramsahay would help this family during times of trouble and to a large extent protect it from the intimidations of the savarnas. He could have chosen to sever all ties with this family after Phoolwati's death, but he did not do so. In any case, circumstances unfolded in such a manner that it was this Bhajjan who turned out to be the real support in my sister's life, even though he was a loafer with an irascible temperament. An irresponsible person who had become habituated to remaining idle, for Bhajjan, education was a waste of time. However, today it is he who is my brother-in-law. It is another matter that this man also turned out to be a wastrel. He was only a somewhat milder version of Bhikari, who opposed the education of his children, and was given to picking up fights and drinking country liquor. Governed by his bad habits, this man sold off his property without bothering to purchase any. Every time I suggested that he give his children an education, pat would come his reply, 'I want my children to lead a happy life and so instead of sending them to school, I'd rather they make and sell shoes. If you think you can improve their lot, take them to Delhi. Get them admitted to a school, get them married, and find a job for them.'

My sister's life wilted like a tree in autumn and she had to put in as much effort as a man in the fields. She had announced her decision to stay on at her marital home to Amma. She was well-acquainted with the consequences of widowhood that my mother had lived through. She was willing to wait for Bhajjan to become more capable. Meanwhile, through sheer hard work and courage she undertook the task of looking after herself, her children, and even Bhajjan. My mother had never been able to take a decision like that. However, the fact remains that after my father's death, my mother did not have any land in her name, whereas, even if it was less fertile, my sister had twenty-four bighas after my Jeeja's death. Therefore, that land proved to be the real anchor in Maya's life and it could be preserved only through the tacit support that Ramsahay gave to her family. Had that not been the case, I wonder what would have been the fate of my sister, her children, and Bhajjan!

Haribhajan is younger to me and our temperaments and values are completely opposed to each other but my sister had chosen him as a solution to the problems of her life. Amma had asked her and she had replied that it was better to live with a bad man than to live alone in a house.

I began to respect him and held my conflicted feelings about him in check. I tried my best to honour this relationship and give it its due but even today, Bhajjan finds it difficult to remain normal and natural, both with me and our entire community. Only those who have led a similarly liminal existence can possibly understand his anguish, the plight of an *akkarmashi* like Sharan Kumar Limbale. But Bhajjan was no Sharan Kumar Limbale, who fought for the right to his father's name. Ramsahay had no other child and he did not hand over his entire estate and the rest of the property to Bhajjan, but at least he gave twenty-four bighas of land to him. However, Bhajjan remains anxiety-ridden and ill at ease about his origins. For how long can he drown his angst and suffocation in a bottle of liquor? Had he been educated, he would have become another Sharan Kumar Limbale and had Sharan Kumar Limbale remained illiterate, he would have become like Bhajjan. This is the similarity that I see in these two contrasting personalities.

The Iron Bracelet

Before going for our treatment to Delhi, Jeejaji and I had gone to Luhamai village, carrying two-and-a-half kilos of jaggery with us as fees for another cure. To cover the distance of several miles on foot and that too with severe joint pains! What a painful journey that was! As was his practice, the ironsmith immediately fetched an iron bracelet and slipped it over my hand, saying 'You can donate anything once you are cured.' We handed over the jaggery to him and returned exactly as we had come. With continuous breaks for rest, we reached our village late at night. That night, the pain and fatigue was so great that I almost despaired of life. Every time that I had stopped for rest, the inflammation in the joints had increased. I was laid up in Gangi Babba's hut for four to five days.

Many people in the basti, who pretended to be close to me, would, in fact, make fun of me. 'He won't get better. Their family is like that. One person is blind and the other is lame. No one seems to be fit and healthy. Almost everyone is a patient. Radhe died, Gangi and Bhagirath's sons also did not live. Babua's Puran and Roshan, both sons are dead. This family seems to have carried over a curse from a previous birth.'

Those days I could find no meaning in carrying on with the burden of childhood on my shoulders.

◆

Summons

In the year 1966, I was summoned to the pradhan's house on a complaint made by my Tai. I went to his courtyard and sat on a stool made of reed which the pradhan, Ramsingh Yadav, found to be unexpectedly defiant. He grew all the more enraged and shouted, 'Sauraj, did you steal Babua's wife's flour?'

'Yes sir. Had Tau been around, I would have asked for it. Since I was very hungry and there was no hope of getting it from Tai, I pilfered it. Whenever I get work and am able to earn, I'll return it to her.'

'Oh! So you were hungry, were you, you scum! If you can steal flour to have a meal, have some knocks from my shoe too!' The pradhan pushed me off the stool and I fell on my back. He got his shoe off and whacked my head with it several times. 'You *chamru*! What do you mean by sitting on the stool when you should be sitting on the ground?'

'Pradhanji, I don't keep well. My legs are swollen due to gout and it hurts to sit on the ground. I will definitely return Tai's flour. I am willing to pull your waterwheel or do any other job you want me to.' I was pleading with him but he was all fire and fury. Just then, pradhan's mother stepped in, 'Gangi is working for us and this boy is also learning to pull the machine. He will be working for us in the future, so don't be so harsh on him. Come on boy, get up.'

Encouraged by her words, I got up and ran off home crying. In the evening when Tau returned and got to know about the whole incident, he reprimanded Tai severely, 'Did he run away with your land? He has no parents and is ill, if you had given him a roti, would you have been the poorer for it?'

Years later, when Tai passed away, I went with my younger brother to the village to perform her last rites. I wanted to cremate her in the same place as that of my mother. I had not been able to make it for my mother's cremation. The people of the basti requested me to take Tai's body to Narora Gangaghat. I did their bidding.

Child Brick-moulder

Once Beedhe Phupha took me along with him to help him with brick-moulding as he had given up working with dead animals. He promised Tau that he would take care of me and also pay me for my labours. I went with Phupha imagining that perhaps there would be fewer difficulties and not much hard labour in that sort of work. Phupha needed one person to hand him the brick-dough when he moulded bricks at the kiln. Bua was nursing an infant and, therefore, was not in the position to help him. Any other person hired in my place would have demanded half the profit whereas a child could do the work of an adult at half the rate.

I was put to work the very next day of my arrival since customary hospitality was not for the likes of me. I learnt to make balls of the clay dough, which I would gather with both my hands and carry in my lap. Phupha would place them in the mould and bring out the bricks deftly. I would quickly place all the dough balls in a row of moulds and then clear the space for the next row. This sequence was repeated everyday. Due to constant contact with mud, the skin of my hands and feet had begun to crack. I developed chilblain in my feet. In winter, my condition worsened and subsequently I fell ill. My face and limbs developed a swelling and I became completely incapable of lifting the dough-balls. My ill health annoyed Phupha and he ranted, 'You've barely worked for three–four months and now you are sick. I have fifteen- to twenty-thousand bricks more to mould. You've become a liability for us.' For four to six days he put up with me and then sent a message about my illness to Tau who immediately landed up in Dhurra with his eldest son, Roshan. The inflammation had not yet subsided and Tau could feel my swelling with his hands. He immediately realized how ill I was.

Maanti, Gangawasi, and the people of Dhurra turned to Tau, 'Baburam, you lost your brother here at the time of your sister's wedding and now you've sent your nephew too to die here. You know only too well how hazardous it is to be moulding bricks at such a tender age and yet you seem determined to send him to his death.' Tau's face went red and he began to shake with anger. I can still recall the ferocity of his anger that day. 'Beedhe, you may be my brother-in-law but I'll call you a butcher. First you killed Radhe and now it is his son's turn. You'd said that you were taking him to help you out but you set him to work like an animal!' Tau refused to stay in Phupha's house. He did not eat the food that Bua had prepared and walked off in a huff. Many women from the village tried to stop Tau and eventually put a cot out for us at the outskirts. We camped there for the night. Next morning, giving in to pressure from the people of the basti, Phupha bought a length of cloth and got a set of kurta–pyjama stitched for me immediately.

Back to the Village

The training I received as a brick-moulder was put to good use to improve Babba's one-and-three-quarters bighas of land, the yield of which was consumed by my Tai and brother's children. I suggested to Tau that if we made bricks of the alkaline soil, then we could not only sell the bricks but also improve the quality of our land.

Fortunately, for us, Niranjan Yadav thought of constructing a home for his first wife, since he had taken a second one. We worked for a couple of months but we received only partial payment for it.

Child labour afflicted me like a disease ever since my father's death and caught me the moment I grew capable of working. I did not stay at any one place on a permanent basis and changed many places to earn a living. Therefore, I gathered experience from several places and came into contact with many kinds of people as well as fell under all types of influences. It is for this reason that my descriptions of these places do not occur in a linear sequence. I have always had to earn my bread and have paid such a heavy price that if society were to compensate for my child labour, then I would have the right to eat without having to earn for the rest of my life. It is my observation that unlike me, those living in mansions in cities and the sons of landlords in villages are children who have grown rich upon the property inherited from their parents.

Once, in a fit of rage, Bhikari slashed Rambharose's cheek when no one was at home. There was a stream of blood flowing from Rambharose's cheek and people from the neighbourhood gathered there. The moment Amma returned, she let out a loud shriek, '*Haai!* This butcher has killed my son!' The people of the basti began to heap abuses upon him. By the time his rage cooled down, he had begun to feel guilty. Rambharose's cheek was shown to the local doctor and the fact that Bhikari had made the gash was covered up. It was told that the cheek was accidentally cut by a sharp tool. If Bhikari had his way, he would have got his mouth stitched up.

His male ego prevented him from apologizing to my mother but at least he accepted the blame and even got Rambharose treated. But Amma had taken quite a fright from this barbaric act and she feared that in anger he might even kill someone. He had not even spared his own son Tej Singh, whom he had once dashed on the grindstone. Fortunately, his head escaped being hurt or else he would have been dead. We always thought of him as another Kansa, who would snatch Devaki's children and kill them. Amma would put up with his verbal abuses but if I reacted, then whoever was at hand received the full blast of his vengefulness.

Despite all his faults, Bhikari Dada had his merits. He never gambled or drank, whereas the people of the entire mohalla indulged in both. He would scrimp and save money in the hope of buying land in a residential area for his son. Since goat meat was expensive, in most homes buffalo meat was eaten. Bhikari was dead against eating any meat except for that of a goat but in a bid to save the consumption of grain, he would allow us to eat the meat even of dead animals. However, he would never bring the meat of the animal that he himself had skinned. Amma would quietly request it of someone else. It was not as if Bhikari did not get to know of it but he never acknowledged it openly.

Many a time, Bhikari would instruct Amma to not cook any food but would feed Roop Singh secretly. Often, while milking the buffalo, he would make his son drink it directly. Sometimes, Amma would find clever ways to feed us. On the pretext of boiling water, she would place a small pot of vermicelli, porridge, or rice in it. At night, we would pretend to be sleeping in our cots but pangs of hunger would keep us awake. The moment Bhikari would go off to sleep, Amma would bring the vermicelli in a glass and distribute it among us. It would appear as if we were drinking water. This act of hers was never caught. Also, Amma would let women of our neighbourhood know that no food had been cooked at our home for two or three days. Thus, pressurized by the people around us, Bhikari would be forced to get the grain ground. Often, he would get it on loan, as he did not have a specific source of income. To get to eat roti and vegetables after many days would greatly enhance its taste for us. Today, when I think about it, I neither relish nor crave for food in the same manner.

Raipur: Todi Tau's Justice

Raipur was a Dalit-majority village. The good thing about this village was that all Dalits owned some land. However, I went there to work as a landless child labourer, on a monthly basis, when I was around ten years old. Todi Tau called me to his home and said, 'Sauraj, you must go to Raipur. You will get thirty rupees a month for harvesting the crop. For cleaning and feeding the cattle, you will get two square meals. Once the grain is cut, you will have to do treading for ten–fifteen days. In all, it's a month's work. After that you can return to the village.'

I sought Babba's advice and he said, 'You can go, Bhaiyya. Even here, you'll have to work to earn your living. The Yadavs extract back-breaking labour here; there at least Doodhon will make meals twice a day for you.'

I had to take a decision, as I was my own guardian. I decided to leave for Raipur. There Doodhon Bua received me with great love and affection. Since I had gone there with the express intention to work, the very next morning we set out early with our sickles to reap the crop. It took us fifteen days and after that the process of treading began.

Raipur had quite a number of Jatavs and all through the months of May–June, one after the other, several marriages took place. In fact, there would be a wedding almost everyday. I got to attend more than two dozen wedding feasts during this period. I returned after two months. My complexion had darkened working everyday in the blazing sun but my health had improved, as I had feasted on good food in the various weddings I attended. Unfortunately, I did not have the good fortune to read a single word and I sorely missed it.

The moment I returned, Todi Tau enquired, 'So, Sauraj! How did it go? Was there any difference between working in Raipur and working here in the village?'

'I had a whale of a time there!'

'Then let's settle your account.' He placed forty rupees in my hand for forty days of work and asked, 'I hope you were not kept hungry over there?'

'What hunger are you talking about, Tau? I went to a feast almost everyday in Raipur. I had a lot of sweets, rice, dal, curd, and sometimes even aloo–puri!' I reported.

On hearing this, he took back the money he had placed on my palm and returned it to me after deducting fifteen rupees from it. 'Why did you do that, Tau?' I asked him. He replied, 'I've deducted five rupees for the sugar and rice and if you had aloo–puri everyday, then that amounts to about eight annas per day. I have given you twelve annas per day after deducting four annas from your wages.' I could only stare at his face. What else could I do? This was indeed the reward for a child's innocence and frankness! He added, 'Your share should have been plain and simple food. Do labourers ever get to eat at feasts?'

The Passion for Reading

Though I had always been very fond of reading, I realized its importance much later. My reading habit played a formative role in the making of my personality. Here, I am offering a very early glimpse of that trait. Whenever and whatever job I undertook, I always had a soiled, slim book that I could read and carry in my pocket or bag. I would pick up and read all that I liked from the school textbooks. I could see no future for myself in the field of education, so I never practised writing. My Jeeja's cousin in Mirzapur, Baburam Swaang, was fond of reading and singing ballads, legends, and classical songs. I had first read Guru Bakhshidas's *Raidas Ramayan* by borrowing it from him in Meerut. We got along very well with each other. He also repaired shoes. He was a man with a noble heart, who lived in a state of complete financial ruin.

In Nadrauli, the song books that could be found on the footpaths of the markets were my source of knowledge. I would buy *Ramcharitmanas, Radheshyam Ramayana, Laila–Majnu, Rohtas, Veer Haqiqatrai, Satyavadi Harishchandra, Aalha, Dhola, The Tales of Hatimtai*, and many other books from the footpaths. I came across a book called *Our Ancestors* in which the story of Dadheech made quite an impression on me. Later, I discovered that it was prescribed in the syllabus for Class Eight.

I was introduced to Ambedkar by my non-Dalit teachers as someone who was a supporter of the British and an accomodationist, who had also spared some thought for the well-being of Dalits. This was what was taught to me. On the other hand, Gandhi was never represented as the leader of only the Banias or Brahmins; he was also that of Dalits and was spoken of as the 'Father of the Nation'. He had fasted for the welfare of the Dalits and had become a Bhangi himself. I was drawn to the semi-clad figure of Gandhi and I believed that he too was poor like my Babba, who did not have money to buy clothes for himself.

My interest in books increased and having no money to buy them, I started stealing as many books as I would buy. I had found a way to pilfer them. I would buy two slim books for four annas and by folding the cover of the book on the top, slip the third in between. This way, I managed to have quite a collection of books, half of which I had bought and the other half were stolen ones. These were primarily three to four anthologies and about ten or twenty books on folk literature. In the village, the followers of Arya Samaj would preach and teach us to sing our prayers. Impressed by their style of oration, I also learnt to sing the historical tales and legends composed in the musical mode. I had a steady supporter and listener in Dayaram Bhagatji. He was so keen to hear me sing that he would wait for me till late at night. He would bring along his container of kerosene oil and sit in Todi Tau's courtyard to hear me sing in my full-throated manner. There were other listeners too, but he was a regular. He also was a supporter of my ideas. He wanted to convert me to vegetarianism and asceticism in the Swami Dayanand Saraswati mould. He had borrowed *Satyartha Prakash* from Yadunath Shastri, who was a self-declared and disciplined Gandhian. He was a Yadav by caste but moved more among Chamars and Bhangis. In order to eradicate untouchability, he would invite many Chamars and Bhangis, along with me, to participate in *havans* (sacred fire ceremonies). I had borrowed two books by Lenin from him, which he had got as a gift from a comrade when he was in jail. However, Shastriji's aim was to convert everybody in the world to become 'arya' (honourable/noble).

I had read these books but then I was not so intellectually evolved to be able to grasp their core meaning. And if I couldn't understand these books I wonder how much Bhagatji comprehended them. However, the Arya Samaj gatherings had painted a barbaric and inhuman picture of Muslims in my mind. In the name of making everyone arya or noble, the songs that we sang in these gatherings would extol the supremacy of Hinduism. Every Muslim would appear to me to be a Babar and a Mohammed Ghori, whereas I would take pride in being a Hindu. Along with the Yadav villagers, I too would refer to Muslims as *kattalla* (circumcised or castrated). Now I wonder at myself. How could I have been so rude? I did not have the knowledge then that it was Hindutva which had engendered and propagated the concept of untouchability and that it had also instituted the caste system on the principle of birth-based discrimination.

Almost about a decade later, when I was returning to my village along with Prempal Singh from Chirori School, I saw the same elderly bookseller in the market at Gunnaur. I wondered if he still sold books. I got a ten-rupee note out from my pocket and handed it to the old man. He wanted to know why I was giving it to him. I replied, 'This is a small compensation for a debt I owe you. I had pilfered some books. Since you never gave them on loan, I would often steal them.' The old man looked incredulously at me, partly because I was wearing a clean school uniform and looked somewhat well-off. I asked him again, 'Don't you remember?'

Once I was able to convince him, he accepted the money and I felt immensely relieved.

My Legacy

Since the Muslims were not part of the Hindu fold, the Yadavs treated them with greater parity than us. 'The donkey among animals', 'The owl among birds', 'The Chamar among castes'—such figures of speech are evidence of the Dalit-hating mentality of the savarnas towards us. These epithets were not coined in a day. The wounds run so deep that instead of wincing with pain, we have grown accustomed to bearing them and it is made to appear natural that it is our fate to endure this suffering. These words of abuse are current in every house of our locality. It is astonishing how Chamars have borne this verbal abuse by the savarnas! Don't the Chamars know that in this world there are such things like self-respect and dignity? Their powers of intelligence and judgement were so severely curtailed that they did not realize their own revolutionary potential. Perhaps they even find these abuses endearing. 'Chamar king of donkeys', 'Son of a Chamar', 'Is this a Chamar panchayat?'—such derogatory proverbs were brought into use time and again to give them legitimacy. In eastern Uttar Pradesh, songs were composed that expressed surprise at the rise of Chamars. During the early 1970s, when I was ten years old, such songs echoed around me:

The Chamarin now struts with slippers on her feet,
The Dhobins are also sandal-shod,
The world has changed indeed, o my god!

This song reflects caste hatred and envy expressive of an anti-democratic sentiment. It is indeed a miracle of Indian politics that Mayawati of this very caste went on to become the chief minister. Just as Dr Ambedkar candidly pronounced himself to be an untouchable Mahar, in the same vein, Kanshi Ram declared to the media that he was a Chamar from Punjab and that Mayawati was a Chamarin from Uttar Pradesh. The Jatavs too derided us and considered us beneath them. They have begun to consider me one of their own only after I have earned for myself a status and a name through self-education. But I have no hesitation at all in saying that I am the grandson of two disabled Chamars—Gangi and Bidharam—who despite their hard and unpaid wage labour found it difficult to sustain themselves without proper food and clothing.

In the nearby villages, our house was known as the home of the disabled. Even today when the elders of the neighbouring villages get to know that I am the grandson of Gangi Chamar, they express astonishment. Many of them think I am the result of a miracle, while others think it is the consequence of a previous birth. However, when someone refers to my having been a Brahmin in the previous birth, I feel enraged. Even the children of Yadavs, Telis, and Banias showed disrespect to my elders by calling out to them in a derogatory manner when they needed them for some work. We had fallen on such bad times that even those of our family who had become marginally better off, like Paiju Tau's sons—Ramcharan and Ulfat—called Babba by his first name 'Gangi'.

I would lead Babba with his stick but his feet knew the roads better. Once he had gone over a route, he would never lose his way. He would manually operate the grindstone for the Yadavs and the flour was not considered contaminated, but after the grain had been ground, the Yadav women would not even let him touch the flour. As wages he would be doled out flour for about two rotis in his sling bag in the manner of giving alms or fistfuls of grain would be put in his shirt that he would spread out for the purpose. A bowl would be tied to the end of his half-dhoti, in which he would receive the food given out as charity. The people of my basti would consider even this hard-earned meal as a form of begging, however, none of them had an answer to the problem of our livelihood. Among them, I cannot forget Ramjeet Pradhan's courteous behaviour. He would address even the young with great politeness.

I must relate an incident which haunts me like a dark shadow from my horrible past, when I was staying with Babba. It occurred on the night when I was running the sugar press at Bade Yadav's place. Sugarcane juice used to be boiled in a large wok and the impurities that skimmed to the surface, in our colloquial language would be called *maili* or *ladoi*. Babba and I would work for such meagre wages that we would accept the ladoi in order to appease our hunger. We were quite a pair—a blind old man and a boy of tender age. I would spur the buffaloes and the old man would keep adding the sugarcane into the press. If the Lambardar was kind, he would also give us some of the jaggery-wash along with the ladoi instead of throwing it to the dogs and pigs.

Some sugarcane juice would trickle into the scum and to that if some jaggery-wash was also added, then our happiness knew no bounds. We would put some water to the mix and filter it into a bowl. We would drink the first few glasses right away and to the remaining we added a handful of grains and set it to cook. These were either millet or maize, for adding rice would amount to having a feast. In those days of paucity, even the smallest things filled us with delight. There was no possibility of getting more and neither did we expect much. That we be given our rights as human beings, such a desire had yet to raise its head. Those Chamars and Bhangis who had learnt masonry as well as those who possessed a bit of land refrained from eating ladoi and those who had it, did so stealthily.

My memory is riddled with so many questions related to my horrific past. I slept in places not worth sleeping, I wore clothes that were not worth wearing and I ate food that was barely edible—the compulsions that dogged me still smoulder like lava within me. In order to fully comprehend my legacy, to not forget my station and to recognize my responsibilities, it is imperative that I do not dress up my past in apparels of gold. There is no doubt that to reminiscence about those days of slavery is to lose some of the possible peace of the present but that which cannot be forgotten should not be obliterated.

We were not given the juice or jaggery because it was believed that it would spoil us and then we would begin to expect more than the few annas of wages and ladoi handed to us. Even our own people thought that we had brought disrepute to the community, though no one was genuinely concerned about our plight. Their only refrain was 'Just give up this slavery and win us some respect.' In the day we would work at the homes of the Yadavs and in the night at their sugar press. People would shun us when they saw us returning from work—an exhausted grandfather–grandson duo, dressed in the dirtiest possible clothes. The juice stuck on our clothes would attract flies and our arms and legs used to be coated by layers of dirt. In any case, they could hardly be called clothes, rather patches of cloth put together. In the eyes of the well-off we hardly qualified as human beings, we were worse than animals albeit with human faces.

Nowadays when I look at the attention a pet dog gets in a prosperous home, I am filled with sorrow and self-disgust. At other times, I am enraged and wonder why I did not rebel against my lot then. However, the social set-up was such that it produced a certain kind of passive mindset. Though there was a submerged consciousness that kept prodding me towards a new life.

That freezing cold night Babba was adding the dried, crushed cane and leaves to the blazing hot furnace. Due to years of experience, despite being blind, Babba carried out his task competently.

Halfway through the task, I heard Babba scream out aloud, 'I have caught fire, Lambardar! Save me, Lalla Sauraj!' It seemed as if his voice had got stuck in his moustaches. I stumbled hurriedly in his direction, but by then the fire had spread and the corner of Babba's half-dhoti had caught fire. He immediately flung it off his body and tried to emerge from the pit of the furnace. I flung my arms around him. The good thing was that the wind was not blowing at the time or else the fire would have spread quickly and caused a lot of harm. All those who were present there doused the fire with mud and water but in the process showered the choicest abuses on us.

Usually, Babba would be enraged if he heard our caste being abused but that night he sat at a distance, crouched in a completely nude state—very much like a woman whose modesty had been outraged. He was struck with fear. Even today I can feel the poundings of his heart as if they were my own and the crouching figure of the blind man is very clearly etched in my memory. I grow extremely restless whenever I recall that scene, as if it had occurred this very night. That night was marked with the contrary consciousness of the freezing weather and the heat of the fire. While at his task, Babba did not feel the cold, but sitting at a distance then, he had begun to shiver. 'Lambardar, please give me a bit of cloth so that I can cover myself.' Mercifully, it was night and there was no woman present. Moreover, the press was located at a distance from the village or else he would have got beaten up for appearing obscene. Even then, instead of showing compassion and cooperating, most people continued to express anger. Anegi Yadav had said, 'If you cannot see, then why do you undertake these tasks and subject yourself to such humiliation? The little boy is not blind, is he? You send him to work in the furnace.' Bade Yadav had said, 'It seems the entire village's ill-fortune has fallen on the lot of these bloody Chamars!' The cane juice kept thickening and gradually sweetened to a jaggery-like consistency, whereas the rising sun filled us with a sense of bitterness and sorrow. What a strange mix of contraries!

As soon as the boiling juice reached the point of acquiring the consistency of jaggery, it had to be immediately removed from the fire. A couple of buckets of water would be used to wash the large wok in which the juice was boiled and that would constitute the jaggery-wash, which would then be stored in canisters. It was a rare day when we would also get the jaggery-wash with the ladoi but that night we felt that we had jeopardized even that.

I had only a torn shirt with patches stuck on it to offer to Babba to cover up his nudity. He tied it around like a loin-cloth to cover up his private parts. Babba continued to ask for some clothes and it was not as if the people around us did not have any to spare. Someone could have given him a half-dhoti or shirt but the problem was that if the cloth touched the body of an untouchable Chamar, then it could not be taken back and there was no custom that permitted the donation of clothes, unless a man was dead. I was shivering in cold without my shirt and meanwhile a dog had managed to put its mouth into the canister of ladoi. I ran towards it to shoo it off but by then it had already left its seal on it by licking it. At the press, people were speaking among themselves, 'Someone must give these people clothes to cover themselves up fully or else once it is daylight and any one of our women were to see these godforsaken people in this state then their entire day would be spoilt. Pack these Chamars off with some ladoi and add a bit of jaggery just for taste! Wonder when these bastards will have some sense! Get rid of them before the light of the day! Off with them to their bastis!'

Babba was acutely conscious of his nudity and helplessness. He felt deeply ashamed. What frightened him more was that if the news spread of him having caused the fire in the furnace. then no one would give him work anymore. I do not want to add any imaginary rebellion on our part or conjure up a passionate rejoinder to the words we heard. The condition we were in has been stated as it is. 'So Lambardar, shall we leave?' Babba supplicated. The answer he got was this—'Will you leave only after you've feasted?' 'Lambardar, at least let us have some of the jaggery-wash. Back home, we'll put some millet in and cook it.' The more Babba pleaded, the Yadav took a harsher tone, 'Today you are asking for the jaggery-wash, tomorrow you'll ask for the juice and the day after you'll want the jaggery!' As Bade spoke in anger, Babba replied with a heavy heart in a small voice, 'You can say whatever you want, Lambardar, do whatever you want. We will have to be patient.' Having said this, he got up to leave, 'Let's go, Lalla.' Bade retorted, 'Why don't you take the ladoi and leave? Is there anything wrong with it?' 'The dog has licked it,' I intervened. 'Give these rascals some jaggery-wash and pack them off!' His son, Anegi, spat out contemptuously. Babba could sense that the Lambardar was angry but would not send us away empty-handed.

I was standing at a distance from the wok in the hope of getting some jaggery-wash. Instead they were handing us some ladoi. 'I am not going to take the ladoi. The dog has licked it.' I stepped back. Babba had sharp ears. As soon as he heard it, he said, 'Lambardar, what are you doing? We have been working for years for you and after Radhe's death, you've been our sole support. We've done all sorts of work in your home and fields. If you give us a bit of the jaggery, our tongues will be sweetened. We work with mounds of jaggery around us and yet have to crave for a drop of the juice. For the huge amount of back-breaking labour are you going to give us just the ladoi, that too which has been licked by the dog! Once spotted, one cannot swallow a fly.'

'At other times you are willing to lick even the pots. I did not let the dog in. Don't forget your station, Gangi. Don't think about getting the juice or the jaggery-wash. Be grateful for whatever you get. In any case, you are blind and you can tell this boy to shut his eyes to eat it up. You can take two sticks of the cane, Saujja.' He signalled to me and after this long struggle, his son's heart melted, 'Here Gangi, you can have half a bucket of jaggery-wash.'

We walked quickly towards our mohalla, as I wanted to hurry Babba into our home. On spotting us, many of our own relatives asked, 'Where is your shirt and the blind man's half-dhoti, Sauraj?' Although Babba was from their community and their uncle, they always addressed him as the 'blind man' or by his first name, instead of calling him 'Chacha'.

Even though we tried to hush it up, news about the fire spread far and wide and our chances of getting work grew dim. We found neither sympathy nor support from the people in the basti, instead it became an occasion for all kinds of reactions. Dori was amongst those who mocked us, 'You are a blot on our locality. You've fallen to the level of Bhangis!' and so on. He had got Babba to sit on the ground while he held forth in this manner. His behaviour was exactly the same as those of the so-called 'upper' castes with Dalits. He continued in the same vein, 'Who will consider the two of you human beings? You have been outcasted from the community a long time back but now you are not even fit to remain in the village.' Shakur Ali also joined the rest in taunting us, 'Arre, Gangi, don't Hindus consider the dog's saliva to be a form of nectar? And you are saying you did not take it because the dog had licked it?' Babba was furious and threatened to drive Shakur off with his stick.

The next day when Rasvan came to summon us to the furnace, Babba told him, 'You can feed the cane juice to your cattle—from now on we'll find some other way to earn our living.'

'That's alright, Gangi, but where will you get work? If not at our place, then you'll be slaving away at someone else's. You'll always remain slaves and hardly turn masters.'

'Yes, Sahab, everyone can see how helpless we are. I wonder which accursed God ordained such a life for us—we have neither land nor property and no one from our family has ever learnt a letter. Slaves can hardly aspire to be masters!'

The next night, a few relatives arrived from across the Ganga and were informed about the incident. However poor their condition, even today the Chamars from across the Ganga, that is from Aligarh and Bulandshahar, tend to boast and pass themselves off as a prosperous lot. A panchayat was called and Babba and I were made to appear before it like criminals in a court or like subjects before a king. No one allowed us to sit on the cots and the judgment and commands were decided in advance—'You better stop drawing water from our wells and give up eating the meat of dead animals on the sly. If we get to know of it, we will blacken your faces and set you astride a donkey to roam through the village.' These were the orders from our own Chamar basti and not from savarnas, Yadavs, and Muslims!

While the prohibitions were being pronounced about us being barred from attending weddings or prayer meetings or partaking of the community meal on the thirteenth day of a person's death, Babba kept listening. However, when it was declared that we would not be allowed to draw water from the well, Babba could take it no more. Enraged, he shouted, 'Who the hell do you think you are to stop us from drawing water from the well? Do you know that it was I who had dug that well and that it is on my land? How dare you tell me that I have lost the right to use it? You people are not Chamars but the bastards of these Thakurs and Brahmins! Go dig your own wells and don't call us for your religious ceremonies!'

Today even though I do not possess a house, land, or any such basic resources, my levels of education and income have steadily improved. I am still, technically, an outcasted member of my community. However, in all these twenty–thirty years I have never felt the need to host a community feast to regain membership of my caste. I am a self-declared Chamar and in place of the earlier abhorrence, I find that now I am adequately respected by the members of the new educated generation. They seem to have expectations from me. I am popular in my entire village on account of my social and literary activities. It will be hard to find even a single Yadav home in which I cannot eat from their utensils or that untouchability is practised against me openly. I am not all alienated. Instead, I have reached out to every home and inspired every child to learn. In the last fifteen years I have also started a movement against superstitions, exorcists, and other such social evils.

I know that no one can be fond of consuming maili or the flesh of dead animals or for that matter jaggery-wash but then even the sages were compelled to eat meat. In Hindi literature, Guru Raidas was a bhakti poet but he was a leather worker too. The famous poet–saint Chokhamela of Marathi literature lifted dead cattle all his life as an ordinary labourer and died when a wall collapsed on him. Dr Ambedkar had once asked, 'What did the Hindus do for the livelihood of those untouchable poets they worshipped?' These days meat is preferred over other food items in prosperous homes but the meat I ate was dead flesh and the maili I consumed was the dead matter of the cane juice and that could hardly be said to contain any taste. Then, should I feel proud or ashamed of what I ate in the past? Should I laugh or cry at the life I did not have? As a writer, I can hardly remain indifferent to the various experiences I have had. Today what I eat is not dictated by compulsions and I have tasted the best of wines and food from many countries but I am slave to no habit. It is wrong to say that people who get used to living in miserable conditions do not wish to change themselves. In my childhood I used to smoke the beedi and draw upon Babba's coconut-shell hookah, yet it never developed into a habit. Right from the beginning, I had no other craving than wanting to read and write!

A poem that emerged from the churning that went on in my mind with regard to my ancestors got published in the Sunday edition of *Jansatta*:

My Ancestors

Returning again and again
To my memories, they loom large
Over my existence—my ancestors!
Transforming my pain into a song of revolt,
That springs from my throat but is
Sung by—my ancestors!
The morning light brings with it the dew,
That falls far and wide, like the tear drops
Of my ancestors!
You could not lead an ordinary life,
But where was the chance of becoming great?
Your religion, your thoughts
Were held in bondage by others,
But you were great souls
In your own way—my ancestors!
Your eyes hid the depths of anguish,
While you remained oblivious
To your own oppression—my ancestors!
I retain not just an element of your selves
But am also the legatee of your compulsions.
Who can tell that within me,
The fiery energy of creation
Emanates from the hot vapours
Of your tears—my ancestors!
'Untouchable'—you were named,
For who could touch the heights
Of your selfless labours—my ancestors!
Those mean in behaviour,
Unethical in character,

Uncultured in conduct
And completely without compassion,
Imposed upon you a silence.
Neither symbols nor metaphors
Can bespeak your humiliations,
Your real struggles.
I am not just your witness,
Your extension too! I am the
Custodian of the limits of your sentience.
I am the negation of all your compliances,
I am the future of all your past experiences.
I am the guide to your
Blocked pathways and lost destinations!
You remain a part of my dreams,
Entrenched in my memories.
I am the true reflection of your
Essence—my ancestors!
Am I forgiven for what I've said,
My ancestors?

◆

Delhi
Small Steps in a Large World

Amma sent me to live in Delhi with my eldest Mausi, Sukhdei, in the year 1968. My Mausa, Devidasji, had a single-room-home-cum-shop at Janta Market, Rajouri Garden, for which he paid a monthly rent of thirty rupees. Outside his room, on the verandah floor, Mausaji would craft shoes out of fine leather. He was indeed a craftsman of the highest order but due to shortage of capital he had taught himself to work within his limited means. He had fixed himself a workstation by digging out a portion of the floor and installing a stone platform in the hollow. He would carry out his tasks under a tarpaulin sheet strung over the workstation, his posture resembling that of a Muslim at his prayers. The one room served as a storeroom for raw material, a workstation for Mausaji, and a kitchen for Mausiji. As for the calls of nature, we answered them by frequenting the municipal toilets.

We would fetch water from quite a distance away, from the municipal taps. My cousin, Nathulal, was five or six years my senior. Lanky in stature, he was like Mausaji, of a weak constitution. He and I would carry two buckets each and not being used to hard labour as I was, Nathulal would tire easily. The water was thoroughly saline but sheer compulsion had accustomed us to its use.

My mind is full of memories of those days. Every Tuesday evening, I would go along with my cousins Nathulal and Naresh to the Hanuman Temple right in front of our house to collect a share of the *boondiya*s offered to the god by devotees. Like them, I too believed that the stone idol in the temple embodied some mystical powers. Consequently, I was ever-apprehensive that Hanumanji would be offended that we partook of his prasad without making any offerings of our own to him. I continued to pay my respects to the spirit of Bangali Baba every Saturday. I would buy a small quantity of jalebis and dedicate them to the Baba before handing them around as prasad. My uncle, aunt, and Nathulal would deride my faith—who, on earth, was this Bangali Baba? Even though Nathulal himself was a student of science, he would fast every Friday for Santoshi Ma and devoutly distribute *gur–chana* in her name. Mausaji tended to denigrate village folk as stupid in comparison to the smarter city folk. It was from this perspective that he viewed my devotion to Bangali Baba. Nevertheless, he himself remained steadfast in his commitment towards Santoshi Ma. She was, after all, the goddess of the cultured and the cultivated.

Mausaji was at once shrewd and frugal in his disposition, and blunt of speech as well. He would neither accept too many obligations from his relatives nor extend too much hospitality to them. He must have learnt these lessons of life from his personal experience. Guests who landed at his house with the intention of sightseeing were, after a stay of a day or two, told directly to fend for themselves. He had told Amma at the very outset that I would have to earn my own living.

A few days later, the three Bhikari brothers also descended on Delhi from Pali and started to stay in the slums of Subhash Nagar. They slung wooden boxes from around their necks and went about looking for customers who might want their shoes mended. My mother worked at sifting grains in neighbourhood chakkis and Rambharose looked after Tej Singh while living with them.

Mausaji tried very hard indeed to find me a job suitable to my age. His friends and acquaintances were ordinary working people—hawkers, barbers, paanwallahs, newspaper vendors, cobblers, and his own customers. One evening, Mausaji took me to meet a labour contractor. I was keen to begin to work, as that was the only condition on which I could stay on in Delhi; otherwise, it was back to the village for me. The contractor, Ballu Teli, was one of Mausaji's customers and had taken up assignments to refurbish buildings in the locality.

Balluji was skeptical about my prospects of getting a job on account of my young age and said, 'At his age, he ought to be engaged in fun and frolic. Why are you sending him out to work? Send him to school instead.' Mausaji narrated my circumstances to the contractor and his own compulsions. Balluji got the point and they bargained about my wages, which were fixed at thirty rupees per month.

Mausaji accompanied me to the site on the first day. Subsequently, I would set out from home every morning at seven and return at six in the evening. Gradually, I learnt to polish floors. I had barely worked for two weeks of the second month that an unsavoury incident occurred, in which I entered into an altercation with the contractor's brother, who had been polishing the floor of another room and had found fault with my work. An argument ensued and upon getting enraged by my defiance of him, he landed a stinging slap on my cheek. I was a child of eight or nine years of age and he a bulky youth. I could hardly slap him in return. Therefore, weeping and cursing I returned to Mausiji's house.

Seeing that I was in a state of distress, Mausiji drew me to her bosom and Mausaji enquired, 'Calm yourself Sauram, and tell me what happened.' Mausaji would address me as Sauram, and never spoke to me in a tone of condescension. He would never talk down to his own children either. It is difficult to fathom how he came to be as urbane as he was. He had a working knowledge of Urdu and had imbibed certain words required for public dealing in the English language.

In between sobs, I narrated the entire incident to them. Both of them exploded in anger and Mausaji immediately took me to the site but by then my tormentor had vanished from the spot. The overseer had come to know about the fracas. Mausaji's enquiries from other workers revealed that the contractor's brother was indeed a lout. After that incident, Mausaji did not send me back for the work of polishing floors. Following my absence from work for a few days, the contractor visited our home with jalebis for me and apologized on his brother's behalf. Perhaps he imagined that being a child I could be won over with sweets and be persuaded to resume work. He tried to reassure us but I declared that I would rather return to the village than work at floor-polishing. Mausaji had signalled to me with his eyes that I should not accept the sweets though I was very fond of them and wanted to taste them, but it was for the best that I did not. Had I done so, I might have been compelled to go to work with the contractor.

The moment my mother came to know about the matter, she arrived post-haste to find out the details. Her excessive anxiety provoked Mausaji to chide her and he asked her to look after her other children and leave it to them to be bothered about me. My mother's affections were dispersed among all her scattered children.

Balluji was a decent person and the very next day, he had deposited my wages for twenty days of labour with Mausaji. Mausaji permitted me a break at home for a couple of days before he started to hunt for a job for me once more. The whole day he would be squatting on his haunches, like Guru Raidas, busy in the making of shoes. In the evening, he would venture out of his shop to stretch his legs and to look out for work for me.

Lemon Seller

In Delhi, I undertook all kinds of jobs that I was capable of doing at my age. Initially, Mausaji had expressed a preference for the job of washing dishes at a hotel, as that ensured a solution to the problem of procuring two meals a day for me but Mausiji was against it. She did not want her sister's son to be washing dishes which were *jootha*. Also, Mausaji had promised Amma that he would find me a job which would allow me some time to study. Mausaji considered education essential for a child. Although he had been a young man during the heyday of Ambedkar's activism, he remained oblivious to Babasaheb's exhortation to Dalits to educate themselves. Instead, he had been inspired by the schoolgoing children of the neighbourhood who had gone on to become 'sahabs' after acquiring education. He learnt from his environment. He had seen both Gandhi and Ambedkar in Delhi at close quarters but was not acquainted with the finer points of differences of opinion between them. All he figured out was that India's independence had been won for the Banias by Gandhi as he himself was a Bania and that he had been against the interests of the Dalits, who were represented by Ambedkar. He belonged to their community and was their saviour. Mausaji was the first person among my relations who had seen Ambedkar in Swami Achchutanand's gathering. He would make it a point to go to the gatherings and listen to the speeches of all the Dalit leaders from Delhi and its surrounding areas. Among the saints he was the follower of Raidas and Kabir and among the leaders he admired B.P. Maurya and Babu Jagjivan Ram. The most he could think of was, to educate his children was till they could aspire for the posts of a school master or a police superintendent and nothing beyond that. It was not as if he did not want to see his children in higher positions but he had realized that higher education required more money. He would relate countless stories to me, of which he would recount Abhimanyu's in particular. 'Sauram, do you know what was meant when it was said that Abhimanyu had learnt the art of archery in his mother's womb?' When I pressed for an answer, he said, 'Children of educated parents acquire a lot of knowledge in a short time, whereas children of illiterate parents do not learn much. Why? This is because illiterate rustics indulge in idle talk, whereas educated parents have an informed conversation.' I heard Mausaji speak with rapt attention and placed complete faith in him since he was my guardian as well as guru.

Mausaji consulted with a vegetable seller who had suggested that I could sell lemons for a living. The preparations for my new task began. Mausaji stitched a bag for me from spare strips of khadi cloth on the leather machine. Nathulal's pants, which were torn at the knees, were altered to make shorts for me and a small purse-like pocket was attached to it, whose long chord went right round my neck to secure it. The next morning, Mausaji woke me up when it was dark yet. I was not used to waking up so early and, therefore, the first day proved tough for me. We took the first bus to Azadpur wholesale market and bought a kilo or two of lemons and also some vegetables for home.

I was sent off with a light breakfast and good wishes. Mausaji also explained the traffic rules to me by sketching on the slab of stone on which he worked. The first day I had managed to finish by one in the afternoon. I was thrilled about my first earnings and poured out all the coins on Mausaji's stone slab as soon as I returned. The next day Mausaji stitched another bag for me from Nathulal's old khaki dress and also bought a new basket for me. By the time the others got up from sleep, I would be back from the Azadpur wholesale market. Since this had become my daily routine, the driver and conductor of the bus also began to recognize me. On my way to the market, the bus would be empty and on my return if the bus was full, the conductor would get me to sit beside him. The price of a half-ticket was five paise and often the conductor would take one lemon and let me get off at my bus stop. In winters this business would hit a low, whereas in summers and monsoons lemons sold well.

I quite liked the job of a lemon seller. The next day when I emptied the coins on Mausaji's slab, the faces of my guardians shone with pride. At that very moment Mausaji got out an old diary and spoke firmly, 'Look Sauram, your mother may someday want an account of your earnings and, therefore, I am putting it down in my diary clearly. Whatever you earn, you must give it to me and see to it that I enter it in your account.' I agreed and then he began to write down my account in Urdu from that very day. His Urdu was as good as Greek and Latin to me but I knew him to be a very upright, honest, and disciplined man. There was no question of him fudging my accounts.

'Every day you will spend a rupee and a quarter on food, boarding, oil, soap, etcetera, and that totals up to about forty-five rupees a month, deducting which whatever remains will be saved for the future—for those days when you may not be able to work. Every paisa that you earn is safe with me.' In this way, I became his undeclared paying guest.

I had begun to like the work, as it was less fatiguing and there was no one to nag me. One could work in accordance with one's own will and with self-discipline. I would work in all for eight to nine hours and then be free by the afternoon. It was during my lemon-selling days that I fashioned my first rhyme. I can still recall it today:

Juicy lemons'n lime, heaped in a pile!
Ten for two, two for fifteen.
Take them with a smile, o brother,
Take them with a smile!

I called out in a sing-song manner as I roamed the well-kept lanes of Rajouri Garden, knocking at the doors of the plush kothis. As I look back at my oeuvre, I find that when I began to compose rhymes in folk style, I could trace its source back to this tradition of labour which gave birth to my poetry. I learnt many good things from others and the process of being influenced by people while also influencing them became a part of the formation of my personality. I was not going to school but was learning from life. I could never remain indifferent or unaffected—my emotions drew me to people as also away from them. Attachment and detachment are the two vices or virtues that continue to be active in the making of my personality.

Once on my visit to Amma, I met my stepbrother Roop Singh. In Delhi too, he had been admitted to school but as earlier, he shirked learning. I would often run into him as he went about cycling on a bike on hire. Even I would sometimes take some money out of my earnings and land up there to learn cycling. Once after a fall from the cycle, I ended up with scraped knees and torn pyjamas. Mausa and Mausiji at first thought that I had perhaps got beaten up in a brawl and were at once angry and relieved to know that was not the case. Mausaji warned me to never go cycling without informing him. He was so angry that I had to seek Mausiji's mediation to bring him around. Thus, for years, this small home became an essential refuge for me. After that incident I never went to Subhash Nagar to visit Amma.

During the course of my lemon-selling days, I got acquainted with many customers and many of them got to know me very well. I carried out my task—the road was clear and life continued at its own pace, while I kept searching out the route to my future. With my childhood upon my shoulders, I was marching towards adolescence. My little steps were treading an unknown territory, the rough terrain of an uncertain future, but the Delhi stopover was an important turn in the journey of my life. I was getting good at my work. Every door opened to a new face, a new voice. Mostly, women and children were my customers. They would often ask about me, especially women would want to know about my personal life. Many women would be filled with compassion as they heard about my orphaned childhood. Some would offer snacks and biscuits while others would say, 'Why don't you work for us? We'll admit you to the government school. You can work at home in your free time.' Everyday I would relate my experiences to Mausa–Mausiji. One Memsahib found it surprising that a child like me who was so eager to study was unable to do so. She held the usual opinion that only those who did not wish to study did not do so. In my case, her opinions had taken quite a beating. The various governments of independent India had hardly ever bothered to open schools for orphans like me, where we could study, work, and not be anxious about feeding ourselves.

That year I saw a Hindi film on television for the first time by peeping through a window of our landlord's house next door. Since Nathulal was a school-going child and also the tenant's son, he had the permission to enter through the main door and watch television but the rest of the illiterate children like me were not permitted to enter. I, too, joined the children who were attempting to look inside. I was stunned at the very first sight! That images could dance, sing, and speak on screen was nothing short of a miracle for me! It was something our Bangali Baba, Bhopur's Chamunda, and even Sayyed Baba would also not be able to pull off. It was a source of unprecedented surprise and excitement. I did not get the title of the film but it its story embedded itself in my memory. Later I discovered it was *Mughal-e Azam* and its songs also became very popular.

One day I did not find Mausiji at home when I returned from the wholesale market. I was told that she had gone to the hospital 'to get a brother for you.' I was unaware about the urban convenience of being able to deliver a baby in the hospital. Therefore, I felt confused that day. In the afternoon we saw Mausiji arrive in a taxi, with a newborn infant in her arms. Mausaji used to consult an elderly retired Babuji about most matters and, therefore, sought his advice about naming the baby. Babuji would discourage people from going to a Pandit for the naming of a child. He would say, 'The child is yours, name him as you wish. But the name should be such that it would have a positive effect on the child.' Such was his belief. Thus, my newborn cousin was named 'Jungi' which meant warrior. It was later that I understood the titles of respect and the derogatory terms that were attached to castes. The Brahmins of my village would insultingly refer to Chamars as *durjan* (bad people), Khacheru, Tunda, Ghuru, among others, while the Yadavs would warp our otherwise well-sounding names—Bidharam would be called Beedha, Gangaram would become Gangi, Radheshyam, Radhua, and Sauraj, Shaura.

Many incidents of those days flash like a lightning on my mind. On a blazing hot June afternoon, I was once summoned by a beautiful girl in a swan-white dress. Not only did she offer cold water to me but also a set of clothes. Perhaps she had noticed that my shirt had patches sewn in places and that my shorts were also frayed. But I was not mentally prepared to wear a stranger's used clothes although I was wearing Naththulal's old clothes and my feet were shod with an old pair of shoes. The cold water quenched my thirst and the cool air from the ceiling fan provided momentary relief. Her kindness was acceptable till this extent, but how could I accept the clothes? I thanked her but refused to take them. However, when she pressed upon me, my mind was torn with conflict. Should I take the clothes or not? I told her that I would have to seek the permission of my guardians. Mausaji would scold me. Even earlier he had taken a hard line. The next thought was—but what was wrong with it, let me take them. By then the young girl said, 'Look brother, if your aunt scolds you then you can bring these clothes back tomorrow or give them away to some hawker.' She stopped there but I had by then made up my mind. I climbed back and folded the clothes under my arm and set out for home. There were still a few lemons remaining but once I had earned about a rupee or two; I would not bother too much if some remained. That day, I was anxious because I did not know how Mausaji and Mausiji would react to my carrying the clothes.

My steps slowed down as I neared home and found Mausaji bent at his work. Mausiji spotted the bundle of clothes under my arm and enquired about them. She turned to Mausaji and said quietly, 'Did you hear? Today Sauram has got clothes from someone.' Mausaji was curious and walked towards me. I placed the clothes before him. Mausiji was angry but Mausaji looked sombre. In fact, I had feared him more but he said, 'Put the clothes aside and let's have our meal. We'll speak about this later.'

For hours, nothing was said about the clothes. It was a source of immense surprise to me that Mausaji had given no reaction. In the evening he came up to Mausiji and asked, 'Do you know why Sauram accepted the clothes? He doesn't have a single dress that has no patches sewn on it. Did we not deprive this child of these things? We should have got some clothes stitched for him of his own earnings. It was a cause for worry that Sauram felt deprived during his stay with us. To wear second-hand clothes unless extremely pressed by circumstances is hardly a good thing. These clothes could be of a sick or dead person. Wearing a dead person's clothes causes a child to have nightmares and seeing ghosts in dreams results in sicknesses.'

He was speaking thus to Mausiji and I could hear them as I sat in a corner. Later, Mausaji called me to himself and explained, 'Look Sauram *beta*, do not hanker after things belonging to others. If you didn't have clothes, you could have asked us.' I decided to return the clothes but Mausaji intervened, 'The person who gave them to you will feel bad. Whether you wear them or not, don't return them.'

It would usually be in the afternoon that I passed that girl's house. I found the girl very beautiful and had named her 'the fair girl'. I also put together a few lines of an incomplete poem for her:

The scorching heat and a sharp thirst
Quenched by a bottle of chilled water, crystal clear.
And the girl so fair, with a voice as pure
As divine nectar!

Outsider in School

Nathulal would return from school by afternoon and spend a lot of time doing his homework, drowning himself in books. Looking at him steeped in study, one could guess that he was deeply interested in his subjects. He aspired to be a doctor, though he studied in a government school but back then education had not been commercialized yet. Naresh, on the other hand, found studying burdensome.

I was very keen to study in a school but it was not for orphans like me, although the municipality school was very close to our home. I would try to read newspapers, usually old ones, or any pamphlet that I found lying on the road. Magazines sold as scrap or billboards were like open pages of a book for me and I read a lot of them. Mausaji would instruct Nathulal to help me study on my own. On Sunday or a day or two in a week, he would explain a few things to me and I would go over whatever he taught me several times in my mind.

It was Babuji who had asked Mausaji to get me enrolled in school. In Delhi there were provisions for child labourers like me to study in evening schools, which were easier to attend than the morning schools in Pali. One day, Mausaji met the headmaster of the municipality primary school and requested him to allow me to meet the teacher. The teacher asked me a few questions from lessons of Class-Four books and, once satisfied, assured us of my gaining admission.

I experienced a mix of happiness and uncertainty with regard to going to school the next day. I had washed my clothes and bought my books at half price. I waited eagerly for that moment when I would become a regular student of a school. Staying and working in Delhi, I had come to realize that one could become successful only through acquiring education. The hope that I, too, would wear clean clothes and accomplish big things was accompanied by the fear that I had fallen behind others and would not be able to keep pace with them. My heart was palpitating with these simple, innocent anxieties. Who would arrange for my upkeep? Where would the money for my daily needs come from? I did not wish to burden Mausaji. As it is, the rubber soles used by Bata had driven the leather sole that Mausaji used out of the market.

I had got used to waking up early in the morning and had even begun to enjoy it. The next day Mausaji reminded me before I set out that I should return earlier than usual, since I had to attend school. I assured him that I would. My customers waited to hear my voice at a fixed time and would call out to me the moment they heard me. My voice could be heard from one end of the alley to the other. That day, I made it a point to express my prospective happiness with all my customers, especially with those women who would encourage me to study. I was freely announcing it to all and sundry. 'Bibiji, you would always insist that I learn while I earn and, therefore, from today onwards I will be going to school. I have enrolled in an evening school. I'll sell lemons in the day and attend school in the evening.'

It was my routine to return by noon but that day I had spent so much time narrating my newfound happiness to my customers that I did not realize it was well past my time. I could reach only after one and found Mausaji waiting for me, fuming; Mausaji scolded me in no uncertain terms while I remained silent. He was right in his own way. He was one for punctuality and I do not recall a single day when he did not send Nathulal to school on time or let him miss school without any specific reason. I glanced at the wall clock and felt a pang. I could have rushed to school but I would not be allowed to go without a meal nor would I be able to study on a hungry stomach. I sat down for my meal and gobbled my food quickly, while Mausaji remained bent at his work. I could make out from his expression that he was miffed with me and his words carried the force of his anger very effectively. In a sad and angry tone he addressed me, 'What a foolish and unfortunate boy you are, Sauram. You got one opportunity to study and you frittered it away. You are not fated to attend school and should give up that thought. You should stick to selling lemons. You cannot turn up on time. Do you think attending school is the same as walking into your Mausi's home, where you will be greeted with a warm welcome? How can one help children like you, even if one wants to? Forget about going to school if you cannot make it on time. It will be a better idea for you to study for a couple of hours at home. If you are fated to acquire knowledge then you will get it.'

Mausi was keen on my joining school so that I could improve my prospects and suggested that he go along with me to school but Mausaji replied angrily, 'Naresh's mother, what kind of nonsense is this? I had to plead for him to be admitted and now should I be begging with folded hands for him to be allowed to attend school after turning up late? What is it that you want of me? If Sauram's prospects in life have to improve, then they will do so if God wills. If God wanted him to study, then why would He take away his father? We tried, but then, that's all we can do.'

Ultimately, it was decided that I would not be sent to school. Therefore, after one o'clock when I had free time, I would enter the school rooms on the pretext of wanting to meet Naresh. In fact, when objections began to be raised, then I would go out and stand close to the outer wall of the school. I would peer through the window that did not have a lattice to observe the teaching going on in classrooms. The window was at the same height as the blackboard and I would jump up to see what was written on it when the teacher's back was towards me. This went on for a few days but one day a student spotted me and complained to the teacher. I was given a scolding and from that day the window began to be shut. The shut window blocked me off from the chatter of the students and the sweet voice of the teacher. I tried once again to enter the school with Naresh but then the teacher took me up on it, 'Look, you may be Naresh's brother but you are not a student of this school. Sometimes you are found peering through the window and sometimes you forcibly enter the school. You had better stop this or else we will complain to your guardians. You will spoil things for Naresh too. You'd better heed to this verbal warning or else the students may just bash you up. Remember, you are an outsider to this school.'

I felt very dejected at having lost this opportunity. I cried my heart out but there was little else I could do. Survival preceded education and I had to make my own arrangements for it.

When it was clear that I would not be going to school, I found no sleep that night. I had no option but to sell lemons for a living. The next morning, I was back to my old routine but with none of the earlier enthusiasm. That day my feet did not feel as light as before nor did my voice sound as sharp. Many of my customers whom I had told that I would be joining school wanted to know about my first day. I felt I was being mocked at by their simple queries about my experience in school. Even their sympathetic words seemed hurtful to me. Who could I blame when I had myself given them the opportunity by publicizing it? Why did I feel I had become an object of ridicule now that I had not been able to go to school?

That I felt drawn to the idea of going to school can be assessed by the fact that I would keep a look out for Nathulal as he set out in his khaki uniform. He would be joined by his friends and mingle among the other school children. I found the school uniform attractive and even though Nathulal wore the same dress as other children, his shoes would be finer than the rest. Mausaji had fashioned them with great skill and care. His shoes produced the pleasing sound of fine leather and the iron sole struck with a rhythmic cracking sound. His steps fell unevenly, because of which the heels of his shoes would incline in one direction due to friction but Mausaji would repair them in such a manner that it would not be visible. I would set out in the lanes and often land up in the school's playground during recess. It was difficult to spot Nathulal among the many school children but I would try to find him. It was a source of constant regret for me that I was not among the school children and would often cry out in the corners of the playground. By the time the bell rang for the recess at 12:30 p.m., my lemon basket would be empty. Hordes of children would rush out of classrooms like sheep and I would watch on. The moment I saw Nathulal move ahead of the crowd, I would fall in step behind the cracking heels but maintain a discreet distance. Since he would be with his friends, I would not join him. Seeing us arrive more or less together at home, Mausaji would enquire, 'Have the two of you come together?', and I would aver, 'No, we met up near home.' Mausaji would hand out practical advice, 'That's alright. Look Sauram, if the schoolboys begin to think that you are Nathulal's brother then they will tease him. Make sure that you are not seen together.'

I would reassure him, 'Don't worry, Mausaji, I will keep my distance.'

Nathulal also did not want me to be seen by his friends and there are many such instances that come to my mind. As my lemon-selling began to progress well, Mausaji wanted Nathulal to also earn a bit on the side. On holidays, he would ask me to get an extra consignment and send Nathulal along with me to sell lemons. We would set out together but he would avoid those places where there would be a possibility of meeting his school friends or acquaintances.

Egg Seller

At the time when lemons did not sell well, Mausaji contacted the newspaper agent in the market and got me the job of delivering newspapers at residences. In the beginning I was shown the locality and homes where I had to deliver the newspapers but I was unsuccessful in aiming my throw to the second or third floor and, therefore, could not continue with this job for long. It was then that I took up selling boiled eggs. Due to his own financial compulsions, Mausaji was keen that Nathulal also contribute to the family income. At one time when the lemons were not selling well, he got us to sell bananas. The first day we bought a basket of bananas and sat at the market square till late evening but the sale was poor. Our earnings were so minimal that far from making a profit, we had not even got back the money we had invested. The skins of ripe bananas had turned black while we waited for customers to turn up. The thought that by the next day they would not be even worth eating, we began to eat the ones that had become overripe. Thus in the entire day we ended up consuming quite a few and returned home with the remaining bananas. Ultimately, we had to consume the rest also. We consoled ourselves with the thought that even if the bananas had not fetched money at least we got to eat them. However, we regretted that we had failed even in this venture.

It was then that Mausaji pointed out that had a Bania been in our place, he would have allowed the bananas to turn overripe but would never have consumed them. He came up with another plan and drew the route to the chicken farm for us on his slab of stone. The first time we could not find our way to it and ended up converting it into a fun trip. Mausaji was obviously miffed with us for having wasted the day and sent us back the very next day. This time we found the farm and did not return empty-handed. Now I began to boil eggs and sell them. Fortunately, the very first day we saved four to five rupees. Nathulal went back to school as soon as it opened and I would set out with a basket full of eggs to sell them exactly as I used to sell lemons. I had fashioned a new rhyme as my call to sell my ware:

Fresh eggs, one for four,
Cash down payment, debts no more.
Eat eggs for health,
For wellness is wealth.

Mausaji would often want to know how I went about selling eggs and when I sang out my rhyme to him, he was very pleased. He felt that my rhyme had some poetic content and would mention it to Babuji. I got to know my customers quite well. One particular person I recall because of his obesity. As a child I would be amused by his rotundity. Whenever I went to his home, I found that he would require servants to lift him from one place to another. These servants informed me that he was not able to carry out the most basic tasks on his own and that there were special provisions for his diet. He would often fall ill and his mammoth size was burdensome to him. It would make me think that here was a man who did not work and had everything and here was I who worked so hard and yet found it difficult to feed myself. I believed in God those days and would complain to Him about why he had made some people rich and some poor.

Once the obese man had wanted to know where I lived. His slim sister had offered, 'Will you be a home servant for my brother?' I had asked, 'What will you pay me?' 'Anything you want.' 'I'll let you know.' But I never went back there.

I had another customer who was very fond of having raw eggs. I recall the scene clearly that she would, without bargaining, pick one, then another, and yet another egg from my basket and crack them open to empty the contents right into her throat and gulp them. I would stare at her red and rather heavy face. Initially I found it very strange but gradually got used to it.

Delhi: Retreating Hope

One incident caused me to leave Delhi for the village. After which I did return to Delhi often, not as a rich tourist or for education but to fend for myself and search for work. However, the first departure from Delhi set my childhood back on the same path of despondency and turned me once again towards my hopeless circumstances.

It so happened that a Punjabi couple who were my regular customers did not have any children and had learnt about my family background, parents, economic status, caste, religion, and related matters in several installments from me. I would wonder why they were so interested in me but even I felt attached to them. The woman's words especially seemed to be overflowing with maternal love. Maybe I fulfilled her need for a child and her soft, sweet tone was a balm to my soul that had always been subjected to a cruel and rough treatment. In those days as I roamed the alleys, hawking my fare, whenever I passed her home that woman would always call me to her place. She bought my lemons and paid me for them but in addition, she also always gave me something to eat. Sometimes it would be tea and at times whatever she had cooked at home. Today, I would find the whole thing distasteful but back then I could not resist her persuasive maternal insistence or just fell prey to greed.

I do not know what the couple thought about me after I had left but to me they would say, 'Can't you stay with us in our home? If you got more money than what you earn from selling lemons and eggs, will you give up this work?' I would ask, 'Why would anyone give me more money and why should I give up this work?' These were the questions that dogged me. More than Mausa–Mausi's scolding, I feared that I would be packed off to the village. I could never speak to my Mausaji about the affectionate manner in which the Rajouri Garden couple gave me things to eat. I feared my guardians and had got into a habit of hiding things from them.

That kind woman had been enquiring about me for a year and a half. On the pretext of getting her shoes repaired, she would make many enquiries about me from Mausaji. Sometimes she would try to forge a bond by bringing me a gift of books. She would express unhappiness about my not being able to attend school despite having gained admission there. One day she came over and said to Mausaji, 'Devidas, if you want I can take this child to my home and give him an education.'

Mausaji felt offended by this noble offer. At first he responded in a dry tone, 'May I know who are you to give him an education? Aren't we there for him? What is your interest in this child?' The woman fell silent at this. However, a few months later, she asked me, 'Sauram, have you begun going to school?' 'No Bibiji, I don't go to school. I just go to the market.' 'If you want, you can stay with us.' I immediately came out with my doubts, 'Do you want to keep me as a servant?'

She replied, 'Whatever you may think about it. As you know Sauram, we don't have a child. We think that if you stay with us, you can be of help to us and can pursue your studies as well. And if you manage to stay on, then you can take the place of a son.'

The woman's offer appealed to me but decisions regarding my future rested with Mausaji. Since she could not take the matter up with him again, I spoke with Mausi, 'Mausi, if I were to stay with that Memsahib and work for them as well as study, would Mausa agree to it?' Mausi was startled at what I had spoken and said, 'Studying is a good thing but is it so important that you are willing to leave your Mausa–Mausi and stay with strangers?'

'Mausi, I want to study at any cost.'

Sensing my determination, her expression altered. She grew so anxious that she did not sleep and spoke about it to Mausa that very night. Mausa explained the context to Mausi by comparing the woman to Putana, 'She is an educated and cunning woman. She has managed to entice the boy with her sweet talk and her display of fake maternal love. Sauram has come from the village and he has no experience about city folk. I suspect this woman will pamper Sauram for a few days and then go to the court and adopt him. What if his mother turns up and demands her son back? How will we compensate for him? Trouble has come unasked, knocking at our door. It is a small mercy that Sauram has asked for your opinion, but later he might just take himself off with anyone who conjures up for him the dream of educating him and making him a big man. What will we do then?'

Mausaji grew extremely anxious and, therefore, the very next day without telling me he dashed off a letter to my mother at Pali. Although she had only recently gone back to Pali with Bhikari, she took the night train back on an emergent basis to arrive in Delhi the very next morning. I had just returned from the wholesale market, when I saw Amma chatting with Mausi in the morning.

'How come you are here, Amma?' I enquired. 'That's rich! I am here because of you and you are asking me why I'm here? Do you know what pains I took to raise you? It was so difficult to bring you up without a father. I did send you away from me but I didn't forget you, did I? You were in my womb for nine months and now you are willing to sit in someone else's lap? God took away your father from me and now a Memsahib is going to take my son away.'

'What do I possess that anyone would be interested in taking me with them? I just want to study a bit and here is someone who wants to help me and that too without any self-interest. What is wrong with that?' I retorted.

'Don't treat the matter so lightly, Sauram. We all know that village folk are such simpletons. These city women don't want to take the trouble of giving birth to babies or raising them, so for them adopting a grown-up child is an easy option. Once you leave us, I don't see you coming back. Now that your mother is here, it is between the two of you. It is no concern of ours,' Mausaji said in an angry tone.

I got scared. I did not wish to return to the hellish life of Pali Mukimpur. I sought permission to sell at least the lemons that I had already bought. 'Okay, get on but make sure to return soon. Mukhi is waiting for you here.'

That day I felt no interest in my work. I kept thinking that the next day I would be returning to the same oppressive environment from which I had come to Delhi to experience some relief. Amma would not be able to keep me in Pali, as Bhikari would chase me away with his beating. She would take me back to Nadrauli, where everyone from my own caste and others would make me work like an animal. Therefore, that day I determinedly made my way straight to the house of the very woman I had been expressly forbidden to visit. I informed her right away about my mother's arrival and that I would be going back with her to the village in a couple of days. I also expressed my fear that I would not be able to frequent the lanes of this locality again. I told them that this would be my last Sat Sri Akal to them. The couple experienced a jolt by my revelations.

I sat with them for a while and then set out again. Once I had earned the amount that I had invested, I returned home only to find the couple sitting and conversing with Mausa–Mausiji. Mausaji's hands were busy at work but his ears were listening to what the others were saying.

'We plead with you, sister, leave your child with us. We'll send him to school and also set him to some light work at our home. We'll send the same amount that he earns by selling lemons to your home every month.' To this compassionate woman's noble proposal, Amma responded in a caustic tone, 'No, Bibiji, I will not leave my child. In fact, I will not let him remain in Delhi. Now he'll be raised in the village.'

Amma had announced her decision, and before leaving for the village, that woman came over and gave me two textbooks of Class Four. Amma took me to Chhotelal and Bhikarilal in Subhash Nagar but they mocked us, 'So, all these days you gave your earnings to Mausa–Mausi. Where were they when you were an infant? They did not come forward to raise you then and now that you are grown, they assert a claim over you!' Finally, they decided for me, 'From now on, Sauraj will work with us and we will not get him to sell lemons.'

The next day, a new work was found for me. I was enlisted as a helper in a nickel factory. There were these plastic drums in which acid was mixed with water and motorcycle and machine parts were immersed in it. We had to rub away the rust from these parts and then they were given a nickel polish. We used rubber gloves to pick these machine parts and the junior helpers were handed down the old ones that had already been used by the seniors.

Our bodies would be completely covered with grime and due to the picking up of sharp nails, tiny holes had bored into the gloves, through which the acid seeped in and cut the tips of our fingers. In about ten days or so, the delicate tips of my fingers developed deep cuts. My requests for new gloves went unheard. Amma was distressed at the sight of my affected fingers but Bhikari was only interested in my earnings. He was dismissive, 'In a couple of months he'll get used to it. After all, other workers also do the same work, why should you be an exception?'

After a month or so, I decided to give it up, 'I cannot do this work anymore.' Amma had to go to Pali and she had to fight with Bhikari to take me along with her. She, too, was convinced that I should give up this work when she saw the deep cuts on the fingertips of my little hands. Bhikari announced his decision, 'If Sauraj won't work here, then he will not go to Pali either and that is final.' Amma had no option but to send me off to my paternal village, Nadrauli. As soon as I reached the village, I took to working on the waterwheel and picking up cattle dung. From accompanying Babba to taking up sundry agricultural tasks, I also undertook the job of passing on bricks wherever a house was being constructed. However, since I could not carry the basin full of mortar, I was not given full wages.

It had become very clear to me once I returned from Delhi that I would have to find good literature to read by any means. But I was not fated to go to school and since a single meal itself was so difficult to procure, the alphabet obviously seemed a distant dream. However, since it was a passion with me, I would read books belonging to school children of my own age group as well as pick up some that were sold on the footpaths. I read without any guidance or specific goals.

Once during winters, I was travelling from Nadrauli to my sister's village, Mirzapur. I walked half the day, then boarded a train, and finally took a bus to Sambhal by which time it got late in the night. It was a rough terrain and quite unsafe. I thought over it and consulted the conductor who suggested that I spend the night in Sambhal itself. He whispered something into the helper's ear and then turned to me, 'Okay, for now you take a seat and when all the passengers get off, we'll talk about it later.' Eventually, the bus got completely empty. The night grew a shade darker and the conductor along with his helpers offered their namaz. One after the other went off to have their dinner. I had not eaten anything the whole day but then I had got used to missing meals.

Would you like to eat something?' 'No, Saab, I'm not hungry.' After some time, he enquired, 'Has your father got you circumcised?' 'Oh yes, a long time back,' I answered promptly. The driver then said, 'Okay, open your pyjama strings and let's check it out.' In a childhood accident, my foreskin had got scraped and it could pass for circumcision.

I sat down quietly, although my stomach was churning with anxiety. The conductor and his helper shut the front door and climbed on to the roof of the bus. In the village I had heard rumours that Muslims would kill Hindus whenever they found the opportunity. This was the sort of image that had been traditionally instilled in us by Hindu propagandists about the murderous Muslims of Sambhal and such illusory fears were deeply embedded in my unconscious. But then why would anyone want to kill me? I did not have on my person any of the markers of being a Hindu. I was just like a Muslim and could easily pass myself off as one. What would I say if they were to quiz me about *roza* and namaz? These questions were plaguing my mind. As the night progressed, I found no sleep lying on the bus seat.

Later in the night, the conductor came down and said to me, 'It's cold up there, I'm going to sleep with you,' and he lay down by my side. I caught the whiff of alcohol on his breath and then felt his hands run over my legs. I grew scared as I guessed his intentions. Just then, Mahmud, his helper also joined him. Before they could seize me I came up with an excuse, 'Conductor Sahab, my stomach has been aching a lot. I need to relieve myself urgently.'

'You bloody swine! Do you have to go for a shit now? Mahmud, give him a can of water and go after him, lest he escape. And make sure you return quickly.' The helper replied, 'He's just making an excuse. Ask him to hold on for a bit, Ustaad.' 'Oh no, he may just spoil his clothes. You better take him. Anyway, he is a rustic who is new to the city and a stranger here. Where will he go?'

I left the clothes that I had decided to wear at my sister's in the bus. The entire city seemed to be sleeping and the roads were deserted. Where could I go to relieve myself? I posed this question to the helper. He pointed to a nearby gutter. I looked everywhere for someone to scream for help. Even in those days I feared the police and, therefore, did not think of moving towards the police station for help. I sat near the gutter to quickly think up of my next course of action. I was quaking with fear and helplessness. Imagining the horrific act that the two of them were contemplating with me, I grew all the more fearful.

I spotted a petrol pump at a distance. The town had no electricity but I could see a dim lamp burning in the petrol pump owner's room. I could clearly see that the person was awake and so with all the strength I could muster, I ran towards him. The helper followed me for a few steps but the hope of finding support made me braver. I picked a stone from the road and threatened him with dire consequences. Now it was his turn to be scared and I raced ahead. The elderly man in the shop was perhaps a Hindu Bania. Seeing me pant with fear, the elderly man enquired, 'What is the matter, son?' I narrated the entire incident to him.

On hearing my tale, he grew angry and lifted his staff to walk a few steps ahead and shouted into the darkness to ward off my aggressor. Turning to me he said, 'You are looking for a place to spend the night? Come with me.' He opened the door of the room, in which there was a cot and bedding. He added, 'Go on, sleep son. You can go wherever you want in the morning. After all, you are a Hindu child.' It was fortunate that he did not enquire about my caste. Had he asked, I would never have revealed that I was an untouchable.

I breathed a sigh of relief and bolted the door, fixing the chain on it. However, in the middle of the night, I faced another problem. I needed to urinate and when I tried to open the door, I found it locked from outside. I grew all the more frightened. I tried going back to sleep and I dozed off towards the end of the night. I woke up to find that I had wet the bed. I got up and had to finish peeing in the room itself. I feared that the person who had given me refuge for the night would now want to beat me up for repaying his kindness with this shameful act. Thus, in a state of wakefulness and fear I spent the rest of the night. In the wee hours of the morning, the elderly man opened the lock and got his servant to walk with me till the bus stop. I kept my distance from him, fearing that he may get a whiff of urine from my clothes. I took the first bus to Daipa and from there walked straight to my sister's village. How I wished I had a fresh pair of clothes!

Procuring a Meal: Working in a Hotel

This incident took place around 1970–1 when we were staying in a jhuggi in Delhi. I had taken up work as a waiter and dish washer at forty rupees per month in a hotel. Amma had taken up the job of cleaning grain at a flour mill nearby. For a few days, even Badi Mausi started accompanying Amma for the same work but she hid this fact from her son who was pursuing higher studies. He was staying in the hostel and was not fully aware of his parents' source of income. The flour mill was run by a Punjabi woman who would often tell my mother, 'Surajmukhi, a woman must have courage. Even I am a widow but I managed to send my children to study medicine and engineering. But you village women are cowardly and always depend on men for everything. Why don't you realize your own self-worth?' Amma would agree, 'Yes, Bibiji, you are right. How can we be brave like you?'

However, the woman never mentioned all that she had inherited from her husband nor could Amma ever analyse it. What Amma meant was that there was a basic difference between a woman who has the material wherewithal for a living and another who is completely helpless. Their claims about self-sufficiency and courage in the face of a crisis cannot be the same. Courage alone cannot satisfy the hunger of children. Without money it is impossible to make a child aspire for the post of a peon, leave alone that of a doctor or engineer. Since Dalits are completely without resources and have no opportunity, even having a father does not ensure education or employment. Amma attributed her troubles to the misdeeds of her previous birth and regarded her circumstances as decreed by fate.

My Mausa–Mausi had managed to send Nathulal to a medical college only by borrowing money in addition to the scholarship that he got due to his merit and hard work. They also found help from a generous Punjabi couple who contributed as well as lent them money. Otherwise, it would have been unthinkable for Mausaji to get his son to do MBBS. Once he had even expressed his inability let him study further than tenth standard.

One day I saw my cousin enter the hotel to buy some snacks. I hid behind the sink and thankfully such an event never occurred again. In any case I lost the job itself. It so transpired that the very first day when I was washing the dishes, I saw some curd left over in an earthen bowl. The supervisor whispered to me, 'It will go waste, why don't you polish it off?' As I sat down to eat it, the owner saw me and grew so livid that he lifted me off the floor by pulling me up by my ears, saying, 'I am not punishing you for eating the curd because there are many things you can eat in a hotel, but it is to prevent you from eating on the sly. Every new boy is tested in this manner, do you understand that? Your name is Sauram, isn't it?'

I admitted my mistake and penalized myself by deciding to never take anything to eat without permission and without it being given to me.

One day, late at night when the hotel had shut down, the head cook set some rice to boil and then the boss of the team brought out a bottle of oil. He stripped down to his wrestler shorts to lie down on the bench and ordered me to rub the oil on his body. I was the new recruit and the youngest one at that, so I had to be given maximum amount of work. I understood that I was a servant here but then I had become the unpaid servant of the servants themselves. I found this extra work unacceptable but then how could I refuse? What if the others also wanted me to service them? By this time, the boss walked up to the dish and found that it had no salt; so he sent me off to fetch it from home and I immediately agreed, 'Yes, Ustaad! I'll be back in a jiffy.'

I walked slowly at first for some distance and then quickened my pace, fearing that I may be called back. I walked fearfully among the barking dogs to reach my home in the jhuggi. My unexpected arrival woke up Amma with a start. As I related to Amma my tale of double trouble, she was struck with anxiety. She expressed her concern about the number of jobs I had undertaken and left, 'You've changed umpteen jobs in one year, will you stick to one job and acquire skill in it or is this how you plan to lead the rest of your life?'

'Whatever happens, I'm not going back to the hotel.'

The next morning, Amma did not wake me up nor did she insist that I return to the hotel. In fact, I did not even go back to collect my wages. Thus, I was unsuccessful even in this venture. You may call it desertion but what happened was as unplanned and indeterminate like my future.

◆

'Swaraj'
The Survivor

Bhikari would drive Amma out of the house with the taunt, 'You live and eat with us but keep harping upon your Sauraj, so you'd better go to his village, earn some money and fend for yourself.' Beating her up was a daily feature, so one day when Amma had had enough, she came over to stay with me in Nadrauli. Here too there were no means of earning a living. Neither farm work nor any other job was available. She was left with no option but to take me to her parents' home in Chandausi. Rambharose was then very young and Rajmala (Manorama) had yet to be weaned. Bhikari decided to keep Tejsingh and Bhura, children begotten from Amma, since they were sons and that too his own. He was happier and keener to look after them than his daughter, though she too was his own child. He did not prevent Amma from taking her.

Even in Chandausi, other than my Nana, there was no other earning male member. Nana had six daughters and one or the other would always be turning up at his place with her children. My Nana was in no position to look after them for more than a few days and so, in Chandausi too, Amma had to look for work but permanent jobs were unavailable.

We had no savings to fall back upon and so it was a case of daily toiling for one's survival. Troubled by these circumstances, Amma began thinking of taking us away with her to look for work elsewhere. Our options ultimately narrowed down to our going to elder Mausi's place in Delhi but Amma was reluctant to take me there. She feared that the childless Sikh couple there would snatch her child away from her. Although she could hardly fend for me and was forced to keep me away from her, she was not willing to give me up for adoption. In any case, my Mausa had by then come away from Delhi and had rented a shop for shoemaking in Chandausi. The onset of monsoon would bring the work of shoemaking as well as boot-polish to a halt and excessive rains also meant that we would not be able to get the work of sifting and cleaning grain with the merchants. It was during such difficult times that Amma met Raama, her cousin Ram Swaroop's daughter. Raama had been married in Rasoolpur (Badaun) and her husband, Baburam, was a landless Chamar, who had taken his entire family to Baajpur where he worked as a bonded farm labourer. Amma enquired about the nature and possibility of getting work in Baajpur, to which Raama said, 'Bua, there is plenty of work there but it is back-breaking labour in the fields. During monsoons, it is sowing time and later the sugarcane has to be peeled, the corn has to be cut and weeding is done throughout the year. However, for workers there is no dearth of food. You can get wheat, rice in advance, and buckets full of lassi are distributed by the Sardars. They have several buffaloes and there is so much lassi that they can't find enough people to consume it. They mix it with the fodder and feed it to the buffaloes or throw it down the drain.'

I was pleasantly surprised to hear the account of such prosperity, plenty, and generosity. In our village we had to work for an entire day at the fodder machine to get one pot of buttermilk from the Ahirs. Babba would constantly be working at the grindstone for the Ahirs and ever since I had got to know that prisoners in jail were also assigned the same task, I had begun to see in Babba the image of a captive. Except that in his case I could never figure out what his crime was. While we could make our escape from the village by looking for work elsewhere to bail us out of trouble, Babba being blind was tethered to his toil.

Raama gauged Amma's situation and suggested that we come over to Baajpur as soon as possible. Before leaving for Baajpur, she gave us directions and the address. Amma returned to Nadrauli to pack her few belongings comprising a few bowls, a glass, a grinding stone, a rolling pin, spoons, and some other items. She hardly had any expensive vessels remaining with her.

Amma arrived in the wetlands of the fertile Baajpur with me, my sister, and Rambharose in tow. This region was entirely new to us. Topographically different and naturally beautiful, it was extremely green and wet, which is why it was called a 'raw' region. All through the year, the weather would remain humid and damp. The natural landscape was fascinating and the station was located in the jungle. Amma decided to wait at the station until daybreak. As soon as it was morning it began to drizzle. 'It is our poverty that has resulted in this exile. The 'upper' castes may have attained Independence for themselves, but we've had to struggle for every meal. Had there been no untouchability, I could have at least opened a small tea shop.' Amma began to cry and as the rain poured outside, tears coursed down Amma's cheeks.

The moment the skies cleared up, the mountains of Nainital seemed to appear right in front of us. But these pleasures were not for us. We had come here to sell our labour, to appease our hunger and we desired no more than this. It was a journey necessitated by the compulsions of poverty and the accompanying grief of displacement. Had we a few acres of fertile land in the village, we would have never come here. From her bundle, Amma handed us each a dry roti with some salt and chilly chutney. We were successful in finding the place that Raama had fixed for us to meet at. It was right at the thoroughfare.

In the market and the town, it was clear that the owners of tractors were Sikhs, Sardars from Punjab, and the rest were workers from the Hindi belt, mostly from Badaun, Shahjahanpur, Pilibhit, Bareilly, Moradabad, and surrounding areas. These were landless people who had left their villages to work as farm labourers here. Out of a hundred, ninety were Bhangis and Chamars, the rest of the ten per cent were poor Muslims. I could not find a single Bania, Brahmin, Ahir, Lodh, or Jat among the workers. To sum up, the agricultural workforce was overwhelmingly from our region. The workers spoke a Hindi dialect and the Sardars spoke Punjabi. The Sardars had pumped-up, mammoth bodies, whereas the hollow cheeks and faces of workers looked like mangoes that had been sucked dry. We were also among those who had come with their families. The Sardars wore lungis, turbans, and roamed around with kirpans. Their women donned bright salwars, spoke Punjabi, and did not work in their homes or outside. One could discern two distinct cultures in the marketplace. The working women would wear a sari and shirt and the men kurta–pyjama.

Like the land-owning Sardars, their women too had full, bright faces with glowing skins. There was a clear contrast between the faces of the prosperous Sardar women and the impoverished labouring women of our community. It marked the relation that exists between master and slave, the exploiter and the exploited. It seemed as if we belonged to two different countries. One was the country of the land-owning masters and the other of the bonded, landless, slave-like workers. The landowners, mainly from the Sikh community, were educated, well-informed about the rules and regulations, whereas the workers were illiterate and predominantly Hindus. And where did we belong in the Hindu fold? Did we have a place in it at all?

The Sikhs had also built a gurudwara in the midst of four or five farmhouses. On the birthdays of the Sikh gurus, all the children would go to the gurudwara. It would be a day free from work and we would get tasty food as well as prasad to eat to our fill. Even among the landowners, there were two sects, the 'upper' caste Sikhs and those with smaller plots of land or the landless Sikhs belonged to the Ravidas or Mazhabi cult. These were considered 'lower' caste Sikhs and they tilled their own lands as well as did the farming work themselves. Their complexion was dark and their marriages were arranged in accordance with their material status. The Sikhs also had a caste system in place but unlike the Hindus, they did not practise untouchability with us. Nor did they observe any irrational rituals or hypocritical customs.

Among the labourers, women worked alongside men and in addition to this, after returning exhausted from the fields, did all the household chores too. Their children also worked with them and they never knew any rest or leisure. Here again there were no schools or medical facilities, in short, there seemed no planning for a better future. All they had was the present. The master-class would go about on tractors and we, the labouring classes, looked after their field and cattle. We would milk their cows and buffaloes and their wives would churn the curds, boil the milk, and bake rotis. They would use expensive soaps, detergents, and eat good food. Their women would dance to the tunes of *balle, balle* and our women would serve them. These were the nouveau queens and our women, the nouveau slaves. Though Amma was very fond of and good at our folk dance and music, she could never be part of this group of women. She would take me along with her to watch these celebrations. We were allowed to be spectators and there was no prohibition against it. Apart from this, there was no observance of the Brahmin-like untouchability or the abominable hatred based on birth. These people did not exploit our self-esteem as much as they did our labour. We could go up to their kitchens and even touch their utensils after washing them.

The labourers could afford to buy mutton and fish but in the market the pig-meat shops would be thronged by the Sardars. Some would even chew it raw and then down it with alcohol to digest it. The indigestion caused by their overeating was held in check by the habitual consumption of liquor and we, on the other hand, were victims of malnutrition. However, at that time, we were neither conscious of our exploitation nor harboured any rebellious sentiment against our exploiters. At the riverside, the Sardars would prepare cans full of country liquor and would go far out into the jungle to ferment the cane juice in drums. Children like us would be assigned the task of carrying utensils, water, and fuel but we received no payment for it. The agricultural work would be given out on contract since the lands were owned by the government. The Sardars had managed a joint ownership or in many cases had captured land illegally and therein lay their strength. As for us Dalits, our weakness was that we were landless labourers.

I can still recall the scene when Raama had found us at the assigned place in the market. She embraced my mother and emotions overflowed in the form of tears. My mother quickly wiped her tears and enquired about everyone after placing her bundle down. Amma moved from place to place with her entire home and legacy tied up in the bundle over her head. They continued chatting with each other and I got the opportunity to explore the market. As I roamed through the market, I saw an old man selling books in a waterproof tent. I was ecstatic to see the one thing that for me was the most important and which I always sought out in a market. I found several books in Punjabi, Hindi, and Urdu. I didn't have any money but made up my mind to earn some first and then buy books of my choice. I quickly finished my survey of the market and went back to Amma and Raama.

Raama took us along to the Kshetriya Krishi Farm which belonged to a Sikh from Punjab called Dr Kartar Singh. He had managed to get his labourers to cultivate about three hundred acres of government land. These Sikhs who had captured miles of government land would always boast: 'The lions of these jungles have fled and now we are the lions of these areas.' And we were clearly their prey!

The Landed 'Power Sardars'

The Sardars had acquired these low-lying plains in two ways—they had come from Punjab and leased these jungle lands at nominal rates. Secondly, they had bought lands from the native Bhuksa tribe at a throwaway price. However, all the agricultural work, from ploughing, sowing, and harvesting was done by Chamars from Uttar Pradesh. Just as the British exploited our labour, these Sardars bled us Dalits. In the name of religious minority solidarity, they organized themselves to prevent land distribution among Dalits. There was complete unity among Sikhs about land-grabbing, whereas the Dalits were divided along sub-caste and religious lines. Those landless labourers who raised their voices in protest stopped getting work and instead of being imported from Uttar Pradesh, labour began to be imported from Bihar.

Recently, when I had gone to Surinam for an International Hindi Conference, I got to know about the oppressed Girmitiyas. It got me thinking that these were our ancestors, who had been transported across the ocean as bonded labourers to various countries, more than a hundred years ago. If I were to compare my past life as a child labourer to the Girmitiyas, it is clear that even after two-and-a-half decades of Independence, my lot was no different. Had I not left the village, I would have been in an even worse state.

The Bhuksas, the indigenous tribe of this region, had a traditional lifestyle. They would catch and dry the *bhur* fish which could be stored for at least six months. Wheat and sugar were the main crops grown here. Even the Bhuksas drank heavily but, unlike the Sardars, the tribals were illiterate. The Bhuksas used traditional farming techniques and knew nothing about newer, scientific methods. None of them possessed tractors and neither were they concerned about ownership of their land. They were oblivious to the rich resources hidden within the womb of their land. Culturally, they seemed extremely backward, but unlike us, they were not slaves to the Sikhs. This was because they belonged to the land, whereas we were outsiders, a migrant, landless community of farm labourers. The Bhuksas, along with their women, would also catch water snakes in the nearby river. They would cut off its hood and tail and eat the middle portion after cooking it. Like the Bhuksas, I would also swim, dive, fish, and catch crabs in the water channelized towards the fields. Meanwhile, the Sardars would eye their land and get work done by them on nominal wages. The Bhuksas had no awareness about modern ideas regarding health, education, and clothing. In other words, the Bhuksas were not developing their land area by cutting down forests but were selling it off to the Sardars.

Raama, along with her daughters, worked on Dr Kartar Singh's farm for the entire day. Her husband, Baburam, worked as bonded labourer on a monthly basis. The Sardar had lent him some money at the time of his marriage and Baburam had been paying off the interest for decades now. His job was to cut truck-loads of fodder and plough those smaller fields with buffaloes, on which the tractor could not be run. He wanted me to learn this work but I was too young for it.

However, we would wholeheartedly participate in the loading and unloading of wheat and cane that was transported to the cities. Dr Kartar Singh's family consisted of his wife Preeto, and sons, Nirmal and Guruveer. His daughters, Harjinder and Parvinder Kaur, were probably studying law in the city. Nirmal Singh drove the tractor to carry cane to the mill and sometimes used it for ploughing too. We were told to build our jhuggi next to Raama's, alongside Lal Singh, who was from Chataari. Lal Singh had leprosy and everyone avoided him. Even his wife had deserted him. Although his fingers and toes had wasted away, he continued to work for the sake of his son, Kishanlal, whom he wished to educate. The Sardar, on the other hand, had been eyeing his son ever since he had grown able-bodied, in order to exploit his labour. It was exactly like a butcher rearing a lamb for slaughter. Not just Kishanlal, even I and Raama's children were like the crores of other children in our country, who were being readied for the killing. However, at that time, we were neither conscious about our exploitation nor did we have an alternative before us.

Amma and I accompanied Raama for sowing and since we were working on the rice fields, we got the chance to eat the rice we planted. The Sardar had many buffaloes and so we got buckets full of buttermilk for free. Of course, we were required to do begaar for it. The Sardars would call it 'lassi' but I wonder why it was so tasteless. We followed the farming calendar by sowing and cutting wheat, corn, and cane at their particular time of the year. Almost a year later, Dori's wife, Bhuri, got in touch with Amma and they also shifted with their family to Baajpur. The Sardar allotted them a temporary place to build a jhuggi like ours and they also joined the workforce. In our cluster, as it turned out, there were five or six other jhuggis inhabited by Dalits from our district and region. We were continuously in touch with dozens of farmhouses.

With Phool Singh's arrival, I found a mate and the hard labour did not seem so arduous since we managed to have some fun. There was another reason for my happiness. I was extremely fond of books and I needed an accomplice in order to procure them. Every week, Amma sent me with a list of provisions to be bought from the weekly bazaar. Before purchasing anything, I would pick up a book of songs or historical tales for myself. After that I adjusted the amount by skimping on the quantity of purchase. Once I bought a book called *The Eyes of Prithviraj Chauhan*. If I had told Amma the actual amount I had spent on it, she would never have allowed me to go to the market again. The book was for two rupees whereas I told Amma that it was only for one and even that had seemed too steep to her. However, when I sang out some of the songs to her, she immediately felt the worth of it. She was a musical woman who loved songs and always took the initiative to gather the working women to sing some wonderfully inspiring folk songs. At weddings, she did not shy away from dancing either. Often, she would hand me a book of songs and request, 'Lalla, sing for me a song in that tune which Chandrapal from Pali had composed.' I can still recall the lines from the book I had bought from the bazaar:

Songs that tell of brave deeds and valour
Enthuse one to break the bed and bedstead,
Failing which, fie the song! Shame on the singer!

The book also contained the myth or popular belief about the blind Prithviraj Chauhan who was guided by his friend, the poet Chandrabardai, in an encoded message:

Sixty hands and thirty-two yards, fourteen measures in all.
At that height stands the Sultan, don't miss your mark, Chauhan.

Deciphering these directions, Chauhan shot the arrow right into Sultan Ghauri's face. The love of books had yet again compelled me to tell lies to Amma, even though her earnings, in a sense, included mine. Phool Singh was privy to my lies and secrets and, later, had even told Amma about them but by then she was hooked on to hearing my songs and trusted me completely.

Hazardous Moments

I can never forget that incident which occurred when we once went swimming near the dam in the river. That day Phool Singh, Khushiram, Rambharose, I, and many others were bathing near the dam. The released water flowed in a swift current and we were enjoying ourselves by diving into it. Islam Ali, also known as Tullan Khan, was posted as government supervisor to overlook the management of the dam. He was an excellent swimmer and would also often bathe with us. That day, he happened to be present when I was performing several antics in the water. As I was at it, a sudden mischievous thought struck me. I asked Rambharose to climb onto my back so that I could show how well I swam in this manner. This drew the attention of the other boys towards me. Islam Ali was furious but by the time he could reach me, I had swum ahead along with the swift current. But the moment I tried swimming further, I found myself sinking under Rambharose's weight. Instead of jumping off my back, out of fear Rambharose clung to my throat with all his might. It was impossible to surface with his weight on my back and by then he had also gripped my hands. Within seconds, I lost my bearings and both of us began to drown. Islam Ali swiftly dived into the water and dragged us out. By then the Bhuksas and their women, who had been standing around, ran towards us and carried us to the fields to lay us on our stomachs, face down to the ground. Islam Ali was a trained person and immediately began the process of pumping the water out of our bodies.

Some children had run off to the jhuggis and broken the news of this mishap to Amma. She began to scream and reached the dam, crying all the way. She collapsed the moment she saw us with our stomachs to the ground. She thought that our life's story had come to an end. She hugged us and wailed, 'You were my only support!' Just then the water spurted out of our mouths and we began to breathe. Amma praised Islam to the skies for reviving us back to life.

After that day, Amma forbade me to swim near the dam and I began to accompany her to the fields. Even though we were surrounded by natural beauty, I had neither the time nor the literary skills to compose poetry in praise of it. Phool Singh and I would be enlisted to assist Nirmal Singh in loading the cane on the trolley and unloading it at the sugar mill. On our way back, we would sit on either sides of the tractor, while Nirmal Singh drove it. Nirmal would pass lewd remarks and tease the working women on the way. We felt disgusted as most of the working girls were from our families. We reported this to our mothers and they resolved, 'If they trifle with our honour or even if one of them touches us, then we will cut them to bits with our sickles and machetes. Let them send us to jail for life imprisonment!'

Sometimes when we went hunting at night, Nirmal Singh would stop the tractor to aim and shoot at animals that emerged from the cane fields and stood immobilized in the glare of the tractor lights. He would hand me the gun too, but I would begin to shake and tremble. Once the animal collapsed dead, he would order me to pick it up. I would lift the animal and hang it by a rope at the rear of the tractor.

Our working hours were not fixed and ranged between ten to twelve hours. Even at night we would be woken up at any time. The Sardar wanted me and Phool Singh to learn to drive the tractor. On the very first day, Phool Singh's finger got stuck in the groove and his shirt got completely blood-soaked. That was the end of our plans of learning to drive the tractor.

Though the Sardars considered themselves lion-hearted, they had ensured that their farmhouses were surrounded on all four sides by our jhuggis. Thus, they secured themselves from any external attack. We had no protection from wild animals or storms and fires. Anyway, our lives had little value—there was no medical help, nor any provision for educating children, though every home had four or five child labourers. The country's law and order did not exist there and we had no sense of being free. Even to this day, Phool Singh reminds me of the satirical lines I had composed on the *aalha* metrical beat:

With kirpans drawn all their lives,
They've not even killed a small rodent!
Those who suck the blood of the poor,
Can hardly be called the Guru's descendants!

The rhyme had tickled Phool Singh and he had danced to it in appreciation.

I had told the Sardar that my name was Sauraj but in the diary in which he maintained the accounts of his labourers, he had noted it down as Swaraj Singh. I was the youngest among the child labourers. He had given my name an entirely new meaning and context but it hardly made any difference to the nature of my work. The irony could not be missed. I remained what I was—a child labourer. After Independence, these landed Sardars were the uncrowned kings and we were their slaves in this so-called free country. Every morning, the children of the Sardars would bathe, don their uniforms and colourful turbans to set out for school on cycles or motorbikes. We wore our soiled, crumpled clothes and set out to work in the fields. If we were alive, it was for the masters and if we fell ill, we would be packed off to the village or the city. If one was dying, they were least concerned. They would rather have one pass away quickly so that a healthier substitute could be found. It did not matter if one was a child, an aged person, or someone ailing—one had to earn one's living.

Artesian Wells and Water Mills

In our village, we undertook the arduous task of fetching water in leatherskin bags from specially dug wells to irrigate Babba's meagre plot of land (of which eighty per cent was infertile). The water was drawn from the well by the waterwheel to the fields but we had neither a well, nor bucket or bullocks to run it. We would have to buy water from Amar Singh Yadav in exchange for our labour. Often the cost of sowing, watering, and reaping exceeded the amount earned by the produce. But in Baajpur, I noticed that tall pipes, reaching well over my head, were bored into the ground all over the place and water sprang out of them, on its own. To see water sourced out of the ground, without the aid of electricity or a motor pump, was nothing short of a miracle for me. It was only later that I learnt about artesian wells in my geography books.

These people could be called truly self-reliant and independent because they were rich in resources, whereas our situation was best expressed in the words of a poet:

Those dispossessed of land and wealth
Are best kept at an arm's length.
Perchance, forced into accompaniment,
'Tis best to keep them in a state of impairment.

Even Shaheed Bhagat Singh's brothers had managed to acquire the government land for cultivation in the Banna Kheda Santokhpur region. Phool Singh always insisted, 'Come along, you must see Bhagat Singh's brothers. They are really very powerfully built chaps!' I wanted to know, 'What do they do?' He would reply, 'They do what other Jat Sikhs do. They plan to get us to work on their fields. What else can they do? Do you think they will ever free us?'

The water-run flour mills held a special charm for me. In the village, I had seen Gangi Babba painstakingly grind the grain manually for the Ahirs. I was filled with awe and a sense of wonder when I saw water-run flour mills here. I was fascinated by the technique of harnessing the speeding current of water for the mill. Similarly, the fodder-cutting machine also caught my attention. Babba would have to manually pull at the fodder machine for the Yadavs and I would also assist him, even though my hand barely reached the handle. I would have to jump high and keep panting through the entire task. As compared to the electricity- or engine-operated flour mills, the water mills would run at a slow speed. Electricity and human fatigue had no bearing on its operation since the water would flow continuously from the mountains for it to run at a leisurely pace.

The Guava Haul

Once on our way back from Baajpur town to the regional farm, Phool Singh and I spotted Sardar Chanda Singh's guava orchard. We got into the orchard but there was no need to pluck the guavas as several of them had fallen on the ground. First, we ate to our fill and then began to fill them in our sackcloth bags, to take some for Amma as well. We hauled the bags over our shoulders and ran out quickly towards the farms. Phool Singh managed to enter the jhuggi but I was lagging behind. Just then, like a lion springing upon a deer, the orchard-keeper, Ali, pounced upon me in the muddy field. Without much ado, he began to slap, kick, and pound me until he grew tired. Suddenly I saw that Phool Singh had returned and jumped into the fray. Phool Singh was twice his size and Ali was not the owner of the orchard; therefore, I managed to secure my release. The next day the Sardar got to know of it and Amma had to apologise with folded hands. I received no sympathy from Amma, instead I was strictly reprimanded 'Did I come here to eat stolen guavas? 'If I had to steal, would I be slaving for the Sardars? In future, be warned ....'

'Swaraj Will Not Be Spared'

Amma was constantly troubled by my adventurousness—once I almost died of snake bite, at another time I nearly drowned my brother and myself. One day she made up her mind to leave—a thought that recurred every other year. This time too, she tied up her utensils in a bundle and said, 'Let's go back to our village, son.' 'Right away? Why, what's the matter?' 'I am convinced that if we stay on here, Sauraj will certainly die before his time.'

The Sardar said, 'We had given a job to Swaraj because we felt that when he grows up he can take Baburam's place for which we could forward an advance. He can look after our farm and cattle for ninety rupees per month. Five to ten years from now, when Baburam grows old, where will we find another servant?' At first the Sardar tried to persuade and then began to threaten us. 'Do you understand now, Swaraj? You have full freedom to choose your work. Eat as much as you want, grow stronger but you will have to work for twelve to fourteen hours.' Amma argued, 'You can shoot us Sardar, but we owe you nothing. Our accounts are clear.' We had barely walked ten steps away from our hut when the Sardar's son intercepted our way with his motorcycle. The fact was that even we were reluctant to leave the place. We had already gathered several bamboos that we had brought from the jungle to build our hut. For this, we were obliged to Lal Singh and would not be able to steal away without taking him into confidence. We also feared that he would betray us.

The Sardar reiterated, 'Surajmukhi, you can go back to the village if that is what you want. You have other children to look after, but you must not take Swaraj with you. You have to leave him here. We will send his wages to you in the village—that much we can assure you. When he grows up, we will arrange a match for him with a labourer girl and marry him off in the gurudwara. You needn't worry about that at all.' This proposal was unacceptable to Amma.

That night we sat in our jhuggi and pondered over the matter. Amma said, 'Even if we do manage to leave Baajpur, what are we going to do for a living? Babba's barren land does not yield even a ser of grain. So it's better that you go to Delhi and earn some money by polishing boots when my sister returns from Chandausi. I'll go to Pali to look after your other brothers and sisters.' I cannot claim that Amma had a political outlook but she certainly possessed a vision wrung out of her experiences. On being harassed by my stepfather, Bhikari, she often enquired, 'Sauraj, you've read many books, can you tell why do men refer to Indira Gandhi's rule as women's rule? If I meet an honest-to-God person, I would certainly like to know as to what a poor Chamar woman like me has gained from Indira's rule.' I did not have an answer.

'The Sardar is not going to let go of me, Amma. Just as Raama's husband and children served him as bonded labourers all their lives, so will I have to be always bound to him. He will not let me leave.' 'Son, even if you manage to make your escape, where will you go? There is no employment in the village, so you'll have to go to the city. Whether in the village or the city, slavery is your share. How will you remain here all by yourself? No, I won't leave you here all alone.' 'If you go away, then on my own I can run away at night.' 'The Sardar will shoot you down and dispose of your body in the jungle. Do you think that these landed people hunt down only animals? The labouring classes are their real prey.' Unknowingly, Amma was passing on to me her understanding of the nature and character of the exploiting, capitalist class. Here was a Marxism borne out of experience. 'The day Nirmal hands over his gun to me, I will run away like a dacoit through the cane fields!' I replied, inspired as I was by the many tales I had read about dacoits.

I did return to Baajpur four or five years later, when I was a high-school student. I had gone there in connection with some matter concerning Phool Singh's prospective brother-in-law. At that time, Phool Singh was working on Janta Farms on Sardar Kundan Singh's fields. Their lot had remained unchanged.

First Literary Attempt

Sardar Kundan Singh had Leftist leanings and was well-acquainted with Shaheed Bhagat Singh's family, which lived in a farmhouse close by. Unlike fanatical Sikhs, he had set aside customary beliefs and advocated family planning. However, even he knew this well enough that if the labourers started restricting their family size, cheap labour would not be available.

I was staying in Phool Singh's mother Bhuri's jhuggi. On observing that I read all the time, the Sardar's wife got curious and wanted to know more about me. I told her my name and address. The next day, the Sardar placed a problem before me. His son, Neete, was participating in a play competition organized by his school for which an original play of half-an-hour's duration had to be written in Hindi. The competition was scheduled for 30 March, the day of Shaheed Bhagat Singh's martyrdom. I got down to writing the promised skit and managed to put it together just a few minutes before the Sardar asked for it. It was called *Lessons from Martyrs' Lives*. I explained the dialogues to the children and added a few finishing touches to ensure a simple and fluent style. In my career as a writer, this was the first attempt at a play which was composed without any serious creative intent. At that time, it was inconceivable that I would ever have a literary future. Everything that I had read about the martyrdom of Shaheed Bhagat Singh, Raj Guru, and Sukhdev had gone into the making of the play. I had also included in it a scene about Udham Singh, entitled 'Fire on Dyer'.

I left Baajpur the very day I had handed over the play and then returned again a month later, for Phool Singh's sister's wedding. I got to know from the Sardarni that the play had been performed in the school's cultural programme and had won the first prize. This piece of information filled my heart with immense happiness. I had forgotten all about the play having once written it. I do not even possess a copy of the manuscript in my records. Sardarji was so pleased that he got an expensive kurta–pyjama stitched for me. This was the first time I had worn such expensive clothes. I continued to wear the kurta for two years, even after the pyjama got frayed. Sardarji was impressed by the fact that I was managing to study by my own efforts, without the help and support of parents or kin. Two or three years later, Sardarji visited me when I was studying in Junabai School and together we went to my village. Phool Singh's father had taken an advance as loan from him and was unwilling to return to work. Sardar Kundan Singh had the address of my school and tracked me down there. In the village, he stayed in my poverty-stricken home and I had to borrow a bed and mattress to put him up for the night.

The Search for Rajju's Father

Now I am going to narrate the event of my third visit to Baajpur. Chunni, who was my friend Rajju's father, had been missing for the past four months. Rajju had searched for him in many places and then it was suggested that he look for his father in the wetlands of Baajpur. Rajju approached many people but they demanded money to accompany him. It was then that Babba asked me to go along with him.

I neither asked for money nor did I want to go with him but when he reminded me of the tragic loss of my father during childhood, something stirred within me. He had touched a raw nerve. Was not my suffering as a child labourer the price I was paying for being fatherless? I immediately agreed. We left the village and headed straight for Baajpur the next day. For many days we looked for him in the newly cleared jungle but remained unsuccessful.

On our way back, the train halted at Moradabad station around midnight. We got off in the opposite direction in order to avoid the crowd of passengers. It was somewhat dark and very few passengers were getting off on that side. A railway constable who observed our shabby appearance began suspecting us of being miscreants and fell in step behind us. He began to enquire in a manner that is unique to policemen. He obviously suspected us of being petty thieves and, therefore, began searching our pockets. He rapped our bags with his staff, 'What's in this? Show me.' I passed my bag to him. It contained four thick rotis, some notebooks, paper, and a towel. That was all, but the constable's curiosity was not so easily satisfied. He took Rajju aside and began to enquire his address. Scared stiff, Rajju did not answer any of his questions correctly. He gave the wrong name of his village and this only added to the constable's growing suspicions and anger. However, Rajju told him that he was a Yadav. After that, the constable took me aside and began to enquire in the same manner, 'Your name?'—'Sauraj'. 'Father's name?'—'Radheshyam'. 'Village?'—'Nadrauli'. 'District?'—'Badaun'. 'Your caste?'—'Jatav Chamar'. 'Who is the older boy? What is his caste?' I told him, 'He is Rajju. He is a Dheenvar. His father is missing and we have come looking for him.' The constable asked for the last time, 'What did you say is his caste?' 'The same as I told you. They are also called Mauryas because in addition to selling fish, they also grow and sell vegetables.' The constable then turned to curse Rajju in a crudely belligerent manner, 'You mother fu…! You call yourself a Yadav when you actually are a Maurya!' He aimed his cane at Rajju's legs and hit them with full force. Rajju began to scream and cry with pain. I kept imploring but the constable was enraged and unleashed an entire vocabulary of specialized abuses for which the police are well-known. He gave Rajju a thorough knocking to stop only when he was completely exhausted and then dumped him on the concrete. Before leaving, he searched our pockets for the last time and walked away with the small change he found on us. Rajju could find only one explanation for this selective treatment. He concluded, 'The constable must have belonged to your caste.' As for me, to this day, I regard policemen as some species of dacoits.

Another incident relates to the time when we were working in the southern part of our village at a Yadav's brick kiln. Pyaare Chachcha and Gangsaay Tau had taken up the work of brick-making. We had prepared the material and were soaking it in water before starting to work. It was the month of May or June and, late in the afternoon, an elderly traveller passing by walked straight towards us to pick the coconut shell-hukkah lying at a distance. He paused only to check if the chillum was warm and, without any further leave, began to puff quickly at the pipe, producing the bubbling sound in the process. After completely satisfying his craving for a smoke, he enquired, 'Are you Thakurs? I mean, what is your caste? You must be Yadavs, like us, aren't you? You are building your own home, aren't you?'

'Thakur? Yadav? Oh, no! We are Chamars. Who are you, Lambardaar?' Pyaare Chachcha asked. The man reacted as if an electric current had passed through him and in a shocked tone, said, 'What did you say? You don't belong to our community?' 'Which community are you referring to? Why didn't you ask us first?' Pyaare retorted. The man repeated his query, 'Are you really not Yadavs?' 'Why should we be Yadavs? We are Chamars, authentic Chamars.' Pyaare reiterated. 'Chamars? But Chamars deal with dead animals.' 'Yes, we do that work too.' By then, the man had flared up and began to fight with Pyaare, 'Bloody sons of Chamars! Why didn't you tell me beforehand? This is sacrilege! You've polluted me.'

Other than those associated with Arya Samaj, most Yadavs are more hypocritical, superstitious, and greater exponents of savarna culture than Brahmins. The lone man was no match for the three of us. He had to give up and when he cooled down, he said, 'Whatever has happened has happened. Please don't tell anyone that I smoked a Chamar's hukkah.' The man walked off towards the village with his head hanging down and we were left wondering.

◆

Here Lived a Mochi

I revisited Kaser Kalan thirty-five years later after Mausaji's death and as I alighted on the railway station, memories of the years 1973 to 1975 crowded my mind. Why did I avoid the platform and exit the station from a rear gate? I had a reserved travel ticket. Did my surreptitious movements have something to do with my old circumstances? What had happened so long ago?

In those days, a young boy would frequently be seen leading a blind man in and out of railways crossings. Nobody would ask them for their tickets. The boy, dressed in dirty and tattered cloths, and his Tau would move on after touching their foreheads to the ground in front of the fakir's shrine at the edge of the station. Who else could that boy be? It was me.

By this time, the landscape had altered quite a bit and some buildings had come up at the crossing. The basti had grown. In the direction of the Ganga, there used to be but one house, that of Babuji Ishwari Prasad. At night, the area would become utterly desolate. What happened to the fakir who would hand us the prasad? Was he alive or dead? Maybe one of his disciples had occupied his post. As the heir to the legacy of my own memories, I move on ahead, wondering … who can tell what invisible shackles fetter reminiscences?

Mostly, we slept on the open verandah facing the footpath and occasionally inside the junk-filled storeroom of Ishwari Prasad's house. The members of this family of ironsmiths had been simple folks and had a daughter, Rani. Ishwari Prasad worked as a signal operator for the railways. On the many occasions he stayed away from home, he would be deeply worried about the safety and security of his wife and daughter. It was a notorious area where incidents of thieving and burglary took place everyday. Before proceeding for work, he would entrust the care of his daughter and wife to Tau and me. I would consequently adjust my weekly schedule of going home to my village, keeping in mind my duties as their guardian. We had been able to win their confidence and in return, they allowed us to sleep in the open verandah outside their house.

I knew that Rani's parents were dead but I wanted to meet her. On reaching Rani's home, I introduced myself to her son who informed me that she too was no more. He and his children were curious to know my relationship with her. I began, 'Now tell me whether Rani ever spoke to you about me. Do you know that your Nana had a roadside shop here and on the footpath a sightless mochi had set up his business? There was always the fear of thefts and burglaries. Under the circumstances, a sense of security was provided by the presence of mochis and dogs. It was in this sense only that they were important.' One of the girls went inside and fetched an old dairy in which my old address was written.

As I stepped out, I began to wonder too. What indeed had been my relation to Rani? Why was I drawn to this place? Neither caste nor community or kinship ties, nor any romantic involvement, yet why did I feel so attached to this spot? Why were these places so firmly entrenched in my memory?

Meanwhile, a familiar-looking sufi fakir, Mohammed Sufi Jameel Ahmedshah Baba, entered into the conversation and enquired about a woman called Chameli and Baburam. He also mentioned my name, 'The boy fought the Lodhs, and that is why he was forced to flee from here. What was his name? He was called Sauraj. Allah had blessed him with some intelligence or else his enemies would have killed him. His nature was such that he would definitely have courted death.'

A little later, I confided to the Baba that I was indeed the same nephew of Baburam, for whose act of retaliation against the Lodhs and confrontation with the goons everyone had warned Tau that it was no longer safe for me to remain there. I did not return and everyone assumed that I had died. Even as I was speaking, Baba grasped me in a close embrace. 'What miracles does the Heavenly One perform! Everyone here thinks that Baburam's nephew was murdered.'

The one other person from the past whom I have not been able to forget is Atiqurrahman. He had had an unsuccessful stint as a tailor in the Bombay film industry and had returned to be established as an expert here. He liked his shoes to be shining bright and would get them polished everyday. Whenever business was low, I would head towards Atiqurrahman's shop to bring back eight to ten pairs of shoes, polish all of them, and deliver them to his shop. He paid me at the rate of ten paise per pair.

Tau used to buy half a kilo of flour each time either from Ashok Lala or Sharafat Ali. Hindu or Muslim, it did not matter, because we never had storage space to keep provisions for more than one meal, which is why we bought our rations just before we cooked each meal. For five to seven years, Tau had survived without a *chulha*. Rani's mother would daily pass on her lighted chulha to us after her own cooking was over.

Adjacent to Babu Ishwari Prasad's shop was the *halwai* shop owned by Mahendra Sharma who wanted us to sleep next to the entrance of his shop. When we shifted the location of our night shelter to the storeroom behind Ishwari Prasad's house, Sharmaji was so annoyed that he brought in a mochi named Ramswaroop and provided him a niche in front of his shop to set up his business. Ramswaroop's work picked up so rapidly that Tau's more-than-two-decades-old trade began to face difficulties. Ramswaroop was a brisk artisan and mobilized clients from afar. Further, to lure them away from us, he charged them less. At this juncture, Tau advised me to set up another stall and eventually two to three mochis' stalls came up on the footpath.

Not having any vessel to store water for ourselves, we would draw water from the public hand pump each time we felt thirsty. Thus, it was this water which sustained us. It was a convenience that did not bear the mark of our touch even if we touched it a thousand times. Mahendra alias Omi Sharma was a halwai-cum-astrologer. He had an income from fees paid to him for preparing horoscopes and for deciphering dates for rites related to births and deaths. Throughout the day, he would be engrossed in calculating his dues, in cash or kind, for the ritual services which he rendered. He had also taken to reading palms, although I never found his fortune-telling very convincing. He was extremely jealous of the fact that I possessed a copy of *Raidas Ramayan*. I do not know why my literacy annoyed him. Sharmaji had kept his impotent brother-in-law's wife as his mistress. This was a source of tension in his household but the quarrels seldom dragged into the streets. Frequently, Sharmaji's wife would appear at his shop to scold her brother, 'You have picked up a street-woman, heaven knows whether a Bhangi or a Chamar.'

Tau knew more about that woman. 'She is indeed a Bhangi, although Sharmaji calls her a Chamarin. If she has been integrated into his family, he might as well have branded her a Brahmin woman. Or else, for the sake of love, he might have become a Bhangi himself, why make her out to be an untouchable?' If I tried to change the topic, Tau would say, 'Son, you do not know the guiles of the Brahmins. They tell lies, write lies and teach lies. All their scriptures are filled with lies.'

We acted as watchmen for everybody but if anybody was unprotected it was us and us alone. Our only guardian was God himself, or those deities in whom we had firm faith. Actually it was Tau who was the one in demand and not me. He was reluctant to leave me alone, although he himself had spent half his life outdoors on this very pavement. On certain days, their food having been cooked in excess, Rani's mother would offer it to us. I would present myself before her with the only bowl we possessed. That bowl, a pan and a tawa were the only utensils which we owned and which would not be touched by anyone even if they remained in the corner of our verandah for over a month. There was, of course, no question of them being stolen. The belongings of untouchables had no value at all for anybody. Even a poor woman such as Chameli Lodhi and her children would not touch them because, though they were as deprived as we were, they were not untouchables. They would say, 'These belong to the Chamars. Not to us. Nobody would buy them even for a fraction of their value if we ever to try to sell them.'

Rani was extremely fond of stories and would get Tau to tell them. Everybody would be oblivious to the late hours of the night till Tau's storytelling went on. He could tell stories from the Mahabharata, the Ramayana, the *Raidas-Katha*, recite Kabir's verses, and extracts from hosts of folk tales. He could sing out his stories, without pausing, for hours at a stretch. It was amazing how much he remembered by heart. Rani's mother, her Tai, and Tau would listen to my Tau's musical renditions in their entirety and even shopkeepers from the neighbourhood would congregate to hear him. This made Mahendra Sharma envious because his scriptural interpretations were so dry, prosaic, boring, and business-like that even the members of his own family found it difficult to sit through his discourses. They represented a form of knowledge which was pedantic and acquired by rote. Nevertheless, he had taken advantage of his fake scholarship to build up a substantial fortune for himself. He kept himself away from strenuous manual work of any kind. As for his disdain towards Tau, which Chamar after all would endear himself to a Brahmin who did not consider them to be learned by birthright or equal human beings, and especially if the Chamar could, at will, adopt the posture of a Kabir? During debates, Tau would cite Kabir and profess to quote him, all the while improvising on Kabir's satire on Brahmins through self-composed verses. I, too, would make my contributions towards embellishing his creations. Our combined efforts resulted in the fashioning of rhymes in the manner of Kabir:

O Peers! The Brahmins ruined our garden,
O Peers! The Brahmins ruined our garden!
Neither any wisdom imparted,
Nor any reforms started.
O Peers! The Brahmins ruined our garden,
O Peers! The Brahmins ruined our garden!
Castes invented, people's unity dented—
Into many pieces our hearts they rented,
O Peers! Backwards our nation they have taken.
The disease of untouchability initiated,
And our own selves they have emaciated,
O Peers! Backwards, our nation they have taken!
On seeing civil strife, the Mughals invaded,
All of Bharat's wealth they raided.
The British watched with huge delight,
Came here and established their might.
Even the dim-witted were allowed Vedas to read,
As for us severe penalties were prescribed indeed,
Severe penalties were prescribed indeed.
Thus the golden bird was put in a cage
And wisdom also was held hostage.

Siblings turned into mutual foes,
The country caught in battle throes.
O Peers! The Brahmins ruined our garden.
They broke the branches and the stems from the tree,
They brought home to us an autumn's decree.
The tree itself, with evil designs, they uprooted,
By heaven, the tree itself they uprooted,
O Peers! The Brahmins ruined our garden.

In the end, Sharmaji would jeer at Tau, 'So, Babu, do you sing these songs on trains to beg for alms?' Tau would reply, 'If I wanted to earn through begging, why would I be mending shoes? God has decreed that it is the Brahmins who should beg.'

Sharmaji engaged with us, but was not transparent in his dealings with us. He did not take kindly to my sense of self-respect. It was difficult for him to tolerate such pride on the part of a mere cobbler boy. One day a man, after getting his own shoes and those of his family polished by me, threw some coins at me from a distance by way of payment for my labour. I scolded him sharply, 'I am not a beggar. Give me the money in my hand.' Sharmaji warned Tau, 'Your nephew will surely be thrashed one day.' He would constantly hope that I get beaten up.

Lodh Rajput: Raining Blows

Once with the help of Atiqurrahman, I had managed to rescue a girl, who had been kidnapped and gang-raped by the noted criminal of Allahbad, Shamir and his goons. Her father had been an Urdu news broadcaster with the BBC. Thanks to our intervention, the girl had a providential escape. Tau would always maintain that it was because of me that the girl's life had been saved. My Tau and I were, however, warned that our lives were in danger from those who had tried to harm her. We were advised to shift our workplace.

Around the same time, another event overtook us. Badani, a politician from the neighbouring village, ran a gambling racket by extending loans at high rates of interest. He was an alcoholic and liberal in the abuses he hurled at others. He had a lot of ancestral property, and that was the real reason for his swollen-headedness. He belonged to the Lodh community. One day he engaged Tau to mend all the old and tattered footwear in his household, who, in turn, passed on the job to me. I dutifully cleaned all the shoes. Tau then told the man, 'Now please pay us. You owe us money from previous times as well. If you cannot pay, why get your shoes polished?'

Scarcely had Tau uttered these words than the man flew into a rage, 'There may be other people who cajole Chamars into doing chores for them. I will make you polish my shoes ten times and then fling a coin at your nose.' Without much ado, he then proceeded to plant a stinging slap on Tau's cheek. 'Bloody Chamar, how dare you ask me for your dues and spoil the day for me? Shall I run away with the pittance I owe you?'

Tau still had the Lodh's shoes in his hand. Notwithstanding his poor vision, Tau dealt a powerful blow with the shoe on the Lodh's skull. His aim was impeccable. Badani was left clutching his forehead. A roadside cobbler, all but blind, and to top it a totally destitute Chamar, would hit a Lodh who claimed to be a Rajput, with a shoe in return for a slap—such rebuttal was beyond the imagination of the Lodh. What he did next was to fell Tau to the ground and began to rain blows upon him. Since I was a patient of rheumatism, I was slow to get on my feet. However, I somehow ran to Tau's aid and never got to know how his walking-stick came into my hands and how many times I struck the gambler-overlord on the back with it!

The swelling crowd of entertainment-hungry shopkeepers and passers-by intervened to save me and Tau. Despite the fact that it was the Lodh who had pulled the first punch, he regarded the personal slight as an insult to his caste. He declared that under no circumstances would he let me survive. It was beyond the ken of this man that even bedraggled roadside cobblers would resort to self-defense and that they too had a sense of self-esteem. He was accustomed to abusing the untouchables in his village almost everyday. But none had the nerve to talk back to him. Those were the days when the Lodhs were aspiring to be recognized as Kshatriyas. They had started to attach the appellation 'Rajput' to their names. An hour-and-a-half later, he returned with a dozen or so musclemen.

Without much ado, his kith and kin pounced upon us but by then Tau had already raised an alarm and shouted to Atiqurrahman for help. I had been pummeled severely by scores of blows by the time Atiqurrahman and his men came to my rescue. The nearest I could appeal to for assistance were Mahendra Sharma and his brother-in-law, Ramchandra Sharma, but rather than attempting to save me, they mocked us with a malicious sense of mirth. They began to instigate the Lodhs. 'This is an arrogant boy. He is too outspoken. Does he fancy that he is the author of a *Raidas Ramayan* and can contest Brahmins in debates on scriptures? Heaven knows from which roadside he picks up his books? Is it proper that scriptures should be read by a mender of shoes?' They were trying to settle their own scores. However, Atiqurrahman and his apprentices soon arrived and the arbitration was successful, but the Lodhs left with the threat that they would kill me while Atiqurrahman countered by swearing to save me.

By evening even though the tensions had eased, we realized that under the circumstances it would not be wise to sleep in the open but we hardly had the option of a secure habitat. Our stay at Rani's house was determined by the family's need and not by our wish. Why not take the night train back to our village? If we survived, we could at least resume our work in some other location. As we started to pack our belongings, Mahendra Sharma, who had been eavesdropping all the while, came out of his shop and enquired as to what we were up to. Tau declared that we had decided to pack up and leave for good.

'I know why you are thinking in this way. It is true that the Lodhs have misbehaved with you. But let me tell you one thing, Babu, it is because of Sauraj that you have come under their fire. If you had tolerated their misconduct and not hit back, how long would the Lodhs have troubled you? Matters were aggravated by Sauraj. Although he is not quite healthy, his young blood is already on the boil. If he had behaved with due consideration of his caste and his status, I might have intervened in the dispute. But if a low-caste boy thinks he can answer back a high-caste man and a landholder at that, on equal terms—where was the need of my intervention?'

Mullaji-Karamtullaji

Another man's profile too is etched clearly in my mind from those days during which I had been a cobbler. The dark, rough, pock-marked looks of that man were fearsome and unattractive but his generous disposition rendered him a gem of a person. This dealer in scrap of all kinds, who remained assiduously preoccupied with his business most of the time, Karamtullaji or Mullaji, had been a friend of my Tau for almost two-and-a-half decades. Or rather, I might say that he was very kind to us since friendship is only possible between equals. How can the rich and the poor be friends with each other?

Tau never took cash in payment from Mullaji, but he never got work done for free. His return for our labour came in the shape of coals, logs of wood, sometimes rice or dal, and sometimes raw mutton. I do not remember any occasion, such as Eid or Muharam, on which Mullaji forgot us. Likewise, it never happened that Mullaji would not send shoes for repair to us, not only of his own family members but also those of his house guests and their children, or that Tau or I would claim payment for the work. Our affections and exchanges were mutual. There was reciprocity in services and help extended. Our relationship was spontaneous and humane. No hierarchy, no quarrel over debts. Mullaji knew nothing about untouchability—I could wash my hands on the same tap as his sons. Occasionally, Mullaji would get meat cooked for us at his home and whisper it as a secret into Tau's ear. I could share the mutton with his son from his plate.

In Kaser, there was a world of difference in the treatment we received from Mullaji and Master Atiqurrahman on the one hand and from the Yadavs, the Lodhs, and Sharmaji on the other hand. Tau's explanation was that Mullaji's forefathers had been untouchables like us. They had converted to Islam, disgusted with Hindu norms regarding touchability and untouchabilty.

Mullaji's house was on the lane adjacent to the masjid. I was a frequent visitor there and the moment I saw from afar that the *namazis* were trooping into the masjid, I would quickly leap across and begin by dusting two or three pairs of shoes and polishing them. I did not require anybody's permission. Everyone knew me—I was the nephew of their well-known Babu who had been working in their area for decades. I did not ask for money from anybody. Some would make the payment right away while others would pay in due time. The devout thought it was sinful to hold back wages. These were not Hindus who skimped on giving just wages for labour, who would extract services and not provide remuneration. Over and above that, unlike Hindus, they would not use pollution norms to distance themselves from us. I could continue to sit outside till Mullaji remained inside the masjid.

That was my daily schedule—head for the masjid if there was a paucity of work. Thus, my wage-earning went side by side with the rituals of devotion. There was no bar to my entering the masjid. The scorn and the taboos associated with pollution norms with which we were met at the mandir did not apply here. Nor was there any abhorrence towards our occupation. Wash your face and hands, sit next to Mullaji, he would even pat you on your head while you spoke to him about your most immediate concerns.

I would work less on occasions like Eid or Muharram, and on those days we were exempted from cooking. On Id-ul-Fitr, he would definitely bring us *sevaiyyan*, and on Bakri Eid send us mutton. He would sometimes personally bring us a ser or half a ser of mutton, concealed under his robe. But what could we do given that our closest neighbours would take offence if they discovered our exploits? Mullaji was alive to these apprehensions on our part even more than we were. He did not want any exposure which would deprive us of our workstation.

We would all shut our shops on the day Mullaji's people took out the Tazia processions. On such days, Sharmaji's business would suffer as the shops run by Muslims would be better patronized. He would come near Tau and instruct him in an imperious manner, 'Babu, we are going home. Sleep lightly tonight. We cannot trust these Muslims. They might break the almirahs and eat the sweets. Everything is now your responsibility.' We were left to guard the sweets in his cupboard and cook our mutton on his *angeethi*. Once the shopkeepers had departed, preparations began for our meal. Since Sharmaji's shop was a little away, the smells could waft outwards and we feared that everyone would come to know that we were cooking meat.

Bare Blade

Tau could shave his beard without soap or cream, by using only water and holding an unsheathed blade between his fingers. I would be amazed at how he managed to leave a thin streak of moustache under his nose. As far as cutting of the hair on his head was concerned, he would merely wet his hair and rid his skull of it. He would offer to do the same for me. I could not get a haircut, as the Hindu barbers would not cut the hair of Chamars and Bhangis. Although the Muslim barbers of Kaser would be willing to cut our hair after a month or two, we would ourselves shave off our hair completely.

Stealthy Gobbler

One evening, I bought three small fish for our meal and, after rubbing them on the sand to remove their outer scales, used the cutter to divide each of them into three pieces. By this time, Tau had kneaded the flour into dough. I liked this variety of fish called 'saunriya' more than any other. In a small vessel, I fried them lightly in oil and allowed them to cook in the spices, adding to them small pieces of potatoes. As we waited for our dish to be ready, Tau began to sing:

There is neither mercy nor kindness in your heart
What then, can your image in the mirror impart?
With a piece of paper I made a boat,
And on the Ganga set it afloat,
On the Ganga set it afloat.
The righteous go across the river,
But sinners drown in the water,
Sinners drown in the water.
If God is in you, your salvation is assured,
Merely by bathing in the Ganga who of sin can be cured
Would not then fishes, that dwell in water, be to heaven lured?

The thought of the cooked fish was making me impatient. There were, in all, nine pieces for me and Tau. I washed my hands and dipped in to eat one. A little later, I ate another. Acts of theft, committed surreptitiously while the rotis were being made. I sat down smugly, thinking that Tau would not have guessed anything at all. As we sat down to eat, Tau took over the task of serving. He used the flat end of the roti-turner to dole out the pieces of fish, saying, 'You take four more and I shall eat three; you can have six as your share.' I trembled because I had been caught red-handed. I felt ashamed and promptly acknowledged my guilt, 'Tau, I couldn't help myself, please forgive me.' It was a good thing that I pleaded guilty or else he would have sent me packing.

One day, my stepfather, Bhikari Lal, landed up and demanded a portion of my earnings as his due. Tau remained silent while I made him tea, fed him *gujia*, and spoke politely to him. After Bhikari left, Tau scolded me for extending hospitality to him, 'Don't permit such a man to sit next to you. He is a mean-spirited man.' But despite his many faults, I remembered that after the untimely death of our father, we had spent a sad, albeit small, period at the home of this person.

Mahendra Sharma had taken a strong dislike towards me, both on account of my caste and because I dubbed him a spurious scholar of the Vedas. In those days, along with my cobbler's implements, I would always have in my possession four-anna worth of books sold on pavements. I had read Guru Bakhshidas's *Raidas Ramayan* in which he outlines the debates that Raidas had with the ritualistic Brahmins of Kashi and had come to the conclusion that Sharmaji operated on blind faith alone. In my own way, through Tau, I was expanding upon my understanding of Raidas and Kabir. Far from regarding Sharmaji as an inborn scholar, I wondered at what ultimately was the measure of the so-called wisdom of the Brahmins? What kind of tree of Brahminical knowledge was this that had produced only the fruit of inequality?

Sharmaji got particularly annoyed with me from the moment he tried to provoke me by picking on Tau as an object of mirth. Once when Tau was shaving himself with his unsheathed blade, Sharmaji, who was preening at himself in a mirror, had mockingly addressed me, 'Here Sauraj, give this mirror to Babu.' What would a blind man do with a mirror? In response, I repeated the lines from Tau's song:

What can your image in the mirror impart?
When there is neither mercy nor kindness in your heart.

Barely had I sung these lines than Sharmaji flew into a rage.

In Kaser

I recall that I had come to Kaser from my village for the first time when my rheumatism had nearly incapacitated me. Many a day, wracked by pain, I would be lying down in one corner of Dori Tau's courtyard. Far from fetching me medical help, this did not afford me even two square meals a day. There was none who enquired about my welfare. It was Tau who, on learning about my ill-health, had advised me, 'Once you become a little mobile, come and join me in Kaser. You will not be able to do hard labour now, you should think of making a living at Kaser by working as a cobbler. Your eyesight is intact and I can operate my hands and feet. We can help out each other. You have nobody to support you and neither have I.' In this manner, he tried to create a bond between his suffering and mine.

Crushed Concoction: Medicine or Poison?

I had become so disgusted with the pain, hunger, and deprivations which marked my stay in the village that I began to desire release from such an existence. I still remember the day when I procured an extra dosage of powdered drugs for rheumatism and in sheer anger consumed it on an empty stomach; it was a dose meant to be had over eight to ten days. I knew it was an act of cowardice on my part. This was nothing but an attempt at suicide. But I felt that I would never be rid of my disease. After consuming the concoction, I went and lay down on a cot spread out on Dori Tau's courtyard. Gradually, the impact of the dose began to tell on me and my condition started to deteriorate as time passed. The news spread in the neighbourhood that Sauraj was about to die. I was not aware who came to my aid and on whose shoulders I was carried to the hospital. Later I learnt that the childless Dayaram couple and Gangi Babba played a crucial part in my rescue. It took me four to five days to recover wholly. The trauma was beneficial in one respect—it reduced my pain. In a month or two, it dawned on me that the only work I would be able to do would be some non-strenuous physical work. I did not have the opportunity to learn tailoring or any other such work. I could only work with shoes, and thus decided to become a cobbler.

How long could I pull along with a debt-ridden childhood? Who would sustain me with loans, and why, and for how long? Debts worth fifty to hundred rupees which I incurred then, now weighed on me as if they were worth ten- to twenty-thousand rupees. One day I dropped a rupee coin from my pocket in the vicinity of Mandoli while returning home from the bazaar at Junabai. I retraced my steps to that spot and failing to find the coin, cried my heart out. My earning for a day's labour at drawing water from the well was a meagre twenty-five paise. The sum of one rupee amounted to four days of labour. With that earning, I could have bought from the bazaar at least ten books priced at ten paise each.

I informed Gangi Babba about my decision and with the intention of boarding the night train, I left home. On learning about my resolution to team up with Tau in the much-detested trade, the boys of the neighbourhood and the more prosperous Chamars berated me in one voice. They were concerned about the reputation of the community, but not about my well-being. The community's responsibility was to raise objections, but not to offer succour. I took them on, 'Did any of you offer me any monetary help? Do you all want that I should die here lying on this cot? Now I cannot do any heavy work, such as drawing water from the well or work in the brick kilns. Should I then not attempt to stay alive by doing some light work rather than maintain the false pride of the community and die gradually in the process? Ever since I grew up, I have had to earned my bread through the sweat of my labour. What great respect have I got anyhow? Who among you has helped me, who has offered me more wages than employers of other communities? As a worker I have found no difference in the attitudes of Banias, Yadavs, Telis, or fellow Chamars. Everyone has exploited my labour and no one has cared for me.'

It was Gangi Babba who spoke in my favour 'Sauraj dear, you go to Dibai. Stay with Babba and earn some money, and, first of all, repay your debts to everyone. Starvation is not going to make a Brahmin or a Bania out of you. We are Chamars, and Chamars we will remain. We do not want anybody else's caste. By mending shoes, you will make enough to pay for your medicines and food, while here in the village there is nothing for you but enslavement to the Yadavs.' Packing my *kathra* into a bundle which I mounted on my head, I set out for Dibai the next morning in search of a livelihood. I had not a coin in my pocket. I was full of dread at the possibility of being caught travelling ticketless on the train.

At a Stranger's Wedding

As I reached the station, a wedding procession had just started. I thought, surely I would be able to eat something if I joined them. I fitted my bundle under the stone bench on the platform. Apart from the kathra, it contained only a few utensils. Nevertheless, I continued to feel anxious that some beggar or like person should get hold of it. The hunger in my stomach drew me towards the baraatis but worry for my bundle brought me back time and again. For a while, I did these back and forth manoeuvres, but finally I joined up with the revellers. Although I had come in clean clothes from the village, my appearance was not appropriate for a wedding procession of this nature. Thus, like a household servant, I stood in attendance, sometimes with the groom's party and sometimes with the bride's. Very soon the groom's party sat down for dinner. I do not know what anybody thought while I hurriedly stuffed myself with puri–sabzi, laddoo, and dahi. Suddenly I heard the whistle of the train. Immediately, I left my plate of food and ran, leaving the people around me astounded. Reaching the waiting room at the station, I looked under the stone bench and received a shock—my bundle was not there. I rushed from this bogey to that, trying to trace my bundle, but in vain.

It was quite late at night when I reached Kaser. I descended on the platform, paid my respects to the mausoleum in front of me and went on ahead. Tau was waiting for me to arrive and immediately sensed that I had come without any luggage. After listening to the account of my loss, he was annoyed at my irresponsible behaviour. From the next day, I began to accompany Tau to his work-station on the footpath. Tau kept all the money that we earned. Whatever was left at the end of each week's expenses on our meals and on the tools and raw materials which we used, we would divide equally between us.

What a life we had! All we had was an iron pan that served for kneading atta, a tin can for drinking water as well as for the dough, a blackened cooking pot and a tawa with two small bowls. We would drink our water straight from the can. We had another can, too, in which we carried water to go to the fields every morning. For bathing we used water from the tap on one side of the road, which we did in full public view, that too, once in many days. In those days, my box of tools invariably carried a book or two. Counting those whom I met at the bazaars, I was acquainted with at least a dozen cobblers in those days but I was the only one who stocked books inside his tool box. Never mind that I only had those books which were sold on pavements, but never any obscene or overtly fanciful literature. I did not ever develop an inclination for such writings. The credit for this should go, perhaps, to the influence of Arya Samaj on me. It is another matter that much later I read some prurient texts as compulsory readings in the name of literature of manners or romance literature in my syllabus.

Someone Like Amma

Since Kaser was the first station after Rajghat, people would travel in large numbers from afar to take a dip in the Ganga. Although not on a regular basis, I would also act as a coolie at the railway station and especially sidled towards old people who came from the towns. On one such occasion, I met an old lady at Kaser railway station, who had come to have a holy dip in the Ganga. I helped her board the train along with her luggage and she gave me four annas for it. I too boarded the same train. Even though the skin of her hands seemed wrinkled, the old woman seemed well-maintained and used to a comfortable lifestyle. She had a snowy white complexion, carried a shiny bright bag, and her clothes were expensive. I could not help comparing her physique and possessions with those of my own mother.

Four annas seemed a large amount for so little labour and I thought, for sure the old woman is wealthy. Before our train reached Rajghat, the old woman requested me to help her take a dip in the Ganga at Rajghat and that she would pay me four annas for helping her off the train and four annas for boarding it again. I would get some prasad as well. Succumbing to temptation, I disembarked with her at Rajghat. Keeping her things in my custody, she reverentially went away to take her dips in the Ganga. Although the old woman would check on her belongings after each dip, she would not even have been able to track my shadow had I decided to make myself scarce from the scene with all her things. But how could I have behaved so in those days? The grandson of Ganga-worshipping grandfathers, I myself reposed faith in the efficacy of bathing in the river. To put it poetically, whether the Ganga, as per mythology, had trailed down from heaven behind the wheels of the chariot of King Bhagirath or not, its waters had certainly flowed from the eyes of my grandfathers in the form of tears. The waters of the Ganga were used to wash away one's sins. How could I proceed from here with sin in my heart?

A thought struck me that ultimately all the money she had must be in her bundle. How long would it take me to rifle through her pockets? No, I could not possibly perpetrate such thievery, such felony, standing on the banks of the Ganga. Was I any less a devotee of Ganga Mai than her? But then another thought assailed me. I could leave her clothes and flee with her wallet. A hundred odd rupees would be enough to alleviate my miseries. She appeared so wealthy; the loss would not matter to her at all. What would she do with so much money, more money than she required? Contradictory pulls and pressures exerted themselves upon my mind. There was still another way out. Instead of stealing from her right in front of the Ganga, I could confiscate what I wanted from her at the station.

At the station, while we waited for the train to arrive, my mind was still engrossed with thoughts of the old woman's wallet and bundle. On the banks of the Ganga, the boat of my enterprise had found itself on rocky waters. Now there was no Ganga in sight. Who was this old woman to me? Who would be able to apprehend me if I picked up her bundle and ran—no, I would not be able to run fast. Afflicted by rheumatism, as I was, what then could I do? Why not push the old woman out of the train without attracting the attention of our fellow passengers? But that would be like murder. What could be in the bundle? The wallet which contained her money was kept close to her chest. Even if I were to push the lady out, the wallet would fall with her. In that case, I should leap out after her as soon as the train started slowing down, but what if that landed me in the clutches of the police? Beset by such contradictory sentiments, I found that we had reached Babrala station. I was to disembark at this station, and was all set to make away with the old woman's bundle. At that moment, my gaze rested in the direction of Chandausi and memories of events in my mother's life were revived.

I remembered a day on which Amma was travelling by train with a consignment of neem fruits with the purpose of selling them in the market and that as I tried to secure a seat for her, her bundle too had got stolen. I remember Amma weeping, as I watched on helplessly. The old woman would also weep like Amma if I were to either flee with her bundle or push her down. Somehow, the features of Amma and the old woman began to blur into each other in my mind. Although the old woman's appearance bore no resemblance to my mother, I found that I could not cheat her. My station had arrived, and I alighted without saying a word to her but she called me to herself and loaded my lap with *batasha*s, adding three more four anna coins as well. 'This is for all your efforts,' she said. She reached out to caress my cheeks and blew me a kiss. As I moved away, she called out 'You are such a nice, decent boy. Do tell me, what do you do? Which caste do you belong to? Do you go to school?' Before I could reply, the train had started moving from the station.

A Cobbler's Legacy

Many years later, when I was travelling with my wife, Rajat Rani Meenu, and daughter, Ajatika, on our way back from Pali, they encountered Bhikari for the first and last time. He had said to them, 'Had I known that Sauraj would not stop studying even though I tried to prevent him and grow up to be a learned person, to whom the Jat–Brahmins would also pay respect, I would have burnt him alive while he was sleeping.' But he adopted a different tone altogether at the moment of our parting. 'I have heard that your wife is from a well-connected family. Do use her contacts to get my children some jobs.'

On the same day, I came across a mochi sitting outside Atrauli station. His unkempt appearance, partially graying hair and white kurta–pyjama looked familiar to me. I told Meenu, 'You wait at the platform, I want to talk to this man. I seem to know him.' Meenu had said, 'It's strange. If we run into a construction worker, you say you have been one yourself. If we go out to buy lemons, you say you have been a lemon-seller. You tell the newspaper-delivery boy that you could never throw newspapers upto the second floor. When we went to dine at a restaurant, you told us you used to wash dishes at a restaurant in Delhi. Now, you claim this mochi is someone known to you. What all did you do before we got married? Why did you not reveal all this earlier?' But I had moved ahead.

One approaching the mochi, I asked him, 'Is your name Ramswaroop?' He said nothing but on persisting with my queries, he revealed that he was Ramswaroop's son. A carbon copy of Ramswaroop, here was the son of a mochi, with no change in circumstances and no prospect of change in social status or economic opportunity either. His children also worked as mochis in nearby localities.

It is sheer coincidence that as I record my experiences as a cobbler at this moment, the only surviving link in the chain of my extended family, my Kalawati Bua, is sitting next to me. She is astounded at the manner in which I am able to recreate the sequence of events. How do I remember each episode, even those which happened during my childhood? As I narrate the incidents of the time during which I was a mochi, she prods my memory further back into the past. For instance, she recalled an incident related to my father: 'One day, your father was carrying some processed leather on his head and was crossing the Ganga along the bridge at Rajghat, the police on duty on the bridge stopped your father and said, "You cannot cross the bridge with leather on your head. The bridge is on the Ganga and it will be polluted by the leather. Our Hindu religion prohibits that."'

'O brother, the leather is on my head, and I am crossing the bridge. How else can the leather be carried across? You and I are both covered with skin of which leather is made and we all cross the Ganga. How can we disown leather? We all have leather on our bodies?'

All of us are covered with skin
That is what makes us all akin.
Skin is the cover which we all wear,
So said Kabir, in your minds please bear,
Does the mark of skin anybody spare?

Even after your father recited this verse, the police persisted with the objections, but relented enough to suggest that Basheer Mian could carry his load. 'He is a Muslim. The rules and regulations of Hindus won't apply to him.' So, finally, the sheet of leather crossed the Ganga, albeit on Basheer Mian's head, though he himself had no use for it. It was strange that the Hindu policeman did not mind leather being carried across the Ganga, merely because the carrier was a Muslim.

At the age of one hundred and four and more, Kalawati Bua's father-in-law's younger brother, Kaare Baba, is still living. All his life, he worked as a tanner, maintained a herd of cattle, used those earnings to acquire land, educate his sons, two of whom have entered government service and the third is a leather contractor. I asked him as to why he did not change his occupation. He shot back promptly, 'If I change my profession, will my caste change? Tanning has altered the complexion of my skin and the colour from it has even seeped into my nails, so how do I shed the skin I now wear? What were the fates of those who did so? They had neither lands nor any business to pursue. They left the traditional occupation of their forefathers and the village too was lost to them. They joined the brick kilns and even put their women folk to work there. Their children could not study nor could they be married off. Their masters took their women and abused them. By the time they returned to the village, the government had taken over their trade and handed its execution to private contractors who were mostly Muslims. Processed leather is now being exported by Brahmins and Banias. Now the owners of Bata Company are not declared Chamars, nor are they treated as untouchables by the Brahmins. And look at me, on the other hand. I have been able to purchase ten bighas of land. Yadram did his

MSc, Omi, his BSc. Both are officers in Allahabad. Bhagwati could not clear Class Ten but because he had been to school he has become a contractor. Not just my boys, I educated my daughter, Kela, as well. Now all their children are studying in public schools and because they have money, they have married into non-tanner, Jatav families. Omi's father-in-law is an officer in Delhi. All have now risen above the tanners' work, but those who had left the work prematurely could not educate their children. Their children now come to us asking for jobs, but we are not so wealthy that we can employ everybody. In this connection, a rhyme comes to my mind:

Does anyone call Tata a Luhar, or Bata a Chamar?
The hatred of our own leather work has kept us below par.

Grinning, he said to me, 'You are the one who knows poetry. Yes, son, you have worked very hard. You reached the lowest depths of misfortune after the death of your father. The hardships of your household started very early indeed.'

Little Hands on a Large Drum

One day as I alighted from the train at Kaser railway station, a man approached me and offered me the job of playing in a band-party. The group had already taken an advance and they were two short of the dozen men they required. I had never played any musical instrument and wondered what I could pick. The band-master instructed me to pick up the big drum but I expressed my reluctance and started to walk away. Immediately, he came forward, blocked my path and persuaded with the offer of three days of wages in three hours. Besides, I would also be able to join in the feast. I informed him that I was a mochi and would not be able to perform but he brushed it aside and took me along with him.

As we approached the procession, we ducked behind the bushes in a park and changed into our bandsmen's uniforms. Even the tightest of the sets was too loose on my body but I managed to adjust my frame into it. I saw myself in the mirror. We had all got transformed into bandsmen. A big drum was slung around my neck and a stick shaped like a fist at one end was thrust into my hand. I was given instructions about how much and how long to beat the stick on the drum and to always keep an eye open for the bandmaster's signals. 'You will receive no less than four rupees, understand?' But how would I demonstrate expertise in an art with which I had never been familiar?

Responding to my self-doubts, the band-master reassured me that I could pick it up in ten minutes. Here was the largest drum in the band and the biggest novice was playing it, but in a group it did not seem to matter. Suddenly I heard a familiar voice. She lifted the veil from her face. I saw it was Noorie, the daughter of Liaquat Teli, our immediate neighbour in the village. She had recognized me and began questioning my presence in the band. Without worrying about the consequences of her conduct, Noorie spread the word about my lack of experience to the women standing near her. Their menfolk, too, came to know and, therefore, began to observe the actions of the bandsmen very closely. They began to find faults with the band. It happened as I feared. When the moment of payment of wages arrived, the master said, 'All the women were saying that you had no skill. Now take two rupees instead of four and get lost.'

I was happy enough to get two. I had had a delicious meal. Two rupees for three to four hours of work, what else did I want? If Noorie had not opened her mouth, I would have got my entire four rupees but she had done so with no malice towards me. However, I also managed to bring home to Tau a few laddoos which I had tucked inside my pocket. Tau was amused by my account but advised me on a more serious note, 'Don't take work which you do not know, or which you might spoil. People have a tendency to thrash young boys over petty reasons. This is my only fear.'

I was always prepared to struggle to safeguard my childhood and my future years. I did not mind doing anything which would fetch me if not coins, at least some food, but I never looked for free rewards. This was the primary merit which characterized my own disposition and that of my family and lineage.

The Pit Hole

It was about three weeks since the episode of confrontation with the Lodh Rajputs. We had resumed our work on a small scale. On a particular morning, I set out towards the pit hole near the pond that served as an ideal location for a public toilet for the likes of us. After sometime, I felt a movement on my side of the pit. Initially I feared that there was some animal but later I began to suspect that there was somebody hidden behind me. As I moved towards home, somebody smacked me hard on the back. As I turned around, a barrage of punches and kicks were showered upon me. A young man, his face covered with a scarf, spoke indistinctly. Immediately I recalled the entire sequence of events related to my confrontation with the Lodhs and their threat that they would kill me and drown my body in the pond.

'You think that you can stay in our territory and raise your hand against our leader, and we Rajputs won't take revenge on you? How could you think that, you son of a Chamar? We will bury you alive today itself. Now call Atiq and Karamtullah. And call any outcaste friends you may have to help you now.' They were three others who were nephews of the man who had threatened Tau. Tau had heard my screams and knew I was in need. He shouted out to Karamtullahji for help but by the time he and his associates came to rescue me, my assailants had fled into the fields.

I was in extreme pain that day and could do no work on the next day too. Tau was happy I had escaped with my life but was nevertheless anxious. Many people spoke of calling a panchayat and reporting to the police. However, most people concurred that I should be sent back to the village.

Goodbye Footpath

Tau had made up his mind to leave and had packed up his stuff even though he had a thirty-five-year-old attachment with everything in Kaser. It might have been a bondage akin to that of slavery, but he would be leaving a long past behind him. Even if he returned to Kaser, he never went to that spot again, though our situation in our own village was no better than earlier. Before long I left the village. I cannot describe in what misery Tau spent the remaining four–five years of his life. Could I have altered the complexion of his fate? It was while I was at the Jawaharlal Nehru University that I got the news of Tau's demise. I could not attend his last rites which were performed by my brother, many of them against my own conviction.

I regret that Tau had to leave his profession because of me and that when he left this world I could not be with him.

Now when he comes to me in my dreams, I find that I am talking to myself. I see him mending shoes, telling stories to me as I sit beside him, and singing in an absorbed manner:

What Fate has destined,
No one can rescind.
When Fate will call, each one will fall.
The pandit will go,
The mullah will go,
The vaid, hakim also.
Fate will take them one and all,
Who can resist Fate's call?
The king himself will pass away,
Nor will the pauper his time outstay.
So Baburam announces,
The power of Fate to kill pronounces.

I recall bits and pieces of his songs:

Karna was born to Kunthi outside marriage.
A fisherwoman similarly bore Vyasa the sage.

Who can take all and die,
Death is our final goodbye
We must leave behind houses,
Whether one or two stories tall,
Why uselessly cry at Death's inevitable call?

In this way, Tau's musicality and sensitivity became a part of me forever.

Once again, after the misadventures at Kaser, I was constrained to leave home to earn my livelihood. It is curious indeed. I left Delhi. I left Baajpur. I even left Kaser. I left my village time and again but my memories held on to everything. I inhabit each of these places in my memories. Now that I have become so happy and successful, I find that my writings are none the poorer for all that I left behind.

Around the year 1973–4, I was regularly hiring myself out as a child labourer on a daily-wage basis. Along with other unskilled workers who lived in the slums of the villages nearby, I too would go out every morning in search of employment and earn a living by working at building sites. For that, every year I paid a commission to one of these skilled masons seeking to get trained in the techniques of masonry. But given my youth, nobody in my village would accept me as a full-fledged professional in this line. Thus, I was compelled to look for jobs as a skilled mason outside my village. During those days, I had already embarked upon my hobbyhorse of cobbling together words into the shape of verses. Invariably, I would carry on my person a pencil and a piece of paper; these would remain with me even as I went about fulfilling my chores in the construction of buildings.

It so happened that a move was initiated in our village to extend the junior school which was located at the eastern edge of the settlements, from Class Eight to Class Ten by adding a few additional rooms. Dalit communities in the village had been mobilized by certain school teachers, who had been touched by the idealism of the struggle for India's independence only three of four decades earlier, with the promise, 'If the school is expanded, then your children too will get the opportunity to attend school.' More or less sixty per cent of the Dalit villagers were on the job as against, only about four of the at least four-thousand strong Yadav community. As I handed out the bricks and mortar, I hummed to myself a self-composed tune, spontaneously prompted by the occasion.

Lets's go ahead and build our school,
For gaining wisdom, education is the tool.
May our village be more renowned still,
O brothers, let's toil together with a will.

The words of my poem caught the attention of one of the teachers of the school, Shri Kanwar Bahadur Singh Yadav, who wanted to know the name of the poet. To which I responded, 'Sir, this is something that I myself authored.' Astonished, he set about establishing the veracity of my claim from those who knew me well. Without hesitation, Dayaram Chacha, Narayan, Munshi, Shishupal, Paiju, Ramchandi, Dori, and others piped up in unison to confirm it.

In those days, not many in my village, not even the teachers, knew that I was a literate person or that I had learnt to read and write through a process of self-study. No one had ever seen me approach the village school, while the sight of me carrying out all sorts of farm work was very familiar to everyone. Hence, my new guise was startling indeed to those in my village who nurtured a taste for song and music. Many might have felt that a divinely ordained miracle expressed itself through my gift for words.

Bursting with curiosity, Kanwar Bahadurji went up to headmaster Khushiram Yadav who also expressed total disbelief and asked me to recite to him a few specimens of my penmanship, a demand with which I complied at once. Following my performance, I was told to go back to my duties but the assembled teachers went into a huddle and I was summoned before them again at the lunch break. The headmaster fired the first salvo at me. 'Would you like to be a student at our school?' He had touched upon a raw nerve. I responded forthwith, 'Of course. I would like to study in your school, sir, but if I study how am I to feed myself? Also sir, to which class shall I be admitted if I am to join school?' Khushiramji took stock of my intense desire to acquire an education as well as of my problems of subsistence, and then, ultimately, pronounced his verdict, 'Don't worry, we shall test out your capabilities and admit you to either the fifth or the sixth grade. Merely let me know whether you have the will to study or not.'

Khushiramji had promised to speak to the School Inspector about me and asked me to keep in touch with him. However, I did not have the leisure to stay in contact with the teachers and I was more than aware of the limitations of the kind of help they were offering me. They might perhaps succeed in formally enrolling me as a student, but my problems did not end there. In addition to food, I would require books, a bag, and sets of the school uniform, all of which I would have to provide for myself.

I had to travel to Lahara for work every morning and return home every evening. I attached myself as a trainee in masonry with Ramcharan, under the condition that I would pay him a commission of two rupees from each day's earnings. Although I attempted to work with utmost concentration, I began to find myself unequal to my responsibilities once the intricacies of craftsmanship were required. My imagination was possessed by the urge to fashion lines of delectable poetry by bringing together words in harmonious arrangement with one another. My pocket invariably contained a piece of paper and a pencil. As soon as a verse sprang up to my lips, I promptly put it down on record. During these flights of fancy, my attention often strayed away from my chores. Sometimes in anger, Ramcharan would warn me that he would terminate my apprenticeship with him if I did not mend my ways. The reason was that he could not envisage any future for me as a poet and he found my obsession with poetry absurd and deviant.

In those days, influenced by the the Arya Samaj, I had given up smoking tobacco as well as non-vegetarian diet. As a matter of fact, I had begun to tie the *kaundhni* around my waist and to sport a *choti* on my head after having shorn it of its hair altogether. I wore a *yagyopavit*, the sacred thread around my neck, too, to signify my allegiance to the Samaj. All the cultivated residents of the village were Arya Samajis. They were naturally pleased at my deportment. I had also begun to refer to myself as an Arya.

It so happened that Mahendra Singh Yadav, who had set up a new grocery store in the village square by breaking into the Bania stronghold, also organized a havan to mark the inauguration of his business. It was graced by the daughter of Raghunath Shastri, Vedvati, who was the pupil of a renowned Sanskrit scholar in Delhi. Sanskrit was her ancestral legacy and she had a fine command over the language. On the day under discussion, I too had presented myself at the havan. Seeing me at the function and knowing that I was the grandson of Gangi Chamar, Vedvati had shooed me away from the site of the havan as though I were a dog. Till today I remember her maltreatment of me, notwithstanding that she perhaps might have forgotten the episode in question which proceeded essentially out of my admiration for her prowess as a singer. In concerts of the Samaj, she would sing praises of Swami Dayanand Saraswati to the tunes of film songs in the most melodious of voices:

The lamp of Vedic wisdom
He had lighted,
And brightened our lives benighted,
Our master dear,
O our master dear.

On the day of Holi, after the hurly-burly of the fun and games was over, a concert was arranged in the commodious premises of the noted Gandhian and freedom fighter, Yadunath Shastri. On such occasions, I would involve myself in the celebrations only for a while and then take myself off to a quiet corner with a book to read. Each day off from work was utilized by me to catch up with my reading and, moreover, I never had money enough to spend on the paraphernalia of the celebrations. So, rather than cast looks of longing at the others, I guarded my self-respect by maintaining a distance from them.

Arya Samaj and Poetry Composition

At the concert, I sat at the back of the crowd, in one corner abiding by the untouchability norms of segregation in public gatherings. Several rounds of songs had been sung. Suddenly Master Kunwar Bahadur's eyes fell on me. He got up and announced to the audience, 'Brothers, you will be happy to learn that a child of our village has developed into a poet. Till today, you all knew him as a child labourer but now I wish to show you a novel incarnation of him who will bring glory to our village; in other words, a most talented poet is coming of age amongst us.' The assembled crowd listened to him keenly and whispers could be heard. The next moment, Kunwar Bahadurji unraveled the mystery, 'That child is no other than Sauraj, the grandson of our Gangi Chamar. I shall request Sauraj to come to the dais and present to us some of his original compositions.'

It was the first time in my life that someone had felt that my self-expression might be of more than private interest to myself and had, with due respect, invited me to present my thoughts in public. It was an extremely significant moment for me and I promptly stood up. Taking out from my pocket bits and pieces of paper, I started to read aloud. The subject of my elocution was Dilman Singh Yadav, our neighbour, who, neta-like, habitually dressed himself up in spotless white clothes that appeared to look like swans' wings. He was a bully by nature who terrorized people weaker than himself and would make a pastime of interfering in the internecine squabbles among the Dalits. He would set himself up as a magistrate and was called a sarpanch by his sycophants. Yet the self-same, self-appointed justice of peace had staked away his wife's jewels, heedless of her lamentations, in wanton bouts of gambling. I made this incident the subject of my rhyme and recited it aloud:

In this assembly he sits in state,
Having disposed of his wife's jewels of late.
Alas what lessons can his children
Glean, from a father who in spirit is so mean?

In this manner, one after another, I read out extracts of my writing, of which some were exhortations against smoking and drinking, some promoted the virtues of vegetarianism, others enumerated the profits of education for children, some assailed the evil of untouchability, while some extolled the benefits of family planning. On the whole, my compositions carried the deep imprint of the Arya Samaj upon my personality.

At the end of the concert, the executive committee of the village unit of the Arya Samaj was reconstituted, and I was unanimously elected its vice-president. The other office-bearers in the executive committee were all teachers, and here was I who had not even started my schooling. Moreover, I was younger in age than everyone else. Thus it was felt later that my election to the committee had been overtaken by emotive factors, and so the results were suitably rectified by Premshankar Shastri, Ramnath Shastri, and Shankar Master who endowed me with the responsibility of serving as joint-secretary on the committee. I was simultaneously made a member of the board of the Arya Samaj journal, *Arya Mitra*, and the designation 'Arya' was prefixed to my name. It was deemed among Arya Samaj circles that those who were Aryas were morally superior to those who were non-Aryas, and from that day I too tried to inculcate that sense of my own superiority. Nevertheless, even to this moment I find it hard to subscribe to this notion of irrational self-commendation that elevates all those who have merely added Arya to their names beyond all those who have not.

That day, my performance was so successful that the audience decided to reward me by putting together a prize amount of three rupees. I contributed the entire amount to the organizing committee much to people's amazement. I had worked on the waterwheel for many of them at the rate of four annas per day. On bright nights, they would make me work harder and it was this reason that I never like moonlit nights. Therefore, one can imagine how important every anna was for me. After that day, the news of my having become a poet spread fast. I wonder what struck people as unique about me but in the eyes of most people, especially students, I had changed. Now I was the cynosure of every enlightened person's eye and had to prove my mettle. Most people dubbed it as no less than a miracle. After this, I took to rhyming with greater fervour and would be completely absorbed in thinking about topics and end-rhymes that I could compose. However, Raghunath Shastri would always find my verse to be lacking in the use of Sanskrit words and poetic form. He found my poetry aesthetically weak and its prosody faulty. He would reason that I should choose end-rhymes without resorting to Urdu and English words and disqualify anything as verse if it did not have a rhythm or could not be sung. But I continued in my own strain and would require him to answer only one question: 'Is what I am writing, poetry?' He would aver, 'Yes, one can call it poetry but it is not in line with the Sanskritic tradition of versification. Moreover, you seem to be deeply influenced by the Muslim Urdu poets. If you continue in this way, then you will neither be a Hindi nor an Urdu poet, you will end up writing mongrel verse.'

◆

On the New Path of Learning

The day after Holi, as I crossed the schoolmaster, Prempal Yadav's fields on my way to work, he called out to me, 'Sheoraj! Sheoraj!' He was the first one to pronounce my name as 'Sheoraj' instead of Sauraj. 'Yes, Massaab, but I'm getting late, Ramcharan will be angry. Is it something urgent?' So saying, I entered his field. He said, 'I was impressed by your performance at Shastriji's yesterday. In my opinion, you should study by whatever means. Masonry and petty labour will crush your poetic talent.'

I was thrilled to hear Masterji's words but in the given circumstances, I felt he was conjuring up for me an impossible dream. I expressed my inability to survive if I were to quit working. On hearing my woes, he suggested that I meet him the next day at his home. That day, I could not do any work properly. Physically I was on duty, but mentally, I was elsewhere. Ramcharan complained to my mother and threatened to demote me from a mason to an ordinary labourer. After he left, Amma revealed that Prempal Master, whom I called Massaab, had come over to discuss matters with her. He had suggested that I join school and could stay at his home and work on his fields during the vacations. However, he had made it clear that he could not offer any wages for my services. After all, he was giving me the opportunity to study. He had also declared that he desired to keep me with him forever. Amma expressed her disapproval to me. She did not want me to think about going to school. She would find it difficult to manage if the two to three rupees that came from my earnings would stop. Both of us sat and pondered over these issues till late at night. Amma ultimately ruled against my going to school.

The next day I went directly to Massaab's residence and since I was conscious of my untouchable status, I stood outside in a corner. Those days, there were only three members in his household besides himself, Anokhia, his wife, and his daughter, Malna. Subsequent to the death of Massaab's elder brother, Anokhia, his widow, had been betrothed to him. For this reason, Anokhia, usually referred to as Bau, exercised a lot of influence on her second husband. She wielded immense power within the household and practised the most stringent thrift. In this context, I often remembered a *shloka* which I had read in the course of the Sanskrit lessons imparted to me by Prempalji:

He who gives nought, nought will he receive.
In guarding his wealth, he wastes his days,
A miser such as this can earn no one's praise.

I was squatting on the floor in the customary posture of a labourer when Massaab entered and asked Bau to give me a *peedhia* to sit on. He also asked Bau to give me something to eat but I pointed out that I had not brought my own bowl along with me. Prior to that day, I had never been served anything in the utensils of a Bania or a Yadav family. No Yadav family, save a few from the Arya Samaj fold, ever allowed a Chamar-Bhangi the use of its utensils. Yes, Muslims could partake of meals from their utensils or smoke from their hookahs, even though some of them were poor and landless like us, but they were not untouchables. Shastriji's household and that of Ramjeet Yadav were exceptions among the Yadavs. They would serve food to Chamars and Bhangis in the same plates that they ate in.

Once the meal was over, Massaab said, 'See Sheoraj, by God's grace we have a lot of land and some livestock but we no longer get farm labour in the village. They all run away to the city to become masons. We need a boy we can trust. We do not want a servant, and nobody will stay with us for nothing. Stay as long as you please, work for us, earn your meals, and study in your free time. But yes, you have to tell your mother very clearly that you will not be able to earn anything for her since we will not be employing you as a domestic hand. Once you have completed your studies, you will find your own means. You will look after your mother and set up home and family for yourself. As such, all worldly attachments are illusory. Devotional bards such as you and me should be unattached to family and home. We should renounce these as soon as possible. Anyhow, you can contemplate upon these issues after you have acquired your learning.' Massaab had outlined his agenda very plainly.

I did not receive support from anyone in my basti and even the members of my family spoke to me in the language of dissension. Thus, relying only on my self-confidence, I declared my deliberate decision with the passion of childish impetuosity. 'I will study. I shall definitely give it one try. If I cannot clear Class Ten, I shall concede defeat, but I shall not give up without trying. Whether anybody supports me or not, I am willing to give every drop of my blood for each letter in the alphabet, but I shall not give up my quest for an education. Since all of you are against me, I shall stop entering the Chamar basti from now on and sleep the nights on Massaab's premises. To hell with the ties of community and of family! I shall procure an education for myself on my own strength.'

If my statement of purpose sounded ruthless, an equal heartlessness reverberated in my mother's reply. 'As far as I am concerned, from today Sauraj is dead to me and to the entire neighbourhood. Now you do whatever you will. When the time was right for you to study, you were unable to study. Now that you are fit for labour, your wish is that you surrender the tools of masonry and hold a pen. If I am alive, I shall see what kind of record-keeper or teacher or soldier you become.'

It was a tough stand for me to take in the first instance, therefore, not surprisingly, Amma's words deeply wounded me. Not that Amma wished me ill, or that I wished to injure her, but I was about to exchange my ancestral residence in favour of the Yadav abode, so her resistance was understandable. She was the victim of abject poverty and also did not see any advantage accruing out of an education for me. It seemed to her that her son was being cheated by Prempal Singh under the alibi of being sent to school. My income was an unknown goal and I was unhappy that on this journey I did not carry with me my mother's blessings. She dreamt of emancipation from the travails of beggary on the strength of my child labour. However, I could opt for only one of two roads. Either I had to settle for an education and renounce my mother, family, and community, or give up my aspiration of learning for their sake.

I was determined to embark upon my education and took up home with Massaab. On my acquainting him with the reactions of my community, he proclaimed, 'I know it all. This is the strain in which people will think now, but once you achieve success these same people will claim you as kin. I shall be forgotten, but you will be cited by them as they seek to inspire their children. You will be hailed for having brought honour to your community. To tell you the truth, Sheoraj, that is what I want too—that you become a role model. One day I shall adopt you as my disciple and we shall proceed on a quest for spiritual wisdom. My plan is that once Malna is married off, Bau has lived through her old age, you have completed your education and I have done enough research in Sanskrit literature to become an Acharya, you and I will leave the village and with the aim of converting the world to the outlook of the Arya Samaj. We shall become ascetics and through our encounter with God, prepare ourselves for the world to come. If you allow your concentration to waver, you will achieve nothing.' He was speaking like a spiritual guru. Each word that he uttered struck a chord in my heart. Till then, I had not turned an atheist. At that juncture, it was Massaab's endeavour to augment my faith in the governing power of God.

Although my own neighbourhood was not far, I had suspended my visits home. All day long, I would work with Massaab on the fields and sleep in his house at night. In Massaab's house, the norms of untouchability were not practised. Still, I was extra-cautious. I washed my utensils and kept them separately but would find them again in the basket. I was not given separate utensils, yet I took care on each occasion to select the smallest of the utensils in the basket for my own use. Perhaps the unit of the Arya Samaj in my village was different from others because its office-bearers and ideogogues were all Yadavs, and among them, mostly educators. However, I cannot say at what stage it shifted from being a noteworthy exemplar of Arya Samaj principles of Sanatan Dharam practices to becoming contaminated by pro-Mandir and anti-Muslim, anti-Dalit sentiments. Today it is an undeclared branch of Hindu Sabha.

Admission to School

Massaab had given me some of Malna's books for Class Six. I began to grasp arithmetic rather quickly, but algebra remained a roadblock. At times, the exercises so defied resolution on my part that I would be filled with apprehensions about the tough mission that I had taken upon myself. Was the path of learning the suitable one for me or should I have continued my journey on the track of child labour? If I failed in my attempt at acquiring an education, what a disgrace it would be for me! As I repeatedly voiced my self-doubts to Massaab, he would say, 'What you already know is enough to get you through to school. Beyond that, you are capable of covering in one month what is prescribed in the curriculum for one year.' He was talking in such a vein at a juncture in my life when I was just about picking up the English alphabet! As it happened, English as a language was taught only after Class Five in the government-run schools of Uttar Pradesh. There were few teachers available to teach English and these would teach through the medium of Hindi. Once a student had cleared Class Eight, the student could leave the study of English.

I had been able to procure for myself an English textbook for Class Six. My days were filled with toil and at night I would devote limited attention to each of my subjects. I was simultaneously becoming a prey to intellectual hunger and to bodily exhaustion. That year the work of reaping on Massaab's fields had commenced the very next day after my arrival at his house. From the threshing of the newly cut crops to their cleaning, I put in more effort than what two servants might have managed in my stead. Till two o'clock each morning, Massaab and I would be engaged in a competitive venture at cleaning bales upon bales of crops. Even today, Massaab reminiscences about those days and nights of the hard work I put in.

Massaab was virtually a Hindu ascetic in the true sense of the term. Yet, all his corporal energy was expended in toiling on the fields. Agriculture predominated among all his interests. He and I got along famously with each other, especially on account of the religious functions organized by the Bania families at their homes. At functions of this kind, Massaab was usually quite reticent, while I inclined towards loquaciousness. On a certain occasion, the pandit in charge of the recital of *Ramcharitmanas* took ill and, therefore, the recitation was suspended for an hour or so. People at once said that I should substitute for the pandit. 'Let Sauraj read. He reads the Ramayana very beautifully.'

As I unleashed a full-throated recital of a section of the *Ramcharitmanas* with all the harmony, passion, and devotion at my command, the audience could not but help being impressed by my feat. As for myself, I got a sense of my success through the altered attitude towards me of Lachman Bania's wife who would habitually shun children from the untouchable castes and treat them with contempt. Since that day she started to welcome me into her husband's shop, did her best to make me sit comfortably on the charpoy and even favoured me with loans on request. She praised me highly to her son, Subhash, with the result that he became my friend and remains so till today.

As the months of my stay with Massaab passed by, I wondered when he would admit me to school, and would time and again ask him. A year elapsed, and March had slid into June. In the month of July, he suddenly declared, 'You have to come to my school with me tomorrow. I shall introduce you to the principal. He is a decent person and, like Gandhiji, fond of untouchables.'

During those days, I did not possess a change of dress. Hence, donning a loin-cloth for the night, I washed my kameez and pyjama. My shorts and vest would stay concealed under my clothes; they would serve their purpose without a wash. My mind was full of thoughts about gaining admission. I would join the ranks of the students and if somehow I acquired an education, I would metamorphose from a child labourer to a child poet. I would demonstrate to Amma, Tau, and my neighbours who felt that I was needlessly submitting myself to a life of slavery, how indeed my efforts had yielded the desired results.

I was bursting with curiosity. That night, I lay awake for such a long time that had Massaab not awakened me, I would have got up late next morning. While bathing I used a piece of brick to remove the dirt off my hands and feet and took mustard oil from Bau to pour it on my head till the slick oil trickled down my ears. I was ready at last, and thought to myself that I was looking as presentable as any school boy. S.P. School in Chirori, Bulandshar, was about twenty-five to thirty kilometres from my village. Massaab and I went together by cycle but on reaching Narora, he said to me, 'If we travel together, I shall be late for my class. You make your way to school via Ramghat. I shall meet you there; the school is on a hillock. It is painted red and will catch your eye from afar.'

Since I was unacquainted with the area, I had to frequently ask for directions from people. After a descent from Bamba, I espied the handsome structure of the school on a sandy hillock, hidden behind a thick clump of trees next to a garden. Despite the simplicity of its profile, the school looked charming under the dense green curtain which enveloped it. As a beacon of knowledge, it had no less significance for me than any architectural marvel in the world.

Fatigue, perspiration, and dirt combined to tarnish my appearance. The clothes I wore were frayed and stained with the marks of my journey. I could glimpse school children running in and out of the gate. The moment I compared their uniforms with my own attire and contrasted my unbecoming tattered slippers with their shining shoes, an invisible bar of an inferiority complex blocked my progress towards them. I could see that all these children were remote from me and especially that not one was like me in the crowd. Countless impediments arose in my mind.

As a result, I could not muster up the confidence to step into the school. I would creep up to the gate and retreat; after a while would once more peep in and return. My gaze searched around for Massaab, but he was not to be found. Disappointed, I sat underneath the tree outside the gate of the school. I wanted to retrace my steps back home, but felt that it would not be proper to do so without informing Massaab of my decision. What relationship with him would I maintain in any case, if I decided to give up formal schooling? It was my aspiration for school instruction that had brought me in association with Massaab. For that I had dissociated myself from my family and community. What reception would I get if I were to renege upon my resolve save heavy chores and light returns?

I continued to sit under the tree till evening and in keeping with my old habit, I penned down a poem in my notebook. The poem, which I have revised several times since that day, included the following lines:

At the open door of the temple of learning
Like a priest I sit all yearning.
Why then the knowledge I venerate
Keeps me far away from its gate?

Towards dusk, Massaab appeared in person and demanded to know. 'Why did you not enter the school?' He fired query upon query at me, but I was silent. Whether he understood my plight or not, he instructed me to spruce up as he intended to escort me to the principal.

I tried to muster up courage for the encounter. Dressed in Western garb and sporting long hair, Principal Sa'ab resembled a hero from Hindi films. His name, as displayed on the nameplate outside his office, was Manoharlal Bhardwaj. Massaab had coached me to touch the gentleman's feet as soon as we entered his chamber. After acknowledging my obeisance, he pointed to the Hindi newspaper which lay on his table and asked me to read out the headline. I promptly read out the sentence to him, 'The government will remove poverty, Indira Gandhi declares.' I read as much, and was filled with an apprehension that I might be ordered to read from an English newspaper as well. Instead, Principal Sa'ab said, 'He can only be granted admission to our school on the basis of having successfully cleared Class Six. Therefore, it will be appropriate for him to come to us after clearing the Sixth Class or get a legal affidavit which certifies to his having studied the Class-Six curriculum.'

I received yet another jolt. How was I to clear the sixth grade? It seemed to me that I was not fated to be in school and would never be part of this institution all my life. Thinking thus, I stepped out of the office. Fortunately, I remembered that about a couple of years back I had made an unsuccessful attempt to clear the exam for Class Six from the Dehgawan as a private student. However, due to unfavourable circumstances I could not study even for a single day. On informing Massaab about it, he exclaimed, 'Then your admission will get done! Get hold of a copy of the result and the Transfer Certificate (T.C.) I know a few people there they will definitely help you.'

After the holidays, I walked fifteen kilometres to reach Dehgawan only to learn that the principal was on leave and the T.C. could not be procured without him. I went over to my Mausi's home to spend the night at Gangurra instead of returning home. Two days later when the college reopened, I got in touch with Prem Shankar Shastri whom Massaab had mentioned and I handed him his letter. Not only did he belong to my village, he was also a member of the Ayra Samaj Committee that had been constituted on Holi. He went into the principal's office and handed over Massaab's letter to him. Then he looked for my results in the two-year-old records and found it. The principal remarked pessimistically, 'You did clear the exam but you did not attend school regularly. I wonder if you will be able to study any further or not. In any case, you can take the TC if that is what you want.'

I took my TC and went back to my Mausi's home. Maaldei and Motini Mausis were my mother's younger sisters and both their husbands did the work of carrying and skinning dead cattle. Not just them but the entire Chamar community of the basti did this work. My Mausi had been very keen to educate her children but her eldest son, Charan Singh, had dropped out after studying a class or two. On probing her about it, she merely answered, 'What could I do, Bhaiyya? As it is teachers of other castes don't want to teach the children of Chamars and Bhangis and if there are a few good teachers who do, then these children don't want to study. They are fated to carry dead cattle. It isn't as if their father has a lot of property that they can sell off and live happily. Nobody would even want to marry them.' The most dominant desire on the part of parents was to get their children married as soon as possible. This was considered as their ultimate duty. Mausaji returned late at night and upon knowing the purpose of my visit, he also expressed great joy at the prospect of my joining school.

The next day I left for my village and from there with Massaab, we set out for school. I gained admission to Class Eight, section B. He then sent me to the principal to seek his blessings. There were a few other teachers present with him. After touching the feet of the principal, I went about touching the feet of all the other teachers. The principal said, 'Remember this day, son! Think that your life has taken a new turn. In fact, this is the day of your new birth. This is the supreme blessing that you can seek!' On the way out of the office, I saw a few more teachers and I kept bending low to touch their feet. In the sheer joy and enthusiasm of the moment, I even touched the feet of the peon! The English teacher tittered as if to say that I did not even know whose feet ought to be touched and who to pass over.

Massaab bolstered my confidence whenever I grew anxious. I was both older and taller than my classmates and would, therefore, be treated as if I was an overgrown child with undeveloped intelligence. However, Massaab would reassure me that things would turn around for me. Those who mocked me would eventually befriend me, 'Look, Sheoraj! Appearances hardly matter. In our country's Gurukul tradition, disciples would beg for alms in order to study. They believed in simple living and high thinking. In a few days, you will begin to adjust with the other children.' I had read the autobiographies of many great men and realized that those who had the will to achieve something, could manage it even in a very short time. Laggards and idlers could spend a lifetime and still not accomplish much.

The twenty-five to thirty kilometres of journey back and forth from school proved to be quite arduous. Of course, when the strip of Ganges would dry up, then the road via Asadpur would be somewhat shorter. If there were a couple of days of holidays, then I would have to miss school for the whole week. Massaab would assign me a long list of farming tasks to do well in advance and almost always leave me behind and go off to school. He would inform me about the portions of the syllabus covered in class and even get my attendance marked. This meant that even though I had gained admission to school, I was still not getting the opportunity to attend it regularly. For my labour I merely got meals. For my clothes and books, I needed to do extra work and when Amma objected to it, Bau explained to her that I was learning while I earned. Nobody could be taught for free. Watching me perform various tasks day and night on Massaab's fields and home, the boys from my community and other relatives would taunt me, 'Look! How well Sauraj is studying! Is disposing dung studying or a form of slavery?'

Teachers' Day

It had been only a few days since I started to attend school and preparations for Teachers' Day celebrations were in progress. Although my admission to the school had been formalized as early as July, I had been able to attend classes merely for a couple of days. This was to be, therefore, the first occasion on which I would witness a school function. Everyone was assembled in the huge building on the west side. Those students who were to take part in the proceedings had been engaged in rehearsals for several days, but Massaab seemed overconfident about me being able to perform without any prior preparation. Thus, instead of allowing me time for rehearsals, he set me to work on the fields, saying, 'You can recite your self-composed poems at any given time.' However, that day my civics teacher, Dheeraj Singh Tomar, handed me the text of a poem which he had composed for the event. I was not at all sure that I would be able to read out the text assigned to me. Tomar Sahab rose to conduct the function and after several performances by other students, he announced my name. I got up from my seat and looked at the crowd of my fellow students in front of me, in their neat and tidy school uniforms, while I was clad in a simple shirt and pyjama combination that was not even quite clean. I did not yet possess the school uniform, nor had been able to cast myself in the mould of the other students of the school. The question of my integration into their fold did not arise and I became convinced that the children facing me were endowed with an intellectual prowess superior to mine and that I could never be like them. A sense of my inferiority besieged me from within. Although I had managed to stand up, my legs were trembling and my tongue refused to utter a word. My right hand, which held the piece of paper, shook uncontrollably; my speech was indistinct and driven by fear. Immediately behind me was the seat of Massaab who sought to encourage me by nudging me on my legs with his toe, but to no avail. I lost my focus and ultimately could not read out the poem despite the fact that I had memorized it well. The poem itself was but ten–fifteen-lines long, of which I still remember a few:

Our perception of the world
Is moulded by our teachers' labours.
The evergreen world that they have bequeathed to us
Proudly proclaims our teachers' endeavours

I was able to say just these lines, and was so scared afterwards that had I not been made to sit down, I might have fallen on the ground. A nameless fear expressed itself through all my features. It was the most unexpected behaviour from me as far as Massaab was concerned. Overcome with a sense of shame, I left the venue. I could not meet Massaab's eyes.

The next day I went back to school, shame-faced still, as though guilty of a serious offence. On that day, I formed a resolution in my mind that any opportunity I was given to speak in public in the future would see me speak without fear. Massaab's high estimation of me had been belied and he wanted to know the cause of my nervousness. I attempted to proffer an explanation but he exhorted me not to be intimidated. During those days, my mind was the site of a tempest whose intensity I can scarcely describe. I was so keen to study that had there been some arrangement for my meals, then I would have devoted all my time to studies. Other boys of my age—and there was not a single girl—were attending school regularly. I had read all their Hindi texts in advance but I lacked practice in writing, since I could hardly afford to buy stationery.

A letter had arrived from Dibai Digambar College about a debate competition. The topic was 'Democratic System Is Beneficial for the Country'. I had raised my hand in favour of the motion. The rival team did not stand a chance and conceded defeat. The other speaker in my team was also not a match. I was chosen by the school as a solo-speaker team and taken to the college. Since my sole focus was on my speech, I did not pay much attention to the rules of the debate and, therefore, when the results were declared, all the three—the first, second, and third—prizes were won by girls, with me getting just the consolation prize.

I was disappointed by this defeat but the teachers who had accompanied me said, 'There is a measure of victory in your defeat.' On returning to school, my classmates taunted me, 'He lost the debate to girls!' I could clearly see my defeat, so what victory did my teachers mean? They said that I had lost because I exceeded the stipulated time of seven minutes and that I had used the incorrect plural for the Hindi word 'neta'. However, they maintained that I had shown great potential and in the future I could hope to be a good orator. In this promise, they saw my triumph.

The First Prize

I managed to clear my eighth grade and graduated to Class Nine. That year the school was organizing a special cultural programme, the announcement for which had been made by the principal two weeks in advance. Among the large audience, the Chairman of the school, Shri Asharfilal Yadav, was also sitting in the row of the special invitees. Tomar Sahab conducted the programme and when the enlisted students had had their chance, he turned towards me and announced, 'If there is any other child who wishes to present something, then he may raise his hand and we will be happy to have him on stage.'

Indirectly, this exhortation was meant for me. From the day of the announcement, I had begun to prepare my rhyme but I was still reeling under the sting of that first day's failure. Despite having prepared on my own, I had not given my name. However, having seen the performance of the other students and being familiarized with the school environment for more than a year now, many of my fears had been assuaged. I took courage and raised my hand. All eyes turned towards my raised hand. 'Come, Sheoraj, come.' Tomar Sahab beckoned. I could see Massaab look very hopefully at me, as if to say, 'You have to come good today.' I began, 'Respected Principal Sa'ab, honourable teachers, esteemed guests, and my dear friends! I am going to recite a few of my self-composed poems. Please forgive me if I commit any mistake.' 'Let's hear it.' Teachers and guests encouraged me to recite. Most of my compositions were issue-based, like serving the nation, against smoking, becoming a member of the Arya Samaj, practising asceticism, and family planning. These topical poems were written out in different strips of paper. I went on reciting and my confidence was bolstered by the encouraging words spoken by the audience. That day I realized that there was no need for me to have been so scared.

As I walked back to my seat after the performance, Principal Sa'ab gestured to Tomar Sahab to send me to him. He handed me a red two-rupee note and even though I protested Massaab instructed me to accept it. As soon as I took the money, Tomar Sahab placed another rupee on top of it. The manager also placed a five-rupee note on it and soon there was no stopping the other guests. The teachers also joined in and in a trice I was holding a prize amount of thirty to forty rupees. This was the recompense for the early failure. I was elated that day. Earlier I had doubted if I would ever become a student and here I was—a student who had won a prize!

I decided to put the prize amount to good use by buying some ration so that I could manage to continue with my studies. I also bought a pen and a few notebooks. Right from Class Eight onwards, I had begun to live in Dhurra as it was closer to school. On holidays, however, I would have to go to the village to work free for Massaab and to thus pay up with interest in advance, the price for the help he had rendered me. As I revisit my memories of those times, I feel I can now sit and hum this song which contains the essence of my experiences:

My little baby steps, wherever they turned,
Found a way.
In sunshine or shade, village or town,
I kept going, as hunger held sway.
The sense of sorrow made me restless—
For a sense of freedom, my mind continued to press.
The world unfolded like the pages of a book—
And I read of it, whatever I could.
A dark legacy was my share
But the lamp within kept up its flare.
I walked ahead while thousands lagged behind,
My life changed, despite my kind.

Torn Shirt and a Coat from the Footpath

I began to pay attention to the neatness of my clothes now that I had gained encouragement from teachers and the attention of my schoolmates by participating in the cultural programmes of school. Dr Nathulal had given me a pair of old, grey-coloured pants which had become tight for him. They required no ironing and would maintain the crease even after they had been washed. Those days I also possessed a black coat that I had bought at an auction. These two pieces of clothing which I wore all through winter suited me so well that I managed to look somewhat better-off than the other students from the village. The credit for this would usually go to Massaab. I had also bought a shirt made of good material from Ulfat who sold it to me after deducting from it the cost of stitching.

After having worked for several days for Massaab, he decided to buy clothes from Ramghat for me for the first and the last time. At the tailor's shop he asked me to get my coat off for the measurements. At that moment, the principal and three or four other teachers were also present. I had staunchly refused to do so. Even when Massaab insisted I did not listen to him. Later, when we had moved ahead, Massaab appeared to be in a huff while I followed behind meekly. On reaching midway, I looked around to see if anyone was watching and then told him, 'Massaab, look I'm taking my coat off.' He stopped reluctantly and turned around to see. The back portion of my shirt had completely worn away due to the corrosive effect of the perspiration of my labours. He was stunned to see a naked back.

In my tenth standard I had sought a loan from Lala Hotilal at the rate of three rupees per month for the amount of three hundred rupees. Anokhia Bau had taken guarantee for me. Every year I would take a loan and work to pay off the interest on the principal amount. Munshiji would keep piling up the interest but when there was no money to be got from anywhere in the village, one would definitely find it with him. However, he would give out the loan only on the assurance of one of his established debtors. Among the Jatavs, Todi Tau, Narayan, Dayaram, Chhotelal, and Munshi were his regular debtors. From time to time, they acted as guarantors for me in order to facilitate loans. In accordance with the spiralling interest rates, I would invariably end up paying six hundred for the three-hundred rupees I had borrowed. As a student, this was hardly a small amount. Other than me, it was Ram Singh's father who took loans to educate his son. Ram Singh was the first graduate of our basti and perhaps the first Dalit record-keeper. In his case, his father, Ramchandi, would pay the loans and in my case, I had to do it myself. In order to maintain my reputation, I would ensure that I paid my debts on time. It was this standing that enabled me to study. I continued to take debts, although the amount of money earned through the extra masonry work I did was not in proportion to the extent of my financial debt.

Caught in the Flood

It had been barely been ten to fifteen days since I had taken admission to Class Eight. I had gone to meet Amma at Pali and when I returned to school I found that not a single student had turned up. Massaab, Tomar Sahab, and other teachers expressed surprised and asked, 'Sheoraj! How did you reach here? The entire place is water-logged. The river is flooded and in such a heavy downpour, no student lands up. It is considered to be an unannounced holiday.'

I explained, 'I saw the river in high tide and realized that there was no other way to reach school without swimming across it. I tied up my clothes and books and placed them on my head, after which I swam across the river.' Both Massaab and Tomar Sahab were amused at my perseverance and merely smiled at me. They informed me that the school had been declared closed due to heavy rains.

During that period, one day Bhikari had come to school. He had enquired about Massaab from the students. He met with him and said, 'Master Sahab, Sauraj's mother does not want him to study. You can get as much unpaid work done from him as you want but please let him go. Let him do some work, now that he is capable of earning some money. Let him earn for his mother's sake. He is past the age of learning, Sahab. I beg of you with folded hands.' He tried his best to cancel my admission.

Massaab conveyed to me Bhikari's intentions and I experienced a mix of surprise and regret. I did not believe it at first. The mere thought of the death of my dream of studying was enough to shatter me to the core. Despite having no desire to go to Bhikari's house, I went to meet Amma and told her about Bhikari's visit. She grew angry, as a consequence of which that night she and Bhikari argued over the issue of my studies. Although initially Amma had opposed me, she became resigned when she saw my self-determination. In Bhikari's mind it was clear, 'I am going to take back whatever I have spent on you and your mother.' He wanted me to work with him in the mango orchards or pick dead cattle but I declared, 'I won't give up studies. Apart from that I am willing to do anything.' Hearing this decision Bhikari grew enraged and declared that I could take Amma along with me if I was so keen on continuing with my studies. Amma thought it best to advise me to make my arrangements elsewhere. Hiding it from Bhikari, she had placed some flour and dried chillies in my bag.

My situation was peculiar. Many savarna and Jat students came from Dhurra-Premnagar to study in the school. Among the Chamars there was only Hardayal, who had been failing in Class Nine for two years. The other one was Ramavatar Jatav. His family had converted to Sikhism and since he was the lone Sikh in the school, both his presence and absence was conspicuous because of his turban. They came close to me the moment they got to know that even I belonged to their caste. Most students were under the impression that I was close to Massaab and, therefore, behaved well with me. Initially, everyone mistook me for a Yadav. Some even thought that I was Massaab's younger brother or nephew, since we travelled together. In order to prevent the students from noticing, he would get me to sit on his cycle only after we had moved away some distance from the school. I knew how to ride a cycle but I was unable to carry Massaab on the pillion, as he had built a strong body like a wrestlter with regular exercise. He would carry me on the pillion and did not leave me behind because he feared that if I went off to my mother's or stayed back at Premnagar, he would have to find a new worker for his fields.

The Sack of Wheat

I had got a set of clothes stitched for myself before school reopened that year in July. I had also deposited forty to fifty kilos of wheat in a sack with Anokhia Bau, saying that I would be taking about ten kilos from it every week with me for my use when I went to school. I could not leave it at my ancestral home, as I was not staying there and in any case it would have been very difficult for me to keep fetching the grain from there while I was studying. I also knew that Rambharose would not go out and work as long as he knew that there was some grain lying at home. However, the sack of wheat that I had placed in Bau's custody has not been returned to me till date. I had asked her about it a couple of times but she had dilly-dallied and said, 'You can come for it later or some other time....' In short, she had filched it, whereas their granaries were filled with grain and the spare amount of wheat was also sold every year.

I felt upset by her undependable behaviour but there was little I could do. I could not insist that she return the goods I had entrusted in her care. Thus, I had to make all sorts of compromises while I was studying, although I found it difficult to put together even a single meal for myself. It would have been better to have left the sack of wheat at my home. At least my poverty-ridden mother could have had something to eat for a few days or I could have left it at someone's place, in order to fetch it easily when I needed it.

Exposing Makhkhan

The members of Arya Samaj would cite non-vegetarianism and alcohol consumption as reasons for poverty and untouchability. Therefore, I declared that I would give up meat-eating though non-vegetarian food was my favourite. After this announcement, I became not only a favourite with Dayaram Bhagat but also the recipient of the exorcist Makhkhan's wrath. I recall an incident of the time when Shankar Master of the village had forbidden Chamars, Telis, Bhangis, and Fakirs from fishing in the ponds and for which reason they would do it stealthily at night. Everyone was petrified of Shankar who would strike terror if seen with his mighty staff. He was an Arya Samaj preacher and taught in the primary school. He shaved his head, wore saffron clothes, exercised regularly, and was also a wrestler. One day in Todi Tau's courtyard, I started a discussion by saying, 'We should give up eating meat and fish' but this statement was turned around by Makhkhan and company to mean something different altogether. He began inciting people by saying, 'Sauraj is saying that he will not allow us to catch fish anymore now that the damned fellow has become a Yadav.' Saying this, he brought his staff out, pulled his dhoti up, and rushed towards me with eyes reddened with anger. He knew he would not be able to fight me alone and had, therefore, raised this issue of vegetarianism so that he could get people to rally around it. Chote, Dataram, and some others also began to say, 'Sauraj should be taught a lesson for trying to be a pandit. Having learnt a letter or two, he seems to have lost his mind.' They came and surrounded me but it was Gangi Babba who rose to my rescue.

The issue of vegetarianism was not the only reason for Makhkhan's ire. He was a renowned exorcist and I was on a mission to expose those who propagated belief in spirits and ghosts. As soon as he would dig his elbows into the ground to suggest the descent of Sayyed's spirit on him, I too would do the same to call his bluff. One day Khacheri Tau placed his hand on Makhkhan Chacha's head and began invoking the spirits, 'Hanumanji is descending upon

Makhkhan! Go quickly and fetch gur and grams from the village!' Whoever saw me would set me to do some unpaid work—here Sauraj, do this, do that! In this way, a lot of work would be done by me for free. Now that Hanumanji was descending, I was handed some money to fetch some sweets and gram. I did not wish to go but it was not considered polite to refuse an elder. I did not wish to pay for the offering either, as I was not doing this out of my own free will. I told my friends, Phool Singh and Ram Singh, as we went to fetch the offering, 'Look, all this is such a fraud. How can Hanuman descend into anyone's body?' They asked, 'How can one tell?' I thought of a trick. I suggested, 'Look, we can taste a bit of the offering beforehand and if Hanumanji has truly descended upon Makhkhan, He will know that the prasad is *jootha* and if he is fooling us then he will eat it without knowing it.' Both my friends feared that if Hanumanji discovered this sacrilege, they would be visited by all sorts of afflictions. They said, 'Bhaiyya, you should be the one to taste it. We are too scared. We will be throwing up blood if we make the offering jootha.' Having said this, they drew back. I tasted a bit of the gur and gram, thus rendering the offering jootha and then gave it to the exorcists. Hanumanji's descent was acted out and no one complained about the prasad being jootha. Phool Singh and Ram Singh kept staring at my face.

I had started living in Massaab's home. Gradually, I became a member of their house. I found the vegetables cooked there very bland and watery. Chamars and Telis ate spicy food and initially I thought I would keep some chillies with me, which I could add on separately but then I decided against it and thought that I should get used to it. In this manner, I trained myself by curtailing these small habits and picking up new things, as has been my nature. Massaab and Anokhia Bau were complete vegetarians. Once she was prescribed a mix of milk and brown eggs when she fell ill and began to have fits following the shock of the premature death of her daughter Malna. Now who would procure the eggs? Consuming eggs was also considered a form of violence. How could good, non-violent people eat eggs? I do not recall clearly whether Bau agreed on her own or that Prempal Singh fed her two beaten eggs added to warm milk, in the morning and at night, without her knowledge. Hens were reared only in a couple of Fakir homes and so I was assigned the task of fetching them in the morning and evening from Revada, which was at a distance of two kilometres from the village. Bau was now like another mother to me though, according to the relations in the village, I would be her father-in-law. However, in her conduct towards me, she sometimes treated me as Massaab's younger brother and sometimes as her son.

Since my mother was now convinced that I would be staying with Massaab, she once again decided to return to her younger children in Pali. Amma kept travelling between Nadrauli and Pali. Her life was a series of transitions. In any case, what options did the village provide to her for her sustenance? She would collect neem seeds or plaster a Yadav's courtyard. She would pick the leftover grain or find a ser or two of sweet potatoes from someone's fields.

From the point of view of serving my mother, my decision to stay with Massaab was not a good one. Instead of supporting her with my earnings, I had put my self-interest first by deciding to study and stay with Massaab. Even educated people like Shishupal Yadav did not consider my decision to be a correct one. He had a bet with Prempal Singh, 'I am willing to lose six hundred rupees. You will see that within a year or two he will give up studies and return to the village as wage labourer. Has it ever happened that you pick an unpaid child labourer, give him an education and he goes on to become a teacher, a registrar, or a soldier! Getting an education is not so easy and Sheoraj can work no miracle.' However, Balbir Master had a different take, 'The day he passes Class Ten will determine whether his decision to join school was right or wrong.' I was not sure I would be able to clear the high-school exams. I had decided to study so that even if I did not pass the Class-Ten exam, I would at least reach that level. Whatever knowledge I could gather would eventually help me to live a better life and only then would I be capable of helping anyone else.

According to the relations of the village, I was my master's uncle but he was my guru and he was taking me to the path of my freedom. There was no doubt that he did not want me to be very educated but he certainly wanted me to learn enough so as to be of use to him. Bau would go to the extent of saying that she would get a poor Yadav girl to marry me, 'Sauraj is hardly a Chamar anymore. He is my child and I will arrange his marriage.'

Decades passed by and life went on but I have not forgotten the past. The day I stepped into school with my endless hopes was a momentous day for me. I do not know whether my education benefitted or harmed my society, my country, or any person but I do know that my efforts did not remain barren. I lost my mother early in life but I also gained quite a bit. Rather I should say that I had everything to gain, since I had nothing to lose. An untouchable proletariat like me—what did I possess that I was at risk to lose? I sold physical labour and satisfied my hunger. By the time I gained admission to school, I had experienced many forms of exploitation of my labour.

◆

Bhai Saab
An Inspiring Role Model

A series of correspondence began between me and Dr Nathulal after a long interval. I wanted to pursue my studies but circumstances were against me. Bhai Saab could not help me in financial terms but would always say, 'Whatever the circumstances, you must study. If you cannot enroll in a school, then continue with self-study.' He was so pleased with my decision to take admission in a school that he came all the way from Delhi to Nadrauli to congratulate me on my passing the ninth-standard exam. His words 'Well done, Sheoraj!' still echo in my ears.

I have always believed that if one keeps the company of people more educated than oneself, one gets to learn something new from them and it was with this in mind that I would visit Bhai Saab every now and then. To converse with him and to see him work with dedication was an amazing experience. It was indeed remarkable that he was pursuing a career in medicine despite the fact that he was from a family without any resources. The journey of his life was an inspiring example to follow.

The World of Letters

This refers to the year 1976–7, when I was a student of Class Nine. I stayed with Bhai Saab for a few nights at his hostel in Maulana Azad Medical College. There I met Comrade Bhagwan, with whom Bhai Sahab had left me for a day. He was a close friend who subscribed to a progressive ideology. I found not just medical books in English in his room but also some literature in Hindi. It was there that for the first time I laid my hands on Gopal Thakur's book on Bhagat Singh's monograph entitled 'Why I Am an Atheist.' I was astounded to read about an atheist and that too a great patriot, who gave up his life for the country! How could one negate the existence of God and in its stead be devoted to one's country? I was completely fascinated and did not step outside the hostel room until I had finished reading it from the first word to the last. The book stirred up a storm in my being and from that day I began to take interest in this kind of literature which was so completely different from the traditional canon. I wanted to read more and more of it. It was only in Delhi that I got to read the Soviet Russian edition of *Yuvak, Soviet Darpan* and the Communist Party of India's student wing magazines *Student Action*, *Yuvavedi*, *Janyug*, and *Communist* in Delhi. I had noted down the addresses of their offices and landed up there. I began to subscribe to them and some magazines had also started arriving by mail at my village address free of cost. I bought a few books one by one. I made a list of the rest of the books that I would be able to find in libraries and expressed my desire to Bhai Saab who I expected would procure them for me. I got to read Kaifi Azmi's *Awara Sajde* as well the collection of his revolutionary poems *Raasta Idhar Hai* through a communist friend of Bhai Saab. When I got back to school in the village, my mind was occupied more with the books outside my course instead of those that were prescribed. I had begun writing down questions related to these books in the form of letters and mailed them to Delhi. I waited for a couple of months for Bhai Saab's reply in which I kept hoping that he would suggest specific books that I could read or buy. On receiving no reply, I grew worried. I finally received a letter from him a few months before my exams. On one side it was written in English and on the other in Hindi:

Dear brother, Sheoraj Singh. I keep receiving your letters and since I stay very busy because of my studies, I am therefore unable to help you. My advice to you is that you should not read anything other than the books in your course. In fact, you should promise me that until you pass your high school exam, you will peruse only the books in your course. Once you are through with that, you can read all the books that you wish to. This is my advice to you. At the moment it is very important that you somehow manage to pass your high school exam. In case you fail, it will be impossible for you to study in a school again. This is both your first and last chance, so don't fritter it away. I hope that you will work hard and study with dedication. More later.

Your brother,
Nathulal

My mind lingered in the precincts of the school while my body grew exhausted by the work in the fields. 'You'll pass, don't worry,' Massaab would always console me, 'You are quite bright, even average students manage to pass.' In his opinion, it was sufficient for me to pass the high-school level and at the most he was willing to support me till the intermediate level but not beyond that. He had planned to set up a flour mill for me and Bau wanted me to marry a poor Yadav girl so that at least she would be able to eat the rotis made by her and my caste would be 'upgraded' from that of a Chamar to a Yadav.

There were many boys of my community, who, inspite of attending schools regularly, reaching till the high-school level continued to be unemployed, even after availing reservation. My friend Ramphool had learned to sing and dance after passing high school. He had taken to playing the roles of female protagonists like Sita in a *Ram Leela* or that of Laila and Heer in plays like *Laila–Majnu* or *Heer–Ranjha*. I would often pose this question to myself: What will I do if I am unable to pass my exams?

There was a deep contradiction between the influence on me of the Vedic thought of the Arya Samajist ideology and the rationalist, socialist ideas that I encountered in my reading of communist literature. My mind would be in a state of constant conflict. My values as well as temperament were those of a believer and I kept the company of people who had a religious bent of mind. What revolutionary change would come about by my just passing the high-school exam? Massaab would say, 'Once we have studied Vedic literature, we'll set out to propagate Arya Samajist ideas by touring the entire country. Like great religious leaders, we'll give up the narrow domestic sphere and dedicate ourselves to God. In this way, we'll be able to achieve enlightenment and improve our chances in the next birth. You shall be my disciple and I your guru.'

I too believed that life should not be wasted away and till I reached the eighth standard, I went along with Massaab's views. Gradually, however, I found that despite being a great devotee of God, who said his prayers every evening, exercised regularly, preached *saatvik* values (of honesty and sincerity) and a vegetarian, he nevertheless extracted back-breaking labour from me. And for my pains I got just food! Even if he had given a tenth of the value for my labour, I could have got by.

Eventually, my exploitation began to be disagreeable to me. Why was it not a sin to exploit labour? How could oppression coexist with devotion to God? Why could I not find a solution to my problem in Dayanand Saraswati's *Satyartha Prakash*? I had harvested the wheat crop for Massaab in the first year and I got just meals for it. I began to think that if I planned to study, I would require rations for at least a month or two for my meals. Initially I believed that since I had been working for Massaab all through my stay, he would definitely make some arrangements for me. However, a year's experience had made it clear that he could only be a facilitator of my education but he had no intentions of rewarding me for my physical labours. He would propound, 'In our country's Vedic system of education, a disciple is supposed to beg for alms to pursue his studies.' I had no answer to this kind of reasoning on Massaab's part. Could a Chamar beg for alms? Would a non-Brahmin get alms? Therefore, I had to enlist as an apprentice mason with Jasram Yadav and worked in the scorching afternoons of May–June so that I could earn money.

I usually did not have sufficient provisions for my meals. If I informed Massaab about it, his response would be, 'A firm determination is all that a man needs. One must have courage and dedication! You are a promising boy, you will surmount all difficulties.' With these words he would divert my attention, but when has hunger ever been satisfied by words? Even if he had considered me as his domestic servant and paid wages accordingly, I would not have starved and managed with a bare minimum. His contribution in my own life was of a contradictory nature. He had set me in the direction of acquiring an education and that was a debt which I could not repay. All the same, it cannot be forgotten that he thoroughly exploited my physical labour. In the absence of basic provisions, I had to find alternative solutions and these interfered with my studies. These difficulties proved to be my trial by fire.

I returned to my village from Delhi with a storm of ideas raging in my head. The reading of Bhagat Singh's autobiography had thrown my thoughts into a tumult. Despite Bhai Saab's advice, I had collected material related to other patriots and martyrs. I was deeply drawn to the reading and writing of poetry. I spent the money I had saved for shoes and clothes to buy anthologies of poetry by Progressive writers. The effect on me of these visits to Delhi and of the people I had met was that I had begun to see and understand that it was education alone that lent purpose to life. This strengthened my resolve to pursue studies. In the ninth grade, when I began to lose hope about being able to make arrangements for my upkeep, I even thought of studying privately. Education was the birdfeed, in reaching out for which, I, like a pigeon, would always be ensnared in one or the other mesh of exploitation.

To Pitampur, for the Love of Learning

Massaab decided to send me to Pitampur village to my geography teacher Chaudhary Raghunath Singh's home to work for him. My work was explained to me. I had to get up at four in the morning, feed the cattle, dispose of the dung, run the tube-well when there was electricity and operate the fodder machine as well as the flour-mill. All these tasks had to be completed the moment I got back from school. Massaab had already made plans for my future. Following my return from the Chaudhary's home, I would be able to run the flour-mill at his home also. He went ahead confidently with his plans as though he had discussed the whole matter with me.

In my presence, Massaab had informed the Chaudhary that I knew all the tasks related to farming and that although I was a Chamar, I had been purified by my association with the Arya Samaj. He also added that in lieu of my boarding and food, he could extract as much labour as possible from me, since for the sake of getting educated I was willing to do any kind or any amount of work.

I also had to maintain the accounts at the mill. I began to like my job. After I got back from school, I would put away my school bag and change from my kurta–pyjama into shorts and vest to get down to work. One of Chaudhary's sons also studied along with me in school. Guruji's son would be busy completing his homework then. I needed time to revise my studies but who would give it to me and from where was it to be found? Even if I had time to study, I would have to continue to labour for my meals. My Guru's wife, Guru Mata, had set aside the bowl meant for my meals as well as a glass in the room in the flour-mill. That I was an untouchable who had been kept on charity was made explicit to the women of the neighbourhood in my presence. This was done to prevent anyone from touching me or being deceived about my caste. In this way, she maintained a distance from me. She would have been happier if I did not touch that portion of grain meant for her home in the flour-mill. She would wake me up at four and assign several tasks to me, whereas I had to reach school at nine. Guruji would wake up at six and he too would want me to do some work, 'I'll take care of your attendance at school, you just look after the crop for a few days. Prempal Singh says that you are good at tackling cattle and managing work on the fields. You are as good as two labourers rolled into one!'

At home Guru Mata would hand me food from a distance as if I were a beggar and this behaviour on her part bothered me. Often, when I was alone and would reflect upon my student life, I would break down into sobs. However, I do not know how but from somewhere within, a sense of hope was gaining strength that these problems, difficulties, and this sense of oppression were merely aspects of my present lot and would soon be a thing of the past. Very early in my stay at Chaudhary's home, I began to realize that I would not be able to study under these conditions and these would soon end up frustrating my sensibilities instead.

In the beginning, Guruji's son would treat me as an equal, but ever since I began to stay in his house, he started discriminating against me on the basis of my caste. Our material status had altered our social relationship—it became one of a master and a servant. He began to consider me as a bonded labourer and himself as my master. This change in his behaviour stung more than his mother's treatment of me. Later, when Massaab found me looking extremely dejected and enquired about it, I confessed to him that I did not want to continue staying there. Pat was his reply 'So Sheoraj, aren't you letting your feelings get the better of you? Have you begun to think of competing with the other school children? If you do not get used to bearing physical hardships, how will you be able to make the sacrifices necessary for an ascetic?' He could not see that it was not the physical hardships that I wished to escape but the mental torture, of which only I knew what I was going through. However, I had made up my mind and Massaab came around.

I reached late for school routinely, panting with exhaustion. I did not have a uniform till I reached high school and it became difficult for me to hide from my classmates, the marks of toil which my clothes would invariably acquire over the week. On the very first evening, Guru Mata had placed a cot in the room near the cattle shed. She handed me a tattered quilt and saddle cloth for a mattress. I would have to wash the bowl she had kept aside for me after my meals and keep it with me. A holiday ended up being a day of punishment for me. I would be set to work for the entire day like a bonded child labourer and it was a matter of great delight for them that I was so well-trained in my work.

On the one hand, my exams were nearing and I needed time to prepare for them. On the other, the crops were ripening and the work of weeding and irrigation had increased. Guruji handed me a list of tasks to be done and went off to school with his son. A strong resentment was building up in me against this uninterrupted form of exploitation. I had not gone to school for several days and when Guru Mata saw me going off to have a bath she stopped me to say, 'Before you go for a bath, dispose of the night soil. The bloody Bhangi hasn't turned up and the place is stinking. Don't mind it, but I'm told that Chamars also do the work of Bhangis. If you get late for school, your Guruji will mark your attendance.' This proved to be the last straw. I had seen their son wearing a clean uniform and setting out for school after having a breakfast of vegetables and curds, while the kind of work I had been assigned had rattled me to the core. Having a bath was now out of question. I asked her to arrange for mud and ashes and walked off to the room near the cattle shed. I wondered what more lay in store for a fatherless child like me. I quickly changed my clothes and stuffed my books in a bag, got onto my cycle, and pedalled away from Pitampur, never to look back again.

A Letter

I once again wrote to Bhai Saab: *Have students like me, who do not attend school and who pursue education for the love of it, ever been able to make a mark in this world like other educated people? As it is, I am already disadvantaged as a student. I think it is not possible for people like me to aspire for an education in a society like this.* In reply I received a long, sealed letter at my school address from doctor Bhai. On the query of my teacher, I felt great pleasure and pride to announce that my maternal cousin was studying medicine in Delhi's Maulana Azad Medical College.

The Reply

Dear brother Sheoraj,
I was very happy to read the news of your having passed the Class-Nine exam. Do not lose hope and continue to work hard with full dedication. Your preparation for the tenth-standard exam should be even better than before. I am in no position to help you financially but I am advising you to either borrow money from someone in the village with the help of your teacher or speak to the principal of your school about your circumstances and apply for a scholarship. If the school has a fund for poor children then you could get some money from there. You could also do a part-time job or give tuitions to a younger child.

Why do you think that even after studying your future will remain uncertain? Even though it's an old saying but the fact remains that there is no age for learning. Listen, I'm going to tell you a story of a boy like you. He was a Russian, who, like you, did not have a father and even suffered a great deal along with his mother. He worked in a glass factory as a child and like you, washed dishes in a hotel. He also polished shoes and did several odd jobs but under all circumstances, he continued to read. Many good people helped him and later he began writing. Many great writers and editors, who saw in him the making of a talented writer, came forward to support him. Lenin, the revolutionary leader, praised him and later he went on to write the revolution of his own country. Do you know his name? He was Maxim Gorky. You can draw some lessons for yourself from his story. I'd advise you to read Gorky's The Mother, My Childhood, My Universities, *and* In the World. *For the moment, I have bought Agnideeksha and a few anthologies of your favourite poets for you.*

Your brother,
Nathulal

This letter, which was written in English on one side and in Hindi on the other, bolstered my self-confidence. Who was Maxim Gorky? How did he live and what did he write? I had never heard of him before receiving this letter and I was curious to know more about him. I was quite the bookworm and perhaps the only one in my school who had read most of the books, that were not prescribed, from the library. Although I could not fully comprehend them, by the time I reached Class Nine, I had already read books like *Nari Niyati* and *A Brief History of the Luminaries of the World*. These lines from *Urvashi* are the most memorable:

'Tis true the iceberg melts and loses its shape and form,
Yet, how boundless it becomes in the riverine form!

Ramavtar

I had gone to Aligarh with Ramavtar, a Dalit student, to attend Guru Gobind Singh's birth anniversary celebrations. As for Dr Ambedkar's birth anniversary, only Jatav Chamars would celebrate it, while the other castes would mock at it, including those from non-Chamar Dalit castes. For the first time on the occasion of Ambedkar's anniversary, I gained precise information about. I had not read anything about him in the school textbooks and I do not recall that any teacher had ever mentioned his name, though Tomar Sahab would keep referring to the Constitution in civics in our course. I wonder why he elided the mention of Ambedkar and told us only about Gandhiji even without any reference to context. For a very long time, I got to read neither any Ambedkarite literature nor did I meet an Ambedkarite scholar. Ramavtar had recently converted to Sikhism and kept enlisting the various advantages of becoming a Sikh. He pointed to the avenues of progress that open up for an individual if the community to which he belonged did not practise untouchability and discrimnate on the basis of caste and to this end, he would take me along with him to gurudwaras. However, by then I had read and acquainted myself with some communist literature and in Bhai Saab's opinion even Ambedkar was not as scientific or rational an intellectual as Karl Marx, or else he would not have converted to Buddhism. Therefore, I, too, did not attach much importance to the idea of converting to another religion.

My mind was in a state of great turmoil during the days of the exams. The exams themselves were a new experience for me. They were to be the basis of my future and I was tortured by my fears of failing in all of them. Some of my exams were scheduled one after the other and I appeared for them sometimes by travelling from Dhurra and at other times from Pali, by spending the night at Amma's. To stay there amounted to compromising my self-respect completely, as I knew that Bhikari Dada could not bear my presence even for a moment. All I needed to prepare for an exam was some time, a place to stay, and some food. But for most of the time, I had nothing to fill my stomach and was compelled to run around for it. Often I would experience extreme pangs of hunger similar to that of a woman who had just delivered a baby. At Pali, I had my mother and I could even earn something for my food but I could not stay there to prepare for my exams.

The Well Mason

For quite a long time, I continued to study as well as to work as a mason. I was the youngest among masons and would undertake the hazardous task of making wells which the others avoided. I have no regrets about the kind of jobs I did as a child. To state it plainly, those who employed me received more than their money's worth. However, I wish to register my complaint against the caste-centred system of this country, which failed to undertake the responsibility of providing education to hapless children like me. This free country did not compensate even a fraction for the exploitation of our labour which has been carried on for several generations. Instead, idlers, hoarders, and land grabbers were the ones who seized the reins of power. In any case, my ancestors possessed nothing that I could have inherited without working. And what could they have amassed since they lived a life worse than that of a slave? Notwithstanding the fact that I was less of a slave than them, I suffered from a greater sense of enslavement, whereas the absolute abjectness of their slavery was perhaps never felt by them. Had they been aware of their wretchedness, they would have revolted or was it that they were in no position to express themselves? They were mute members of an indigenous community who were oppressed for centuries in this country. Ignorance and lack of education and resources were the factors that prevented them from feeling fully human. There was a conscious attempt to keep us away from education, literature, and the arts so that we led an animal-like existence.

I was extremely happy when I cleared an exam. It would seem like a victory in a war. That year, I worked enthusiastically through the whole of May and June. I slaved away on Massaab's fields, but I was happy. The hope that I could learn while I earned was gathering strength within me.

The Praiseworthy Bullocks

Even though from the point of view of scoring marks my eighth-standard result was undoubtedly not very encouraging, I was consoled by the fact that I was going on to the next class. I was all the more satisfied because I felt that I would be one student among other students. I did not know then that the division of marks and choice of subject were also matters of great significance. For me, to pass my exams was to gain the world and to fail was to be reduced to a nonentity.

Massaab had bought ten bighas of land and I was instructed to plough it. In those days, I had been newly struck by the poetic muse. I believed that suffering was the stuff that went into the making of great writers and, therefore, had begun to regard my problems as the necessary precondition to my qualification as one. The encouragement I got at school had added fuel to the fire. I would compose lines even while working in the fields, as I hardly got any moment of pure leisure for creative pursuits. I had little practice on the newly arrived harrow and was ignorant about the precautions necessary for sitting on it. I usually stopped the harrow for a while to quickly note down a few lines since I always feared that I would forget the lines if they were not written down immediately. One day the moment I put my hand in the pocket to bring out a pen, my attention got diverted from the bullocks and the discs of the harrow struck a solid lump of soil and toppled over. I lost my balance and my left foot went under the disc of the harrow. Two-and-a-half inches of the flesh over my toes got scraped off and flipped over. The bones of my foot lay exposed. The moment my foot got stuck, I had pulled the ropes tied to the bullocks with all my strength to bring the harrow to a halt. The bullocks were well-trained and followed every instruction of mine. Had it not been for their tremendous observance of my commands that day, my leg would have got completely entangled in the discs of the harrow. I would have lost my left leg and become handicapped for life. I managed to somehow wrench my leg free from the harrow with great force and wrapped my foot with a towel by straightening the flesh back over the bones. There was blood all over the place.

On my way to Massaab's home, I kept recalling my own statement which I would often repeat to the brethren of my community, 'I am willing to give every drop of my blood for each letter that I learn.' However, in this case, it was not for learning but for tilling that my blood had been shed. I still have a deep scar on my foot and when the entire sequence of events unfolds itself, I realize that my blood was not shed in vain. Even though my foot was wounded, I continued to make progress with my work. I did not look back. I cannot say that I've reached my destination but I've certainly achieved a few milestones. The journey, of course, is endless—one that goes beyond death.

Once I reached Massaab's house, Bau was harsh in her reprimand, 'Looks like you've deliberately got your foot injured so that you can sit back and eat some freshly made food by me for about fifteen days or so. Well, you'd better give up daydreaming because I'm not giving you a sip of water without your working for it.'

The vaid was not home so I limped back to my home in the basti to find both my mother and brother missing. Even Tai had no word of sympathy for me. I heated some water for myself to wash away the mud from my wound and urinated upon it in a corner and finally bandaged it tightly. Those who had opposed me found in this an opportunity to hold forth and the entire mohalla began to speak in a mocking manner.

With the vaid of a stick I went back to Bau and once again she merely taunted me. Had I been working independently, I could have managed to make provisions for food for four days in lieu of a day's work. Bau knew that I needed a meal but she injured my self-esteem by using hurtful words and so I quietly returned home. Ultimately I had to borrow some flour from Siyamania Mausi's home and after adding some salt, I managed to bake a few thick rotis on Babba's stove for myself.

Some people suggested that I apply some mustard oil mixed with water in a brass or copper vessel to my wound but Bau refused to give me even a drop of oil, even though there were about four canisters stored away at her home. It was the large-hearted Todi Tau who gave me a little oil. I stopped going to Prempal Singh's home. Bau claimed to be like my mother. Would a mother act like this?

I had hoped that Massaab would undertake the responsibility of getting my foot medically treated when he returned but his selfish unconcern dashed my hopes to the ground. He could only think about his field that had not been ploughed. From that day, a knot had formed in the skein of our relationship. Even today I can recall clearly—how miserly, greedy, and exploitative he appeared that day! It was a complete contrast to the image of a saint-like teacher.

However, when he got to know from other people that my foot was indeed deeply wounded, Massaab arrived at the Chamar basti and expressed concern. He also instructed me to go to a government hospital for treatment. He offered me his bycyle for hundred rupees and advised me to stay with my Bua for a while. When I raised the basic questions about how I would manage to survive without work, Massaab said, 'Don't lose heart, show courage and all your problems will be solved. I have full confidence that you will be able to surmount all impediments.' I was troubled and wondered as to how courage alone would provide a solution to my basic struggle for a meal.

I managed to pay off the money for the old cycle from my wages as a mason in a few days and packed my belongings to leave for school.

Thwarted Expectations

At my Bua's place in Dhurra, I found an old woman posted outside their house. I thought that my Bua had given her the keys to the house and that she was waiting there especially for me. Bua had left with Phupha and her children for the brick kilns. The old woman had another tale to tell. 'Chhoti has asked me not to give the keys to their home to you. She's said that you've got it into your head to study but her advice to you was to join them in the kilns. Instead of merely turning the pages of books, you should think about earning some money.' Bua's decision to not let me have the keys got me extremely agitated. Where could I go now? Would Maanti–Gangawasi also not spare a corner of their house for me? I could put up in a hut outside their home but if I stayed with them, the people of the community would raise objections. Even the teachers would get to know and once the boycott began in school, I would not be able to continue with my studies. In any case, I decided to go to Maanti's house.

Maanti confirmed the information I received from the old woman. Even she advised me to go to the brick kilns. I had never ever heeded any such advice or gone back on my decision to pursue learning. I was in tears as I ultimately got on my cycle to go back. It was that time of the day when even strangers would not turn away someone from their homes. I had built so many hopes about being able to stay and study there. I had intended to look for a part-time job as a mason during the ten days of my holidays and also skin a buffalo or bullock with Gangawasi during the dark hours. I did not wish for more than a roof over my head. I was left with no option but to go back to my village in the dark of night.

As I prepared to go back, I felt as if I had just buried a dear one. Meanwhile, some elders began to discuss that it was a matter of great shame that I had not been allowed to spend the night at anyone's home. It struck me that I could spend the night in the school as I crossed it on my way. After all, untouchability extended only to matters related to food. I could sleep on a bench in any of the classrooms and leave for my village the next morning.

The Large-hearted Hardayal

It was Hardayal who came after me and brought me back to his home. Hardayal was the lone Chamar in Dhurra who went to school. He was not related to me but had come forward to help me as a fellow Chamar. He offered his brother's tenement to me to stay till he returned. I was moved by his words and protested feebly but breathed a sigh of relief, having found a refuge. I stayed on for about three months without a care in the world.

Hardayal's mother offered to cook for me and his sister, too, considered me as her brother. He was a year senior to me and had been failing the Class-Ten exam for the last three years successively. His mother felt that my proximity to Massaab would help Hardayal in clearing his boards. I had passed the Class-Eight exams with a third division. The English exam had been the least satisfactory, but how could it have been otherwise, as I had learnt the alphabet only recently?

That year I cleared my Class-Nine exam and Hardayal also passed his tenth. It was sheer coincidence because I was hardly in a position to do anything for him. Except that by my studying and reading on a regular basis, an atmosphere conducive to learning had been created and he may have benefitted from it. However, his mother always gave me the credit for his success but the fact remained that he had managed to pass by his own efforts.

During holidays or after school, I worked in the fields and studied at the same time. During moments of leisure, I would go to the *chaupal* to hear anecdotes recounted by the elders and examine the slates of school-going children. It was my daily routine to find out what they had studied in school. I mixed very quickly among these people. I would make my own food, grind the grain, and fetch the fuel from the jungle all by myself. I got so caught up in my studies that I could not reach from school on time for Hardayal's sister's wedding. She waited for me at the time of her farewell ceremony and when I finally reached, she hugged me and wept on my shoulder in the same manner as she had done with Hardayal and her other brothers. I had nothing to give her, so I just handed her a rupee and a quarter and touched her feet.

Oh, for a Scholarship!

In those days, scheduled-caste students would get scholarships in schools. Money-wise, it was a very insignificant amount but both the teacher and the clerk who disbursed the scholarship would think that it was going from their own pockets. I did not know of a single teacher who thought of the money as a form of compensation or a partial payment of a historical debt. Even the teachers of history were ignorant of the history of Dalit oppression. As for me, even one rupee was a big amount then, bigger than what hundred rupees would be today.

In the year 1975–6, Massaab got me to fill up a scholarship form for the first time. I signed the form, but it was hardly a signature! I had merely written down my name. I never had the good fortune of availing the stipend all through eighth, ninth, and tenth standard. I would fill the form every year and it would be made out as a favour that I was studying at subsidized rates. I did not receive a single paisa of the scholarship but I would hear the clerks say, 'These SC fellows study only to avail the scholarship.' I had once taken it up with Massaab and he had replied, 'Stop worrying about getting money, it is a material thing, knowledge is metaphysical in nature. Therefore, you should not allow any other ambition to flourish in your heart, other than the attainment of knowledge. Lakshmi, the goddess of wealth, and Saraswati, the goddess of learning, are inimical to each other. You must worship only the goddess of learning.' He held the belief that learning and devotion to God in this birth would come to good use even in the next birth.

There was such sweetness in his tone that it was difficult to believe he was a Yadav. In my village, Yadavs were mostly found to be rude in speech and querulous in temperament. Since I was always seen with him, many people of the neighbouring villages thought that I was his brother and even my schoolmates thought so. That I was a Chamar belonging to the Chamar community was discovered only belatedly.

The Untouchable Leaf-plates

At Massaab's engagement ceremony, Bau commanded me to set the row of leaf-plates for the guests as they came for their meals in groups. I was overly mindful of the fact that many guests may not like my touching the leaf-plates. On the other hand, I also thought that the Yadavs of the basti knew that I stayed with Massaab and was now an Arya, a purified person. I was no longer untouchable, like the rest of the Chamars. A person is purified by the work he does even though he may be fundamentally pure or impure, such were my misconceptions those days. I must have laid about ten to fifteen plates when I looked back to see that the guests were not sitting down to eat; in fact, those who were seated earlier had also got up. Ramjeet Pradhan, Khushiram Master, and Yadunath Shastri were the only three persons who remained seated while the others stood up and with stiffened postures said, 'Are we to completely cast away our religion and faith? If you wish to become

Chamars, that's your choice but do not contaminate us. Are you holding a feast or bartering our faith?' The Ayra Samaj preachers, who would constantly speak against untouchability, this time too, tried to handle the situation—'Your faith will not be jeopardized by touching these leaf-plates. The plate itself has been made by a Chamar and their women are the ones who have plucked the *dhak* leaves. At the most, if you want, you can wash them.' But the guests became angrier and were speaking in enraged tones. It was then that Bau lost her temper and snapped at a boy, 'Eat if you want to or else go back to your home! You can be a pandit for all you want at your own home! Sauraj is like a son to me, I don't believe in your ideas about untouchability.' Even though she was addressing one person, it was meant for all those who were present. Her bold speech and outspokenness was known to everyone in the village. She could be equally good humoured and very strict at the same time. I can still recall clearly her words that day, which have stayed in my memory and strengthened my belief in human ties over and above those authenticated by blood. There are some aspects of her personality that invoke respect from me even today. 'Bau' was merely a form of address; my feelings for her were more like those for a mother. When she was amiable, she would treat me like her son, when in the mood for some fun, not just me, she would not spare even an eighty-year-old from her incisive humour, and when saddened, she would get me to sit by her side and cry her heart out, peeling open the several layers of pain within. She kept ill quite often and would go on for several hours about her sorrows. Along with all the other tasks, it was a part of my compulsory duty to hear her out for an hour or two once a week and when she was pleased with me, she would feed me some curd or milk. I have already spoken about her shortcomings but her essential goodness and fine qualities far outweighed them.

As part of the preparations, I had to run around handing out invitations for Massaab's wedding. I had got his elder sister on a bullock cart from a nearby village as well as Bau's niece, Bhuri Devi, from her village. Bhuri, who stayed on for several days would say, 'Just as you've done now, you must always fetch me from my marital home in this manner.' However, after the wedding when I met her walking along with her husband at the Rajghat Ganga bridge, she turned her face away from me as she passed me by. I stopped her to ask, 'Why Bhuri, don't you recognize me?' She replied, 'It took me some time. You see, you aren't a Yadav like us. You are a Chamar.' I kept staring at her face and she moved ahead.

Later that night, as I slept on Massaab's terrace, the women began to sing wedding songs. Bau woke me up, 'Look, who's dancing below!' I saw that it was Amma, who could sing and dance very well: *Come to me, my golden bird/ Come into my lap....*

Amma's song continued. Bau had thought that the sight of my mother dancing would embarrass me but that was not the case. In fact, I wished to join her. After Amma left for home, I heard the tinkling of bells and the beating of drums and the tune of a song reached my ears. A woman dressed up as a man was singing:

The sly harlot entices with her enthralling dance.
The elder brother-in-law grabs her
And the father-in-law also wants her,
The younger brother-in-law doesn't have a chance,
The sly harlot entices with her dance.

On the day of the wedding, the baraat was also made to sit in a row. The bride's father, Shri Asharfilal Netaji, went around, welcoming the guests with the customary invitation to eat. I was standing in the corner and he recognized me the moment he saw me. He knew about me and would always congratulate Massaab on his noble deed of lending support to a fatherless child like me. He invited me to settle down to the meal. I sat down at the end of the row. Netaji called out to someone to heap my plate with goodies. I was hungry and impatiently polished away the meal. I could hardly ever wait to eat and, moreover, the opportunities to eat a good meal were so rare!

While I was eating, I kept wondering whether I should carry the leaf plate with me or leave it there. If I was the only one to be taking away my plate in the presence of such a large number of people, would that not make everyone think of me as someone different? It would draw the attention of even those people who had not noticed me earlier. Till now, I was being considered as one among the other Yadavs. The custom was to wait for the others to finish and then get up to leave together.

After everyone finished their meals, like Muslims at their prayer, they got up together to leave. My mind was in a state of conflict—if I were to leave the leaf-plate, some baraati from my village would raise an objection as to who would pick up my plate. And if I were to carry it with me, the people of this village would think, who is this untouchable amongst us Yadavs? Even though he was standing at a distance, Asharfilal Netaji intuited my dilemma. He was a man of sharp intelligence who was extremely enlightened and sensible. He came up to me and said, 'Son, will you have some more?' I replied, 'No, Netaji.' He enquired further, 'Have you had to your fill?' 'Oh yes, completely.' 'Then you can get up, what are you thinking?' I turned the leaf-plate over and began to pick it up. He stopped me and said, 'There is no need for this, after all you are a guest, Sheoraj. If you want, even I can pick up your plate.' 'Oh no, in that case, I'll carry it.' 'No, you leave it there.' He signalled to some young boys holding a basket, 'Here, pick this up too....'

Out in the Cold

As soon as the bridegroom's party returned to its quarters, the music and drama programme began in the courtyard of the school. I got to hold the mike for the first time in my life that day. Before this, I had spoken a couple of times in the village's Ram Leela but then the mikes would hang from the curtains. That day when I shifted the mike from one place to another, the speaker came off from the stand. I thought that I had done some irreparable damage to it, for which I could never compensate. I felt so frightened by what I had done that I gave up my plans about participating in the programme and sat behind the spectators who were farthest from the stage. The programme got over at around midnight and the baraatis went into the big hall of the school to retire to their warm beddings for the night. I stood outside the hall in that extremely cold December night and peeped in to look for Massaab, to ask him as to where I had to put up for the night. My situation was exactly like that of a loyal dog which had been left outside the house by its owner. At least the dog could make sounds and draw attention to itself, whereas I had to keep quiet. I kept roaming for an hour in the hope that I would catch Massaab if he stepped out to go to the toilet and inform him that there were no arrangements for my sleeping. Locks hung on all the doors of the classrooms in the school and only the hall had been kept open for the baraatis. Very soon the windows of the hall were also closed and the mercury dipped. Ever since I had turned an Arya Samajist, I had given up smoking the hukkah and beedi and, therefore, did not possess any matches to light up a fire to warm myself for the night.

The school was located in the jungle and I feared that if a wild animal, snake, or insect were to emerge from the wild foliage, I had no weapon to defend myself. It was growing colder each moment. I climbed a tree but it felt colder up there and my limbs began to shiver and my teeth chattered. A tractor and trolley stood in the corner of the assembly ground, so I got into the trolley to look for something with which to cover myself. I found a soiled raincoat to spread beneath. It was extremely dirty because the baraatis had sat upon it. I sank into the corner of the trolley, gathering my limbs about me, and began mustering up courage to face any eventuality. It struck me that I should cover myself with the raincoat. It was better to stay alive in a dirty state than to die due to squeamishness about cleanliness. However, around four or five in the morning my body began shivering tremendously. My participation in the programmes of the Arya Samaj and my reading of its literature had freed my mind of the superstitious beliefs in ghosts and spirits. I had grown more rational in my thinking. However, I continued to believe in the existence of a God who could protect or destroy anyone He wished and who was the sole saviour of the helpless. Massaab had ensured that I knew my Sanskrit shlokas by heart and even I believed that the Gayatri Mantra I had memorized was my only life-saving weapon in this hour of need.

I began shivering all over but reticence, fear, and the acute consciousness of my untouchability prevented me from thinking up of an alternative course of action. My body had turned numb and I came to life only at the sight of the first rays of the sun. I thought Massaab would have to take my dead body along with his bride back to the village in the trolley. He could hardly be blamed, as he probably knew nothing about my whereabouts. In the morning, it was Bau's nephew who informed Massaab about my weird appearance. On hearing this, he came up to me immediately and, upon hearing the entire account, scolded me about my foolish behaviour.

There are several such significant incidents that occurred when I was studying in Class Nine. For instance, I had already spent three years and was well-settled in Massaab's home before Ashaji came into it as a bride. I would hang my coat and pants, which were particularly dear to me, on the pegs inside the verandah. On the very first day, Asha took them off to fling them to the place where the saddlecloth and sackcolths were kept. She received a severe ticking off from Bau who clarified my status to her. I had not expected this of Asha; for one, she was the daughter of a social leader and also because I would often run into her during school time. Once I had even gone up to her and introduced myself. Perhaps she had not understood that a person with a name like mine might also be a Chamar. Moreover, her father's exemplary behaviour in dealing with the issue of the leaf-plates negated any belief in untouchability. Did his daughter believe in a different set of values? On hearing about it, Massaab came up to me and said, 'Sheoraj, you know this is a very common attitude. When I'll explain things to her, she will stop finding you offensive. Don't hold a grudge against her. Any reform can take place only very gradually. Today, Bau does not practise untouchability with you but you recall there was a time when I had given some vegetables in a brass vessel to Matru Bhai who was a Valmiki working for us in the fields, and then she had burnt the vessel so long on the fire to purify it of his touch that the polish had worn off and the metal had begun to melt. However, now all Jatavs, Valmikis and Muslims eat in our vessels and it is Bau who serves the meals to them.'

Winter in a Saddlecloth

I had to vacate Hardayal's brother's home because he was retuning for his sister's wedding. I wonder why, but one day the woman staying in my Bua's home had a change of heart and she suggested that I shift in with her. The old woman stayed with me for a couple of weeks and then left for her home. I continued to stay there and cooked my own food.

I managed to manually grind a ser or so of grain all by myself for my own consumption but I never forgot that my Gangi Babba ground grain and cut fodder for the Yadavs for a living. The women and children of the neighbourhood would find it strange that I ground my own grain, cooked my own food, and also kept studying. More so because even in a state of utter poverty, most men would never be found grinding grain. In fact, any form of hard labour was hardly ever assigned to anyone who was studying. The women would express sympathy and be full of praise for my efforts at independent living.

By the time I returned to Premnagar, winter had set in and I once again applied to Massaab for provisions, since the lack of warm clothes would impede my studies. He repeated his standard advice to have courage and be devoted to God, 'You'll manage, I'm sure. Look, suffering is a prerequisite for greatness. Even Lord Krishna was born in a prison. Have faith in God and show some courage.' It became clear to me that apart from expressing verbal sympathy he had no intention of extending financial help, even as a form of wages for the work I had done on his fields.

I told him, 'I think I have shown courage but that alone might not be sufficient to pass the cold winters. I'll have to do something to provide myself food as well as warmth.' Massaab then offered me an old, spare saddlecloth which had spent many a winter on the buffalo's back. I agreed to take it but I kept wondering if it had to be used as a blanket or a mattress. Had he given me a fraction of the wages for my labours, I could have bought a new blanket and mattress. The moot question was this—why would he have taken me into his house if he did not wish to take advantage of me? He could have got anyone to work for him by paying wages. There was no dearth of poor labourers in the village.

I would exercise in the morning and shave my head regularly. These were the two things that I had imbibed from Massaab. I would also read Sanskrit but only for its cadence, otherwise I found it a waste of time. The study of civics was an eye-opener, especially the portions related to Rights, Duties, and Directive Principles of the Constitution. Tomar Sahab's teaching methodology was also very effective. That winter when the cold winds blew into Bua's home, I would settle down to studying in the light of the lamp after dinner, covering myself with the saddlecloth. I was haunted by the fear of the ghost of the Board exam and to be successful in it was proving to be a great challenge for me. My self-study turned into a form of meditation. I was not able to sleep much, partly because of the cold and partly due to anxiety. There was no one to guide me, neither in the daily affairs of my life nor in my studies.

One day, I had a surprise visitor. It was my geography teacher who wanted to leave his cycle at my place because its tyre was punctured. Some non-Chamar had informed him that I lived there. He came in at a time when I was working on the grindstone, dressed in shorts and humming away merrily. My face was powdered with flour and I felt extremely embarrassed when he walked straight in because I wished to hide somewhere to cover up my pitiable condition. He parked his cycle inside and I felt that he could see how poorly I lived.

A saddlecloth instead of a mattress! He saw the grindstone too. I was troubled by the manner in which my poverty-stricken state lay exposed before him and more so because it was so much in my nature to hide it. But can poverty ever be hidden? Just as a photographer captures the scene of an incident in his camera, Masterji took in all the details of my room in a single glance. I gave him my cycle and he did not return it throughout the monsoon season, even though he had got his own cycle picked up by someone. I remained a pedestrian throughout this period.

Buffalo Hide

During vacations, I had gone to Pali to show my ninth-grade mark sheet to Amma, when news came about a buffalo that was lying dead from Tochhi village. Dalchand suggested that I join them and earn a few rupees on the side. Thus, no sooner had I arrived, I was on my way to the job of lifting a dead animal.

We took the buffalo out of the owner's house and carried it far away from the basti to the barren land in Mukimpur. After some time, I grew breathless and wanted a break but Chacha mocked at me, 'Come on, put some muscle in that body. This task is not the same as carrying books in a bag under your arm like an accountant. I know that you are going to school so that you can escape hard work. You seem to have no strength in your body but today you have to prove your worth. Come on, heave it up a little more.' I tried once again. I wanted the bamboo rod to be shifted a little more towards me so that I would be able to balance the weight of the animal according to my capacity but it seemed like an impossible task to me. For them, it was something they did everyday, but I had lost my nerve.

I looked towards Dalchand Chacha hoping he would relent but he growled at me and let out such abuses that they still seem to be stuck as thorns in my consciousness even today. That is also one of the reasons why I could never forget that incident. He began by abusing my mother and I was forced to keep quiet but then he went on to abuse my sister. He was extremely irritated by the fact that I went to school and he wanted to use this moment to teach me a lesson. Having trapped me in this situation, like Abhimanyu stuck in a *chakravyuh*, he was waiting to strike out at me. As he spat out, 'You sisterfu…,' the other two men, Gendalal and Veerbal spoke up, 'Hold your tongue, Dalla. Don't lose your head.'

There was no getting away from the task. The weight of the animal was back-breaking. I felt like a prisoner serving a rigorous imprisonment and my crime was that I was not Dalchand's own nephew and that I was studying in a school. It was certain that Dalchand would not let me go without beating me up first and when I stumbled, Dalchand kicked me, swore at me, struck me with several blows, and left me lying on the road. The men pushed one bamboo rod over the other and carried the buffalo off on their own. His beating hurt lesser than the bamboo rod boring into my shoulder.

As the men got down to skinning the buffalo, I walked away towards home. On reaching home, I spread a sack cloth to lie down under the neem tree. The moment Amma saw me, she was full of concern. In the summer afternoon, lying thus, I regretted coming here to share the good news about my passing the exam. Perhaps for everyone else, other than Amma and me, it was an unwelcome piece of news, something unexpected and unnecessary. 'Pass' or 'Fail', these were the two words that mattered. Neither I nor my relatives were aware about the importance of scoring a good division. For many, my pursuit of learning was like an experiment. Not many saw any future in it. At that time, even I thought I would continue studying till the time I kept passing my exams.

Amma must have been happy to see me but she did not express her feelings. The only consolation for her was that perhaps I would get a regular job before I reached Class Ten. My Mausi's son, Shriram, had joined PAC as a soldier and Amma would always cite his example. The next day I intended going to my Mano Bua to tell her about my result. Amma had prepared the food and was calling out to Bhikari. I greeted him when he came in but he ignored my greeting. The news about my clearing the exams had already reached his ears. Without saying anything to me, he addressed Roop Singh, 'Look at him, he managed to pass the ninth grade, didn't he? You've been studying in the school for five to six years now and you've not been able to read five books! You wretched fellow, like us, you will also die skinning dead animals. Today he has passed the ninth grade, tomorrow he'll clear his tenth exam, and one day he will be installed in a seat of authority. So there's something to an education after all.' He went on speaking in this manner.

I had not eaten anything since morning and Amma was about to finish cooking when someone came with the information that a buffalo was lying dead since the night before and we should go quickly to lift it. He took a rupee for giving us this information and went away. Within an hour, another piece of news arrived that a calf had died in a nearby village. In those days, the contract for cattle lifting was not allocated at the district level. The villages were allotted to the Chamars who traditionally carried out this task. I would be reluctant to go to Pali, as meeting Amma meant associating with all those who were not in sympathy with me. It was a case of mutual disaffection. I would be saddled with the same task everytime and at all times I found it beyond my capacity. Bhikari instructed me to accompany the men for the task, not heeding Amma's protest that I had had nothing to eat and was also out of practice.

I changed out of school shorts and shirt into Roop Singh's old pyjama and shirt. The cow was lying at the lower level of the house. Once brought down, no one had even bothered to change its position. A foul odour emanated from the dung and water that had gathered beneath it. Covering his mouth with the end of his dhoti, the Chaudhary stood in his doorway and called out, 'You were asked to come in the morning and you turn up in the afternoon.

Are you related to the cow? Bloody bastards, turning up like guests for a feast! And here we are all dying of the stench. For eight days now the dung has not been cleared, why must you be so slovenly in your work? No wonder you are so poor, you good for nothing!' 'We'll just carry it off, don't be so angry,' Birbal Baba apologized as if he had committed a big crime. The Chaudhary added, 'Take away the cow but also tell the Bhangi to clean up the dung.'

A lot of our energy was used up in carrying the cow up from the lower courtyard. The Chaudhary called out to us to say, 'Listen, one cannot say how long the Bhangis might take to come, why don't you clean up the dung and spread a basketful of mud over it? The whole place is stinking and the children may fall sick. Come on, hurry up!' Dalchand got down to the task immediately by gathering the mud and Birbal picked up a basket while Gendalal lifted a spade. 'What are you looking on for? Clean up the dung and urine. Get down to it,' Dalchand commanded me. And I too fell in line. I did not utter a word of protest then. I was conscious of a rebellion rising within but when I reflect back now, I realize what a cowardly and compromising person I used to be! I had accepted my oppression as my fate.

We quickly cleared up the dung and urine to rid the house of the stench and went back to lifting the cow. I began to totter as soon as we were out of the village. I felt the pole bore into my shoulder and I felt as if it rend through it. As Dalchand got down to skinning the cow, I held its legs. He nicked the skin between the hooves and drew the knife along the length of the animal's body. A white film appeared the moment the knife went over the stomach. With a slight pressure from my hand, the skin became detached as if it was not joined to the body but was stuck on it. After skinning it, pieces of meat were carved out and filled into the skin. This heavy load was placed on the carrier of the cycle and we set out. Hardly a mile had been crossed when the tyre of the cycle burst. I had been trailing behind when Dalchand called out to me by hurling an abuse and then I knew that I would have to carry the load on my head.

Fortunately, Gendalal and Birbal, who had left earlier, had reported to Amma that I had fallen while lifting the cow and that Dalchand had again abused me. Amma grew restless and complained to Bhikari who took Gendalal's cycle to set out for us. He spotted us from afar, Dalla pulling the cycle and me carrying the hide. Irascible by temperament, that day he took my part and scolded Dalla for loading me with so much weight. They took it off my shoulder to put it on the cycle, after which they set off in the direction of the village.

That evening I grew extremely vexed and felt like running away from Pali but could manage to have my meal only by late afternoon. I ended up spending the night there and set out for my village in the morning. I had seen the consequences of my wanting to show off my ninth-grade exam result and had I stayed on longer, these people would have shown me the way to my death. I came away. Amma also wanted me to stay safe, even if it meant staying away from her.

A Teacher Practises Untouchability

This anecdote relates to the time when many teachers had decided to stay on in the school rooms for a few weeks during monsoon. The school peon helped in the preparations for their meals and Massaab desired that I should wash their clothes and gather firewood for cooking. For my services, I could have my meal there. On one of those days when I had been able to attend school, I was informed that Massaab was running a fever. As soon as I heard about it, I went straight to his room and found him lying on a cot. After the initial queries about his health, he called me to him and spoke in a lowered volume, 'Look, you know I don't believe in untouchability but the others cannot change their beliefs instantly or else even you could have stayed on here. You could have cooked for the other teachers and had something to eat yourself. You hardly need anything more than a square meal.'

It got quite late as we got talking and the rain also began to pour heavily. Massaab began to insist that I stay put for the night, as I would be completely drenched if I set out for Dhurra. He also suggested that I could help Chandrapal, the peon, with the preparations for the meal. I went ahead and picked up the bottle gourd to begin peeling it. Just then my Sanskrit teacher, Siyaram Arya, used his stick to strike the gourd out of my hands and said, 'It's better if you leave this alone. What if someone were to see you peeling it? Who would then eat it?' In a lowered tone, he addressed another teacher, 'Is it right to eat a vegetable peeled by a Chamar? Will you be able to bring yourself to do it, Tomar Sahab? At least I cannot gulp down any food prepared by an untouchable. Prempalji may have turned into a saint but I am an ordinary teacher.' To Massaab he said, 'You can help this boy in some other way but don't expect us to eat food cooked by him. If there were no laws against inter-dining, what would be the difference between Chamars and Yadavs?'

I could wash their clothes, clean rooms, and collect firewood and peel it but was forbidden to touch food items.

Before he could turn me out, I had made up my mind to leave. I had to cross the river to reach Dhurra and the way passed through a dense thicket of trees. It was pouring and lightning struck as I walked on all alone. My bag contained some books that had been covered with a piece of polythene to prevent them from getting soaked. The fear of the unknown led to the quickening of my pace and I quickly covered the distance to eventually reach Dhurra.

In the course of time, when Siyaram Arya was contesting as an MLA from my constituency, he had approached me through his nephew, who was a doctor, to campaign for him. 'Will you campaign for me?' he had asked, to which I had replied, 'Certainly and spread the word far and wide—that this khadi kurta–dhoti- and cap-clad man is no leader but a worthless Yadav, who practises untouchability! Do not vote for him!' He kept gazing at me in astonishment.

In the meantime I had made up my mind that I would first work somewhere for a couple of weeks to earn some money and only then go to school. Otherwise, it would be very difficult to continue my studies. The day my name would be struck off the rolls, I would give up studying. What could be worse than that? However, so long as my name was still on the rolls, I would not give up. I decided to go to my Bua's brother-in-law, Gangawasi, and seek his help. I said to him, 'Phuphaji, find me some work.' His prompt reply was, 'I have some work but you are a school-going child, why would you do leather work?' I answered confidently, 'I'll do it. Just tell me what has to be done?' Then he explained, 'Look, you have to pick the carcasses of dead cattle and skin them. You can come along with me. One buffalo hide will fetch you money that will provide for meals for ten days.' I nodded in agreement and said, 'Okay, Phuphaji, I'll do it but I have only one fear that if it is discovered by my schoolmates, then no one will want to have anything to do with me. So I'll do this work in the night or in another village.' The fact was that in the entire region, any student could have easily spotted me but until that happened, I could get on with this work.

Phupha spoke of his own experience, 'The moment people see me from afar with my cattle, they turn their faces away. Who's going to come up close to see you? In any case, you don't have to wear your school uniform. Moreover, you can always cover your face.' While we were discussing these matters, Maanti served me two large pieces of buffalo meat, saying, 'Here, have some. Even knowledge and concentration cannot hold up to an empty stomach,' whereas Gangawasi was saying, 'Eating the meat of a dead animal will harm his head and even the Goddess of learning will shun him.'

I was ravenous and hunger shattered my observance of the Arya Samajist purificatory routine as well as my vow to be a vegetarian. Consequently, I made a meal of it. It was a painful moment for me. For more than a year, I had given up meat, fish, and tobacco under the influence of Arya Samajist ideas and that oath was forsaken that day. I had sworn that I would abstain from not just dead meat but also fresh meat and all forms of intoxication. I would regard every woman either as a mother and sister and not allow any lustful thought to enter my head. But hunger had consumed many such vows of purity. In order to be able to survive, I was willing to submit myself to any condition.

The Scraper

I began to go to Dhurra after school hours. Gangawasi would give me some money as wages for picking carcasses of cattle and with that I was able to manage my expenses. One day on my way to school, I found vultures hovering at a distance in the jungle. I went towards them and discovered a dead buffalo calf in a ditch. I was adept at the art of skinning, having learnt it from so many masters but that day I was donning the role of a school-going student. In my bag I was carrying texts and copies but for skinning I needed a scraper or a knife.

I came back halfway from school, as I thought that it was better to arrange for some money first and then go back to studying. I picked a scraper from Gangawasi's home and returned straight to the spot where I had found the calf. I tied its leg to the cycle and pulled it lower into the ditch. This had to be done very carefully, as even the minutest tear would reduce the price of the skin to half. No one was watching and most people would turn their faces away from such a spectacle. I thought it was a good opportunity. Whatever happened, no one should get to hear of it at school. If Massaab ever got to know of it, I feared that I would be completely exposed. There was no greater fear than this. Books, food, and a place to stay—these were my basic minimum needs. I desired little else. Had I found some good job that gave me time to study, I would never have done this forsaken work. However, at that time I did not regret doing that work, as my focus was on my future prospects.

With great skill and care, I nicked the skin in between the hooves of the calf's forelegs. Then I made a slit from the neck to the middle of the stomach. It took a little longer to remove the skin from the legs but over the stomach the skin was as easy to remove as a film stuck over the mouth of a drum. All it required was the slight pressure of my fist to peel off the skin over the stomach and ribs. I tugged the skin over the tail and tied up that end. I drew great satisfaction and pleasure at having accomplished the task so successfully. I folded the skin and put it away in the sack to head for Dhurra. The moment Gangawasi saw me he said, 'You've earned this, go sell it at Atrauli. It may fetch you seven to eight rupees. You can use it for your studies. For the time being, apply some salt to it and put it away. Wash your hands and have something to eat first.' I got up to go inside to have my meal. Gangawasi had decided not to claim his share, as that was not his collection area.

The next day I went to Atrauli to sell the skin. This episode had made me think that I could look for such opportunities every morning and evening in the surrounding areas and in this way earn something on the side. During the icy-cold winters, the weaker calves would die more frequently. Their skins would also sell at a good price.

The very first day of school, I had managed to hide the scraper wrapped up in a cloth among my books in the school bag but my attention was completely taken up with it. The other fear that bothered me was that the goddess of learning, Saraswati, would make an exit from my books, repulsed by the tool used for skinning dead animals. I would console myself with the thought that, after all, God had created human beings to carry out all kinds of tasks and He would look to their welfare. Why would He not take care of me? Even when I went to the toilet, I would be scared to leave my bag behind. When I stood up to read in class, I worried that one of my classmates would put his hand in my bag and discover the scraper. Beset by all kinds of fears throughout the day, I worried more and studied less. My drawing teacher ended up asking me, 'What is it that you are carrying in your bag, Sheoraj, you seem to take it with you everywhere?' I felt like a thief who had been caught red-handed! My heart fluttered but I got hold of myself. I pretended to not pay attention to his question. Since I was not behaving in my usual way, my movements and actions appeared unnatural and different. The moment I got a chance, I got away from school. I even got a scolding for it the next day. When the complaint reached Massaab, he wanted to know, 'Why did you run away from school?' I could not furnish a satisfactory reply and to have told him the truth would mean that I would have to leave school forever. I was petrified of losing this opportunity, as getting into school had been such a struggle.

On my return from school, I would be on the lookout for a buffalo or calf during the twilight hours. For this reason, I carried my scraper with me everyday. Now, I would reach school either earlier or later than other children, after having hidden the scraper in a hole that I dug in the bushes or garden. I would then saunter into the school with a freer mind.

That day I sat slightly apart from the rest of my classmates. My teacher thought that I was not being able to adjust to the environment in school because I belonged to the 'lower' caste and had remained deprived of school education. He kept asking me, 'Why do you keep shrinking and shifting to the back?' But that was how I wanted to be, I could hardly concentrate on my lessons that day.

However, it was a problem that I alone had to deal with. If I went to drink water, I would take my bag along with me. If I had to pee, I would keep turning back to look at it. My classmates could guess that there was something special that I was carrying in my bag. What had made the bag so dear to me? Some of them even enquired about it and wanted to peep inside. Jaipal thrust his hand inside my bag and also got hold of the scraper. My heart beat fast. He tried to unwrap the cloth around it but I snatched it away from his hand. Massaab found this to be rude behaviour on my part. Finally, when the bell rang to signal the break, I did not stay back for my remaining classes and came away to my place at Dhurra Premnagar.

I recall that once when I heard on the radio that Babu Jagjivan Ram was coming to Narora, I ran all the way to hear him speak. I had also hoped that I would benefit from the schemes announced by the government about allotting fertile lands to the Dalits. I would then be able to have Amma with me. Unfortunately, he did not turn up and I returned disappointed.

◆

A Milestone in Life's Journey

In Classes Nine and Ten

Tomar Sahab used to teach us civics and as a student I can vouch that he was a very good teacher. I drew great strength from the awareness gained by my study of citizen rights and duties. He also taught me about the lives of poets. He would get us to write the biographies of poets and also composed a few lines of his own as an introduction. He expected us to do the same. I too was not content with reading just the poems in my course and would also try something original, fancying myself to be a learned writer or an established litterateur! After all, I did possess a restless heart and a critical perspective!

These were the lines I composed as an answer to an explanation of a poem in my Hindi paper:

Neither is there any feeling in it nor reason sound,
The poem lacks a message and with verbosity compounds.
No poem is this, except the poet's arrogance abounds.
It only displays a mind unsound.

I wrote these lines in bold letters like a sketch on the answer sheet. The invigilator, who came up to sign the answer sheet, stopped to read what I had written and enquired, 'This is not in your course; from where did you learn it?' I replied, 'I didn't pick it up from somewhere, I've got it out of my own head.' As soon as I spoke, the principal, who was on his rounds, came up to me and on reading the poem, patted my back and said, 'Good! Very good!' My chest swelled with pride.

Even though I had prepared for all subjects to the best of my ability, I could spare only as much time as would prevent my name from being struck off the school register. Despite my absence, my teachers would mark me present for minimum attendance but my own irregularity was a source of unhappiness for me. Although I was part of an institution, I was more like a private student. I had put in a lot of hard work for my ninth-standard exams and other than mathematics no other subject posed much of a difficulty. Though Massaab had a sweet, sing-song manner of teaching and would explain the shlokas in simple language, there was no fluency in my translation till Class Nine.

The day my exams got over, I wanted to leave for Dhurra but Massaab, as usual, wanted me to go back to work. I had half a mind to tell him to get the work done on hire. But then he would throw me out of school and if I once committed to finish the work, I would have to keep my word. I told myself that I had been doing this work for about two to three years, so it would not matter if I did it for yet another year and a half. There would come a time when my bonded service would be in accordance to my will and I could live the way I wanted. Then I would render my unpaid service to Massaab. To say 'no' now would mean to rock the foundation on which the structure of my dreams rested. Therefore, after much thought, I agreed to go the day after.

Dhania

The year I reached Class Ten, I began receiving proposals of marriage. Dayaram had also come up with a match with one of his relatives. He had assured me that once the marriage was formalized, the bride's father would meet the entire expense of my education. But I knew my position only too well and, therefore, remained firm on my decision of not accepting proposals. Another proposal came from a Dr Bhagwandas from Bilsi who seemed to be booking me in advance. He believed that once I passed my tenth class, I would qualify for the job of a record-keeper and, therefore, there was no risk in getting his daughter married to me.

Ramcharan's wife called her sister Dhania over from the village. She wanted me to have a look at her. Tai called out to me as soon as I reached the village, 'Come over for a bite.' I was stumped. Tai had never been so generous. She would not even offer an ember from her chulha and here she was inviting me for a meal! I saw a girl baking rotis on her chulha when I went over on my way back from school. Tai introduced her, 'That's Dhania, she cooks really well. She has cooked for us many times when you were not here. She can clean the vessels to such a shine that you can see your face in it.'

'So?' I wanted to know.

'What else? Marry her. None of your family members are here. You have studied till ninth and even she has read a book or two. She is tall and fair. Her father will be very happy if you agree.'

'What will she survive on if she marries me? I've not even finished my studies. No one gets a job with such qualifications.'

'You'll manage. Marry now, when you have the chance.' Since I was only too aware of my financial condition, I refused this offer in no uncertain terms, 'Look Dhania, I wish to study ahead and I don't even have money to buy books. I can't even guarantee two meals a day for myself and, therefore, Tai's advice seems irresponsible. If we get married, it will be a burdensome life. I don't want to think about marriage now. I can't even ask you to go to your father's home and wait until I finish my studies and get a job. My future is uncertain and even you have given up your studies. I can't promise you anything. It may be that you are a good cook and homemaker but how can a student turn provider? Please do not nurse any such feelings for me in your heart.'

She burst into tears and sobbed like a child. I stuffed my books in my school bag and stepped out of the house. A few days later when I returned, she caught hold of my hand and demanded, 'So why did you refuse to marry me? Am I not good enough for you? I can survive on an empty stomach. You can continue to study and if you wish to go to the city, you may. I'll stay with Tai in the village.'

'No, Dhania, I don't think you understand. One cannot survive on sentiments alone, one needs food, shelter, and clothing first. If you stay back here, I'll not feel free to move ahead.' We spoke for a long time, standing alongside the road. It was dark and so no one could see us. In the village, everyone was curious about the other and when Ramcharan's wife came close, she wanted to know what we were talking about. 'Find out from Dhania,' I replied.

No Girlfriends Please!

As I came of age, I found myself drawn to good-looking girls and had never interacted with girls from other castes. In the rural context, boys and girls were clearly segregated. Unlike the fashionable, well-to-do classes, there was no trend of acquiring girlfriends and boyfriends in our village life. While among them it was commonplace to hug and kiss, we could neither touch nor speak to an unmarried girl. In fact, one could not even have a glimpse of one's betrothed and this is true even today.

I can recall that Ramcharan had abandoned his not-so-good-looking wife and had got married to another good-looking girl from Bilsi. I had to fetch her in a bullock-cart and during our journey Ulfat challenged me, 'Sauraj, if you can somehow manage to let us have a glimpse of the bride, I'll give you four annas for it.' I immediately thought up of a plan, and said aloud, 'Did you know the best thing about these long stretches of barren land? Aeroplanes and helicopters can easily land without making much noise. Look! Here is one landing now.' The bride raised her veil out of curiosity while I pointed to her face and said, 'Look Ulfat! What a beautiful airport! The aeroplane is as bright as the moon!'

On another occasion, my friends and I cycled fifteen kilometres to Senjna to catch a glimpse of a bride passing by in a tonga but failed in our efforts. Her in-laws had led her away at Babrala station and we returned disappointed.

During my stay in Pali, while playing, we children would end up imitating our elders. We would make a tambourine out of a cask or an earthen bowl by covering it with a film of buffalo or bullock hide. Then we would get one of us married and take a marriage procession out. One day, I was made the bridegroom and Uttam's sister was my bride. She was willing to be part of the marriage procession but when it came to entering the makeshift 'home' with me, she flatly refused. Then Maluki was persuaded to be my bride and she entered the structure we had built with bricks, which was then covered with a wooden plank and cloth. 'Now, Maluki you lie below and Sauraj, you above her,' were the instructions given by the rest of the children, who clapped their hands and ran away. We had barely entered the structure that our feet struck against it and the bricks fell over us.

In the evening when her elder brother got to know of it, he was furious. Amma too scolded me and twisted my ears and got me to do hundred sit-ups—'Promise me that you'll never speak about marrying any girl!' The rest of the elders began to say, 'Let them be. They're kids, they are innocent.'

Makkhan's daughter, Jaldhara, was as haughty as her father, so I hardly spoke with her and the rest of the girls were as good as sisters. However, they could not play with us like the other boys. Amitiya was my age and, therefore, I would get the opportunity to speak with her. In winters when her mother would invite me to sit by her chulha and recount stories, even if I happened to touch her finger, I would feel as if I had committed a grave sin.

In Premnagar I had merely suggested to Seeto's elder daughter, 'If you bake my rotis, I'll get some sweet potatoes for you.' She took great umbrage at this and said, 'I'll tell Amma that you were offering me sweet potatoes.' I had to appeal to her with folded hands, 'Oh God! Please don't bring disrepute to my name. I have come here to study, sweet potatoes be damned. I can cook my own meals.' Two days later, she taunted me, 'So, you took fright at such a mild threat! I was only testing your guts.'

A similar episode occurred during my stay at Pali. Lalchand Chacha's daughter was an eleven-year-old girl with a very sweet temperament. One evening she got her cot next to Chhote Chacha's to lie down on it. Holi had just gone by and I stroked her cheek but without any colour in my hand. The next day she complained to her mother, 'Sauraj was touching my cheeks.' Then all hell broke loose and her mother came up aggressively towards me and began cursing me. Chhote Chacha rose to my defense, 'He just stroked her cheek affectionately. He is like an elder brother. Don't blow the whole thing out of proportion. The little one was lying next to me, I saw it.' Amma kept quiet but I feared Lalchand's arrival. However, when he returned, the usually strict Lalchand heard his wife out and even enquired from his daughter. Afterwards, he reprimanded his wife in such strong terms that she retreated into a corner. He said, 'You fool! After all, he is her brother. He can show affection, can't he? I may scold him otherwise, but I know that Sauraj is a gem of a boy.'

I was greatly bolstered by the clarity of his perspective and his progressive attitude. Even Amma's eyes brightened but she drove home the point, 'Look Sauraj, do not compete with the spoilt brats. They have money. You don't even have a father. There will be no one to take your part. Whatever you do, you alone will have to bear the consequences.'

Many girls came into my life's journey and went out of it. A nascent sexual desire was held in check within the bounds of propriety.

Sundariya

My Bua had a neighbour whom I called Sundariya. In terms of relation, she was my Bhabhi and her eldest son was a couple of years my senior. Even though she possessed a few acres of land, she would take her children along to work at the kiln. That year, she had stayed back to look after the land and her husband had left with the two sons for the kiln. Sundariya was a Jatav but whenever Gangawasi got buffalo meat, he always shared it with her, and when Sundariya cooked pork she called him over. Their intimacy was interpreted by some people to mean that the two were lovers but I never saw them in this light. Sundariya was a beautiful, well-built, sharp, and garrulous woman, who could be called a 'bold and strong lady'.

The pledge of vegetarianism that I had taken in Class Eight under an Arya Samajist influence had been undone by starvation. A smattering of Marxist literature had changed my outlook. Why should one not eat meat if nothing else was available? Therefore, when Sundariya offered some pork to me, I accepted it on the condition that I would make my own rotis. However, she insisted on making them for me, so I persuaded her to at least accept the flour. From then on, Sundariya would often make rotis for me.

My house was cut off from the rest of the village and this often led me to feel like a prisoner in solitary confinement. Since I was extremely passionate about my studies, I bore this pain of deprivation stoically. I had endeared myself to everyone in the village with my scholarly fervour and every mother pointed me out as an example to her children.

The fact that I had passed my exams two years in a row had pleased everyone in Nagla. In a way, they saw my success as their own. The reason for this was that till then only two or three children from this village had gone to school and there was not a single child who had not failed several times before reaching the eighth class or had dropped out before high school. For them, I was a guest scholar who was amiable and spoke well, sang songs, and got the children together to recite poems and tell stories. What more could they expect from me?

One day, I told Sundariya that I required a place to stay as my Bua was returning home. Sundariya had reassured me, 'Remember that you will always have a place to stay in my house, whenever you wish, even if you turn up in the middle of night!' I left my stuff at Sundariya's and returned to school, after which I went back to the village with Massaab and other teachers.

That winter I was studying for my tenth-class Board exams and it posed a huge challenge for me. My existence and identity were at stake, as my entire future depended on its outcome. Even during this preparation period, I continued to work at Massaab's home and fields. I got time only at night to prepare for my exam and then I was so fatigued that I was unable to decide if I should study or rest.

It was during this period that Sundariya cooked for me several times. Often she would come up to me and say, 'Sheoraj, how do you manage to study for such long hours for days together all by yourself, like a sage in meditation? I am fascinated by you. What is it that is so absorbing in these school books?'

Like a Strange Dream

That winter, when her sons had gone along with her husband to the kilns and her daughters were sleeping in the other room, Sundariya came up to me and said, 'Sauraj, let me put your cot inside. Then you can light your oil lamp and study for as long as you like.' Thus, I began to sleep inside. One night when I had just dropped off to sleep, Sundariya woke me up, 'Sauraj, Sauraj, wake up! Here, have some warm milk that I've got for you.' I asked her sleepily, 'Milk and me? No Bhabhi, you can give me some buttermilk in the morning.' Placing the bowl on the canister, she held me up with her hand on my back and said, 'I'll give you some buttermilk too. You can have whatever you want but first drink this warm milk that I've got for you.' The milk was sweet but not sweeter than the manner in which she spoke with me.

I drank the milk and went back to sleep. She drew up her cot close to mine. Well past midnight, Sundariya woke me, 'Sheoraj!' 'Yes, Bhabhi?' 'Have you gone off to sleep?' 'Just about.' 'Are you going to sleep all by yourself? Has the warm milk left you cold? Must you sleep apart?' My heart thumped in my chest. She continued, 'Shall I come over to you?' 'No, Bhabhi. You remain where you are.' I was not prepared for this unexpected turn of events. I had never experienced this kind of intimacy with any woman. I could barely cope with it while she kept saying, 'If you don't come to me, then I'll come to your bed.' I did not know much about man–woman relations; as a child labourer, I had hardly any time for such things. My natural curiosity was purely theoretical as any discussion about sex was a taboo in our society.

In fact, as someone influenced by Arya Samajist ideas, I felt under tremendous pressure to maintain my chastity as a celibate. Whether Sundariya came to me or I went to her, the vow of chastity would be broken. I felt certain that God would punish me for this sin by failing me in my Board exam. Then all would be lost! She went on, 'Arre, what are you thinking? After learning so much, don't you know anything?' 'No, that's not the matter, Bhabhi. After all you are a woman.' 'So! I'm not asking you to do anything about it. Just come close to me and lie down next to me. Or, if you want, then I can come over to your cot. Don't be scared. I just want to express my affections for you. I like you a lot and I just want to hold you close to me ….' This elderly woman, who was as old as my mother, was someone I was very fond of and she had supported me through my student years. But to see her in this light was shocking indeed!

'Bhabhi, you are so much older to me!' She replied, 'Am I passing myself off as someone young? Come to me as my young one,' 'So, are you like my mother?' 'Yes, you can say that. Just let me hold you close to my chest.' How was a piece of wood to remain unaffected and untouched in such close proximity to fire! This was going to be a tougher test than the Board exam for which I was appearing those days.

Fortunately for me, she stopped after caressing and kissing me just as a buffalo would lick and tend its young calf. It was on her insistence that I had gone to lie down by her side. But was that the truth? Was I not stirred by a desire to know and do all that was forbidden? What about my vow of chastity? That year, I had read Gandhiji's autobiography. He would sleep with two young women at the same time, who were not compelled by anyone to do so. He had continued to experiment with truth till an advanced age. Would my integrity be undone by sleeping once with a woman? Such was the conflict that raged in my mind that night.

My thoughts were overpowered by the feeling that contact with women was the root of all evil. If I committed this sin, I would certainly not be able to clear my exams and that was tantamount to failing in life. God would be displeased. Later, by the time I reached high school, under the influence of progressive writings, I began to negate the concepts of gods–goddesses, the soul and super consciousness. And here was Sundariya, who continued to lie by my side, with my hand held to her chest, free of any conflict. I both hoped and feared that she would not stop at this. As I lay close to her, I enquired,' Is that all?' She immediately replied, 'Of course not! I want to go all the way. Are you not a man? Or are you a eunuch?' Saying this, she held me in a close embrace and caressed my cheeks. Kissing me deeply, she said, 'How dedicated you are to your studies! You continue to study under any circumstances and look at my children! They studied four years in school and then dropped out.' Then she added, 'You needn't sleep on your own from on. You must lie with me for a few nights and only after that will I take any step further.' I could not comprehend what she was trying to say. My mind was in a state of turmoil while she was calmly planning for the week ahead. I asked her, 'So why did you come to me tonight?' She held my head close to her bosom and fell into peaceful sleep, saying 'If you don't know, then just keep lying close to me by my side. You'll understand later.' But my sleep had fled. I had seen some blood-stained pieces of cloth on the trash heap but I had no idea about menstruation then. There was no sex education at school and none at home. The reason behind her reluctance to go ahead became apparent to me much later.

The next morning, I got up early and resumed my routine activities. The previous night seemed like a strange dream. I repented my unsteady feelings. Had something untoward happened, my vow of bramhacharya would certainly have been broken. The other nagging thought was that should I have gone through that experience? A week later that day would arrive and then would I sleep with her? That would distract me from my aim. The only way out was to sit for the rest of my papers from the village or Pali. Perhaps God was testing my character and He alone could be my saviour at this moment.

By evening, her husband turned up unexpectedly. He had received his wages from the kiln and had come to spend a couple of weeks home. After the exam, as I packed my stuff and set out on my cycle, Sundariya held its handle and said in a whisper, 'When will you be back?' 'I can't say but I'd like to return once.' Here is a song I composed for her:

Sundariya! O Sundariya!
Let not the sea of your emotions run dry—
Your shores will always be remembered by
A thirsty, hungry and dependent boy.
Sundariya! O Sundariya!

Although I never went back to Premnagar again, its folk culture is very clearly etched in my mind. Once a competition was held among singers of many villages and a line was given to each to compose a song from it. A folk poet had sung this song:

Ravan did not Sita beguile,
It was Ram who fell to his vile.
The real secret was kept hidden
From a world that remained mistaken.

That's how I developed a critical perspective towards Ram, among other epic characters.

Back in the Same Village

During my two-and-a-half-month break, I worked very hard on Massaab's fields harvesting the crop. Had I been free of this labour, I could have earned enough as a mason but I never got the chance. When school reopened, I was constructing a well along with Dorilal Tau. As the chief mason, he expected special treatment from the landowners but the meals we got were very miserly, so he said, 'Sauraj, the bugger gives us neither paranthas nor curd. Let's push a few bags of the bastard's cement into the well.' That was his plan to punish the well owner. I disagreed, as I was against the abuse or wastage of things. I thought of a different way of punishing him. My suggestion was that we use up a large quantity of his cement that day so that his loss would be heavy but at least the walls of the well would become doubly strong. Dorilal did not see eye to eye with me and, therefore, refused to take me along for any other future assignment. Ultimately, the two of us ended up wasting a lot of cement. I repented my deed but Dorilal was known for his wicked ways, so I too made up my mind to never work with him.

As the new session began, I was hopeful that Massaab would give me at least five to ten sers of wheat and some dal too, but no provisions were made for my meals at the time of my departure. Perhaps they thought that if I took some wheat and dal, I may not return soon. Who then would work on the fields and look after the animals? This happened time and again. I spent the entire vacation working for Massaab and always remained empty-handed.

Many people from the village were under the misconception that since I stayed with Massaab in school, I did not have to bother about my meals. Once, on seeing me return empty-handed, Master Balbir Yadav asked, 'What arrangements have you made for your meals Sheoraj? You must be staying in Chirori School with Prempal?' On discovering the truth, Balbir Singh said, 'Prempal is a good man but he is extremely miserly. He is my childhood friend and I am well aware of his merits and faults. Why don't you take some wheat from me and return it when you can?' He lent me about ten kilos of wheat and made this act of generosity conspicuous to Bau as he owed Massaab some money.

Later when I paid him the money and offered him the interest, he refused to take it, saying, 'If you really want to return the favour, you can work on our fields for a few days.' Can a Chamar or Bhangi incur a debt from a Yadav and get away without paying it back? In many cases, these Shudras were more feudal in their dealings with the untouchables than the Thakurs, Jats, and Jatavs. They could not bear to see a Chamar walk with his head held high or a Chamarin–Bhangin wearing good clothes.

At the Right Time

One day as I entered the house, I was shocked to find Massaab lying completely naked on his cot. I wondered why Massaab did not get up on seeing me. Why did he not react? I stepped out hesitantly but then I thought maybe he was unwell and that I should have checked his breath. So I went back into the house. I first covered him up and on touching him I discovered that he was running a high fever. Such a fever had claimed many lives in the village. My cousins, Roshan and Puran, had also succumbed to it. I panicked. I did not know when Bau would return and in any case, she was hardly a vaid or doctor. I ran up to vaid Raghunath Shastriji's home. It was at a short distance but on reaching I discovered that vaidji had injured his legs and was unable to walk. I pleaded with his wife that vaidji should check Massaab, as his condition was very critical.

His wife protested that he could barely walk and added, 'Why don't you fetch Prempal here?' I replied, 'How can I lift him? He is heavily built, like a wrestler.' 'Then you'll have to carry vaidji to him,' she said in jest. She had barely finished saying this than I slung vaidji's bag of medicines round my neck and lifted him with both hands on to my back, to walk off to Prempal's home. 'Arre, arre! I said it only in jest. What if he falls?' But by then I had reached Prempal's cot.

On checking his pulse, vaidji instructed, 'Get some cloth soaked in cold water and my bag of medicines.' And then addressing me he said, 'Had you delayed in coming to me, Prempal would have lost his life. I will hold a havan in your name. You must bring along children from the Valmiki and your own community for it.'

On learning about Massaab's condition, Bau was all concern. The next day, vaidji told her, 'You must give him a pat on the back. Sauraj lifted me and brought me here.'

The Heap of Wheat and Massaab

Anokhia Bau had gone off to her parental home and had entrusted me with the twin tasks of feeding the cattle and guarding about forty quintals of wheat which she had stocked up in her house. On the many occasions that Bau and Massaab were away, I had to miss school to stay back home and look after the cattle. Then the entire house was under my charge. Where was the question of untouchability and to be practised against whom? The point that I am trying to make is this—though I had stayed hungry for days, in Premnagar, during the course of my studies but the sack of wheat that I had given Bau to keep was never returned to me. I continued to guard their wheat without taking even a few sers of wheat for my own use. I wonder how I managed to remain honest in this very village where I had been kicked and scolded by the pradhan for stealing two rotis worth of flour!

As for Massaab, he had his own share of sorrows. Though he prospered materially and went on to acquire the largest tract of land in the village, a tractor, a large house and courtyard, his life remained tragic. I was witness to his niece Malna's death, whom he had raised as his own. She passed away the year she was engaged. He gave away the dowry meant for her to the girl who married Malna's betrothed. I recall pouring canisters of ghee on to Malna's funeral pyre. Massaab had lost consciousness and Bau was in a worst state. I did not know whom to console.

His wife, Asha, died during childbirth, two years after their marriage. I had composed a narrative poem in her memory called 'Ashasmriti'. Massaab was married a second time to Asha's cousin sister, Urmila. It was a quiet affair and poetry was read out on that occasion. Asha's father, Asharfilal Netaji, asked me to recite my poems. Tomar Sahab and an English teacher had also participated in the poetry-reading. Massaab's poems were the most moving, as they reflected his own heartfelt experience. The entire school was moved to a stunned silence on hearing him. Even on that joyful occasion, he had intoned mournfully: 'How do I cope with the punishment dealt by God's hand?'

Massaab has still preserved the manuscript of 'Ashasmriti' and considers it to be my biggest *gurudakshina*. He knows almost eighty per cent of the text by heart.

Sadly, he could not complete the journey of life even with his second wife. Two years later when I was at Chandausi, I got the information that Prempal's second wife too had died after giving birth to a child. I rushed to the village as soon as I heard the news. On reaching Massaab's home, I found Bau lying on the cot and

Massaab in the barn. He looked miserable and he clung to me and wept in such a way that I was moved to the core by his grief. We sat in silence for a long time.

Though he spoke just once his glance seemed to convey, 'Perhaps you were right. You had asked me to settle down in the city like Sharmaji, Guptaji, and the other teachers. You had said that then my children would be able to study and even their mothers would survive.' However, I had no wish to repeat my advice to him on this occasion. I thought of all the other people living in villages. How many could one advice to leave for the city? Had I been able to save the life of my brother-in-law after taking him to Delhi?

I did not go back to the village for good fifteen years on account of my studies and work. I enquired after Massaab from those who came from and went to the village. He had once come to meet me in Ambedkar College and in Jawharlal Nehru University. He also had his meal with us. Ten years later when I was on my way to Vancouver for a literary programme, I got to know from Meenu that Massaab's son had died in a road accident. I kept thinking about him as I boarded the plane.

A Failed Relationship

One day, Dayaram Chacha's Mausi came with the bad news about the death of my cousin. I recall that she had converted to Sikhism and lived in a gurudwara in Delhi. She cured many women with her homemade medicines. Although in relation she was our grandmother, we called her Mausi. She was a short-statured, heavy-faced, fair-complexioned woman with silver hair like washed hemp. Always dressed in white, she seemed like a snow-woman to me, solid as a rock. She was a childless widow who had been a huge support to her nephew in his straitened circumstances.Whatever she earned through curing women's diseases or by singing bhajans, a part of it was always sent to Dayaram and his mother and sister. She visited us once or twice a week when we were staying in a jhuggi in Delhi and invariably got some portions of mutton for us. She got along very well with Amma and though I do not know much about her, I do remember her as an altruistic, humanitarian, and hard-working woman.

She informed us that Baburam's eldest son Roshan had died suddenly. We were shocked to hear this sad news and began to weep. Roshan had been a couple of years younger to me. His younger brother, Puran, had also died prematurely. Both the children had contracted fever while working on the fields of the Yadavs. For my blind Tau this was an unbearable tragedy. The two had been eyes for the blind man.

My grief-stricken Amma made up her mind to go to the village that very day. We were not sure if we would return to Delhi and, therefore, Amma sold off the jhuggi for half its price at thirty rupees. We went back to village the very next day. Amma consoled Tai, 'You can adopt my Sauraj. As it is, he is used to staying in the village.' That was how it was for a few days. I began to work for Tai and Amma too supported her (I had to tend to the one-and-a-half bigha of land and the cow). Ultimately, in order to support Tau–Tai, I began to work for others.

It was during those days that I was laid up in bed for about five days with cold and fever. Then the arthritic pain began. The joints of my feet swelled, after which the knees bloated to the size of a football. The pain, swelling, and stiffness kept increasing and even the joints of my toes got affected. My condition deteriorated to such an extent that I could barely lift myself from the cot. I stayed there for about a month and a half during my illness. For Tai, adoption meant that all the money that I earned from farm work would go to her. On returning from Mirzapur, Amma had handed to Tai the prescription from the experts—home-bred hen's eggs, crab soup, and a 'vishgarbh' oil massage to provide some relief for my arthritic pain. However, Tai made it clear on the very first day, 'Mukhi, you have to look after your own son. I won't be responsible if anything were to happen to him!'

This was the same Tai who was willing to take my earnings as an adopted son but was reluctant to provide even a single meal to me during my illness. This was how I was returned to Amma whose heart ached at the sight of my swollen limbs. She fed me roasted eggs bought by her own hard-earned money as a form of medicine. The spicy eggs that she made for me for those few days were a source of temporary relief but the pain did not go away completely. It was also clear that I was no substitute for Roshan or Puran and that Tai could never be a mother to me. Ours was a failed relationship.

A Promise Kept

I wrote a letter to Bhai Saab after my high-school exams got over. He had promised to buy some books for me and called me to Chandausi to pick them up. On reaching Chandausi, my entire focus was on getting hold of the books as soon as possible since they were such a rarity for me. Among them were Anil Rajimbal's books in simple Hindi on 'What is Imperialism?,' 'What is Capitalism?,' 'What is Monopoly?,' and other basic books on Marx, Lenin, and Mao. I also found Harivansh Rai Bachchan's *Madhushala* among them. Bhai Sahab informed me that he had heard Bachchanji recite 'Madhushala' when he was doing his pre-medical in Kirorimal College.

I picked up *Madhushala* and began to recite from it to a rhythm. In the evening when Mausaji returned home, I held forth to him too. These were the lines he particularly liked:

The one who has set ablaze the holy books with his soul's fire,
Brought down mosques, temples and churches' spire,
Cut down the shackles of priestly cant and broken away,
He alone is welcome to my tavern today.

However, Mausaji changed his mind about giving me the books when he heard me recite these verses. He told Bhai Sahab, 'Son, when you go to Bekainia tomorrow, you must carry this *Madhushala* to your cousin brother, Gulab. Sauram has already been given many books.' Bhai Saab replied, 'Bhai (he addressed his father as *Bhai*), Gulab is hardly interested in reading poetry. He is a tailor master and Sheoraj is a student. He even composes poetry and if he reads other poets, he will write better.' But Mausaji had made up his mind and before I could request him again, Bhai Saab signalled me to remain silent.

That evening, Bhai Saab introduced me to some Leftists who were active in Chandausi. First, he took me to Comrade Bhagwan Das Sharma's home. Since he was not in, he went ahead and one after the other introduced me to Arvind Saxena, Comrade B.K. Dutta, and advocate Madan Dikshit.

We went to meet Comrade Dulhe Khan who lived in Janaita village near Chandausi. The purpose of these visits was to encourage me to interact with these people if I intended to pursue my studies in Chandausi. Even though all the comrades were non-Dalits, belonging either to the Brahmin or Kayastha castes or were Muslims—they did not believe in untouchability. Dulhe Khan was a true communist. He was born into a zamindar family, who went on to become a lawyer and formed the Communist Party of India in Moradabad. He organized the sweepers in Aligarh and in the Belari region and also took on the land-grabbing Rajas to claim some land for the Dalits, which was later distributed to them. In Nagaliajat, he got Nathu Chamar appointed as the village pradhan. I am going to digress from my recollection of the memories of his life to say that the man breathed his last in my arms.

The next morning, Bhai Saab decided to drop me to the station. As soon as we reached, he opened his briefcase and the first thing he did was to hand me the copy of *Madhushala* along with the other books before I boarded the train back home. Had not a Marxist friend taken away *Madhushala* from me later, I would still have a copy of it.

The news of the death of Angola's president Agostinho Neto, along with his photograph, was published in *Yuvavedi*. The caption beneath the photograph said—'Angola's President was a great revolutionary poet.' It was very encouraging to think that a poet could also be a president. Until then I had always thought that a poet could wield a lot of influence but was always dependent on patrons. He could be a bard or a minstrel but never a leader.

I cut out the photograph from the newsletter and scraped off the polish from the back of the looking glass to use that as a frame for it. I hung the photograph on the wall, right in front of the door. For years, it continued to hang on the wall. Since I never had the spare money to buy a proper glass frame, I would hide away all the photographs of my childhood in this makeshift frame. My younger brother did not take care of these photographs when I was away for a couple of years and when I returned, I found that, barring Neto's photograph, all the others had been destroyed by the rainwater that had seeped into the wall. For my family, my books, photographs, and newsletters were merely scrap. In fact, my brother's wife sold off my entire trunk full of literary material to a scrap dealer. She thought that I was wasting my time on these books.

After reading a lot of Communist literature, I had begun to debate over the existence of a God or gods–goddesses, heaven–hell, rebirth, and avatars. I would get into a direct conflict with the worshippers of spirits. Once I wrote slogans on all the walls, both inside and outside of the chaupal—'Away with Capitalism, Save Socialism!', 'Only those that receive education will prosper in this nation.'

Everyday I recited this Sanskrit shloka which I had translated into Hindi to the people of my basti—'Parents who do not provide education are enemies of their children.'

Faiz Ahmed Faiz's poems were often published in *Yuvavedi*, in which I saw his picture and read about his passing away. For a long time after this, I kept humming his verses like a crazed person. I was deeply influenced by Sahir Ludhianvi's poetry too. I remembered many couplets by heart. Faiz's famous poem:

So what if my slate and quill have been snatched away,
I have dipped my fingers in life's blood.
And—
Though your beauty still enthralls with its charms
But shall I add, there are other sorrows in this world,
Apart from love!
And Sahir's song—
I have drunk wine but what about you?
You've drunk human blood?
If I am abominable, then what shall I call you?

I would keep repeating these verses to myself. However, there always existed the danger of my being influenced by sentimental and romantic poets, as they were prescribed in the syllabus, whereas I believed in realism! My favourite poets, Kaifi Azmi, Ali Sardar Jafri, Sahir Ludhianvi, Faiz Ahmad Faiz, and others, had vehemently raised their voices against communalism and capitalism but did not touch upon the predominance of Brahminism. Perhaps this was so becuase they also belonged to a privileged and powerful class among the Muslims. Moreover, they had become songsters who peddled their ware in the film industry.

I got to know later that Shailendra, who also worked in the film industry, was a Dalit. No wonder his songs seemed closer to my reality. These lines from his song still reverberate in my memory:

If one is alive, one must believe that life triumphs over death
If there is heaven somewhere, it must be brought down to Earth.

The Sanskrit Question Paper

During my tenth-class board exams, I always wanted some leave from the gruelling routine of physical labour so that I could prepare for my papers like other students. Barring the day of my exam, I got no leave from the work at Massaab's home and fields. In my community, I would always be greeted with sarcastic barbs, 'So, are you done with your slavery for the Lambardar? What about your Guruji?'

On the day of my Sanskrit paper, I got dressed early in the morning to leave with Massaab for school. We had travelled twenty kilometres past Narora when we met the Art teacher, Thakur Ramvir Singh Raghav. Massaab requested him to drop me to school on his motorcycle, as I was running behind time and would not be able make it for my paper. He agreed to take me but we had barely travelled for a couple of kilometres when the chain of his motorcycle came off. I put it back on and we started once more but a little later, it came off again. Thus, instead of reaching early, we got further delayed. I ended up pushing the motorcycle for the rest of the way. Eventually, Raghav Saab had to say, 'Sheoraj, if you want to make it for your paper, it is better that you leave me to my own devices and run off quickly to the school.' I ran fast but reached quite late. An hour had already gone by and I felt that I had missed my chance to sit for the exam. It was as if a swimmer had drowned at the shores even before entering the sea. I was sweating profusely out of fear and ran to the classroom but the invigilator on duty did not allow me to enter the room on the grounds that the rules of the Board exams did not permit such a late entry. I panicked and related the entire episode with reference to Massaab. The teacher then asked me to seek permission from the principal who was on the rounds. I finally got the permission to sit for my exam but as I began my paper and looked around, I found all the students laughing at me. I soon divined the reason for it—the repeated attempts at putting the chain of the motorcycle had blackened my hands with grease and I had been wiping the sweat off my face with the result that it was completely black. The students found that funny but I did not care and got down to solving the paper so that I could save my future from turning dark.

I was busy with harvest-related work when Massaab got two additional rooms constructed and I had to work hard on them too. I took up some masonry work to earn some extra money. I paid back two-hundred rupees to Hotilal as interest and as part of the installment of the debt of four-hundred rupees that I had incurred from him. I still owed three-hundred rupees to Munshi Shyamlal. I sold off the little plot of land, which I had got as part of the Government Housing Scheme, to Happu Dharmpal for three hundred rupees. I intended to pay off all my debts once and for all but I still had to think about getting myself admitted to school. That was when I received the letter from Bhai Saab exhorting me to continue with my studies. I have preserved Dr Nathulal's inspiring letter for the past twenty years and it proved to be a guideline for me.

The village was abuzz with the news that Gangi's grandson has passed his tenth-class exam. It was discussed not only in my community but also among the Telis, Fakirs, Valmikis, Banias, and Yadavs. Shishupal Singh Yadav and Mohkam Singh Yadav had a bet with Massaab that I would not be able to clear the high-school-level exam. I had been working since early morning on Massaab's fields on the day the results were declared. I saw Ulfat Master cycling towards me. He called out, 'Sauraj, the results are out.' I got up with a start, 'In which newspaper?' He replied that he had seen it in the *Amar Ujala* newspaper's examination supplement being sold at Ramesh Gupta's bookstore in Babrala. The man was taking a rupee to show the result.

'You wouldn't know my result since you don't have my roll number?' I asked him, to which he replied, 'There is no need to bother.' 'Why, what has happened?' I enquired anxiously. 'The government has cancelled the S.P. School's examination centre and the results have been held back.'

There were two implications of Ulfat's statement. One was the desire to see me unsuccessful in my exam and the other was to imply that the only way I could have passed the exam was through cheating. However, I knew that that even though our school did not have a good reputation, it was not known to allow cheating. I felt that Ulfat was hiding something. I may have passed or failed but the school's result could not have been held back. But the ground had slipped beneath my feet. I felt as if my dedicated efforts of so many days had been wasted. If I had indeed failed, it would mean that I would never be able to embark in this direction ever. Another attempt seemed impossible. To fail would mean that I would remain a day labourer forever. No, I told myself, there was no question about that, I had to move ahead.

'If you don't believe me, let's have a bet for five rupees.'

The moment he mentioned the bet, it struck me that something was wrong. My heart was beating fast and I felt I had to find it out for myself. I immediately rode off on my cycle in the direction of Babarala. I was panting by the time I reached the bookstore. I asked the shop owner about my result and he showed it to me only when I placed a rupee on his palm.

I had passed in the second division. My happiness knew no bounds when I saw my results. But the question was—how would I be able to study further? I would have to make arrangements for myself. First, I felt it necessary to pay off the debts I owed to the villagers. That year I worked with double the enthusiasm on Massaab's fields. After all, I had managed to reach high school only with his advice and support. I was overwhelmed with sense of indebtedness. Barring a few exceptions, almost all of my blood relations had constantly hurt me but some people with whom I had struck bonds of the heart and humanity had considered me their companion. My aim and determination never wavered. And to those who were my partners, I owed a deep sense of gratitude.

Whichever alley I passed, Master Lekhpal, and other junior as well as senior students kept asking me about my result. People were congratulating Massaab more than me. He was heard saying, 'My mission is over. Now to study further or not is up to Sheoraj.' A remarkable teacher had unconsciously laid a good foundation for the future. The grandson of the blind Gangi Chamar, who had passed his tenth class, belonged to a family which did not have a single literate person in its entire generation. This was noted by persons of every caste and community.

Anyway, now the second phase of Gangi's grandson's journey had begun. He had now to pursue higher education, serve the country in the field of literature, and live amongst farmers, communists, Dalits, and students. After all, Gangi's grandson had passed his tenth-class exam! Now he must find ways to study ahead, let's see what he does! He now has to sing the song of his new journey.

This life narrative has taken the reader along with me only till the point of my reaching high school. I would now have to tell you how I managed to study ahead, preserve my identity, and fight the battle for my progress. I have thought of writing about the new ideas I had with regard to my cultural and marital life and the scientific and rational aspects of the making of myself. The reader will also get to know of my role in the world of education, media, and literature. If I keep good health, I hope for an early fulfillment of my aims; until then, I take your leave on a poetic note and with the hope of another rendezvous:

Life's journey is replete with memories of people and places traversed,
My strength has been gained from those who were weakened by circumstances.
I have closely watched my own people and others, friends and foes for long,
All too human they seemed, although to different castes and creeds belong.
For centuries I have been cursed to silence—
Many have spoken on my behalf, all to no consequence.
There is no point in speaking of my moment of arrival—
It's the experiences of the journey of my life,
Benefit from which many people may derive.
Like the hapless multitude, my childhood epitomizes their strife
It belongs to those who nurtured my life.
The few breaths that I had, have got me to where I now stand
I shall see you again, for it seems, I'm much in demand.

◆

Names

The names of Sheoraj Singh Bechain's relatives with a short note on the kinship connections of each to the author:

Beedhe Phupha	The husband of his father's sister
Gangawasi	The younger brother of Beedhe Phupha
Maanti	The wife of Gangawasi
Baburam	The elder brother of his father
Gangi	The younger brother of his paternal grandfather
Bhagirath	The elder brother of his paternal gradfather
Bidharam	Paternal grandfather
Radheysham	Father
Maya	Sister, who is elder to him
Meenu	His wife
Ajatika	His daughter
Ayush	His son
Kalavati Bua	The eldest of his father's sisters
Mano Bua	The second of his father's three sisters
Mukhi, or Surajmukhi	His mother
Nek Singh	His younger brother
Ramlal	His mother's second husband
Rambharose	His younger brother, after Nek Singh
Bhikarilal	His mother's third husband
Chhotelal	Younger brother of Bhikarilal
Tej Singh	His step brother from his mother's marriage to Bhikarilal
Roop Singh	Bhikarilal's son by his first wife
Rajmala/Manorama	His stepsister from his mother's marriage to Bhikarilal
Gangawasi	His sister Maya's husband
Phoolwati	The mother of Gangawasi, his sister's husband
Matru Chamar	The father of Gangawasi, his sister's husband
Chandro	The sister of his sister's husband

Mandro	The second sister of his sister's husband
Bhajjan	The younger brother of his sister's husband
Nathulal	The son of his mother's sister
Vinod	The son of his sister, Maya, by her first husband
Sillu	The younger son of his sister, Maya by her second husband
Ramsahay Jat	The illicit lover of Phoolwati, the mother of his sister's husband
Puran	Son of Baburam, his father's elder brother
Roshan	Younger son of Baburam, his father's elder brother
Sukhdei	His mother's sister, the mother of Nathulal, his cousin
Devdasji	Nathulal's father

About the Author and the Translators

SHEORAJ SINGH BECHAIN teaches in the Department of Hindi at the University of Delhi, India. A prolific writer, Bechain has several publications to his credit, the most notable of which, apart from his bestselling autobiography, are a collection of short stories *Bharose ki Behen* (2010), two anthologies of poetry *Nai Fasal aur Anya Kavitaayein* (2014) and *Kronch Hoon Main* (2011), along with several books on Hindi journalism and Dalit discourse. A prominent voice in the world of Hindi Dalit literature, Bechain is the recipient of several prestigious awards: the national Subramanyam Bharati Award, Dr Ambedkar National Award, and Rashtriya Hindi Gaurav Sammaan, among others.

DEEBA ZAFIR teaches in the Department of English at Lakshmibai College, University of Delhi, India. She has translated essays on literary criticism and fiction from Urdu and Hindi into English. She has also written on and reviewed works of Urdu and Hindi literature.

TAPAN BASU teaches in the Department of English, University of Delhi, India. He is the author of *Khaki Shorts and Saffron Flags: A Critique of the Hindu Right* (1993), and the editor of two anthologies on caste, namely, *Listen to the Flames: Texts and Readings from the Margins* (2016) and *Translating Caste* (2002).